shyness
what it is
what to do about it

Philip G. Zimbardo

Research in collaboration with
Paul A. Pilkonis, Ph.D.
Therapy in collaboration with
Margaret E. Marnell, R.N., M.A.

Addison-Wesley Publishing Company
Reading, Massachusetts • Menlo Park, California
London • Amsterdam • Don Mills, Ontario • Sydney

This book is dedicated to

Margaret, my mother,
Christina, my wife,
Adam, my son, and
Zara Maria, my daughter,

who have given me the gifts of trust,
unconditional love, and gentle tenderness—
and taught me how to appreciate and share them.

acknowledgments

Preparing to acknowledge the contributions of all those who have enriched me, and hopefully this book as well, I am struck by the size of our "family" of kindred spirits and pleased in my memory of each of them.

Robert Norwood was one of the first shy students bold enough to force me to tackle the problem of shyness as a serious subject to investigate. To Paul Pilkonis I owe a special debt of gratitude for organizing reasearch teams, directing the analysis of our voluminous data, and adding his creative intelligence to the experimental analysis of shyness. Christina Zoppel has carried on the computer programming and processing of our thousands of surveys with a competent efficiency and wisdom I have come to rely on heavily.

This work on shyness has also benefitted from the observations, interviews, experiments, and personal insights provided by the following students: Nina Hatvany, Trudy Solomon, Jeff Wachtel, Debra Tong, Miv London, Terri Macey, Mel Lee, Susan Reilly, Carol Frey, Tim Botello, Steven Cohn, Judy Leventhal, Christopher Counihan, Scott Fink, Colleen O'Beirne, Gopal Gupta, Alex Armour, Michael Broderick, Judeth Greco, Joel Kabaker, Angel Mayorga, Cecilia Pacheco, Carolyn Sanders, Christina Sousa-Silva, Robert Blake, Jeff Prater, Susie Malouf, Hilary Davis, and Zehra Peynircioglu.

Cross-cultural data collection (including translation of questionnaires and all arrangements) was volunteered by colleagues whom I thank for their generosity and research support: Francesco Gaona Lopez (Mexico), Larry Leo (Taiwan and personal observations of the People's Republic of China), K. L. Sindwani (India), Karl Minke and Richard Brislin (Hawaii), Helmut Lamm (Germany), Charles Greenbaum (Israel), and from Japan, Giyoo Hatano, Michiru Sugawa, and Hitoshi Fujisawa. I add a kiss to my expression of thanks for Ayala Pines whose infectious enthusiasm for understanding the nature of shyness resulted in her supplying an impressive set of data on Israelis from little kibutzniks straight through to men and women in the military.

Acknowledgments must go also to teachers and others who shared their resources and ideas about shyness: Sharon Bower, Marilynne Robinson, Dorothy Holob, Jean Davis, Mimi Silbert, and Christina Maslach. From Jordan Junior High School, I thank Chuck Moore, Elizabeth Lillard, and Mary Kushnick for their help, as well as Ruth Miller and Dora Buntin from Green Gables Elementary School, and from Synanon, Brooks Carder, Elizabeth Missakian, and Linda Burke. And there are others whose contributions, though not singled out, are appreciated.

To get the Stanford Shyness Clinic off and running took courage, tenacity, hard work, sensitivity, and a good sense of humor—for which I thank Meg Marnell.

All these efforts also took money; funding came from research grants from the Office of Naval Research, the Boys Town Center for the Study of Youth Development at Stanford University, and the National Institute of Mental Health. Their funding does not in any way signify endorsement of the conclusions, ideas, opinions, or values presented in this book.

Sitting atop a pile of research data or on the floor of a shyness clinic is a long way from getting it all together in a book. To do so, Warren Stone of Addison-Wesley lit the fire under me, and editor Ann Dilworth generously fed and sensitively fanned it to keep me going when the writing got cold. My wonderful secretary Rosanne Saussotte did her usual best in separating the heat from the smoke in my illegible writing (with able assistance from Joyce Lockwood and Annie Edmonds).

Finally, the words in my head could not have continued to reach the paper were it not for the combined efforts of the crew at the Palo Alto Massage Center—their ministrations kept my right arm moving late into the night after all sensibility was numbed.

I hope each of these contributors to this book will also delight in the tangible consequence of our "family affair."

San Francisco   PGZ
February 1977

contents

introduction

F or the past four years, I have conducted psychological research to increase our understanding of a fascinating aspect of human nature—shyness. As a parent and teacher I had long been sensitive to the inhibiting impact of shyness on children and adolescents. But it took a curious set of events to direct my interest as a social-science researcher toward the systematic analysis of shyness.

I was lecturing to a large class at Stanford University about the power of certain social situations to alter profoundly the ways in which we think, feel, and act. To illustrate the point, I described an experiment we had recently completed in which students played the roles of mock guards and prisoners in a simulated prison setting.[1] Although these people were chosen because they were normal on all psychological tests we gave, they began to behave in strange, pathological ways after only a few days in that prison.

The mock guards moved from being initially domineering to acting in brutal, often sadistic, ways toward "their prisoners." The mock prisoners reacted to this display of power with emotional distress, feelings of helplessness, and, ultimately, by sheepishly complying with all the rules. The experiment, planned for two weeks, had to be terminated after only six days because of the dramatic alterations in personality and values that were taking place in that prisonlike setting.

How was it possible for these boys, chosen by a flip of a coin to play the role of either mock guard or mock prisoner, to slip so easily into those roles? They had no training. But they had already learned what it means to be a prisoner or a guard from a variety of experiences with power and injustice in their homes, schools, and through the media. Guards control by creating or maintaining the rules of the institution—rules that usually limit the freedom of action. The rules specify all the things you might want to do but are not allowed to do, and all the things you have to do that you don't want to do. Prisoners can react to these coercive rules by either rebelling or complying. Rebellion brings punishment; so, most give in and do what the guard expects of them.

In discussing the mentalities of the guard and prisoner with my class, parallels were drawn between this relationship and those of husbands and wives, parents and children, teachers and students, doctors and patients, and so forth. "But can you imagine these two mentalities in one head, these two ways of thinking in the same person?" I asked. The obvious example was the extremely shy person.

"There are some shy people who have both the desire and the know-how to do a particular thing, but are held back from taking action," I said. "They go to a dance, they know how to do the dance steps, yet something within keeps them from asking anyone to dance or accepting an invitation. Similarly, in the classroom, there are students who know the answer and want to make a good impression on the teacher, but something keeps their hands down and stifles their voices. They are inhibited from acting because of inner commands from the guard-self: 'You'll look ridiculous; people will laugh at you; this is not the place to do that; I won't allow you the liberty to be spontaneous; do not raise your hand, volunteer, dance, sing, or make yourself obvious; you'll be safe only if you're not seen and not heard.' And the prisoner-within decides not to risk the dangerous freedom of a spontaneous life and meekly complies."

After class, a couple of students came to ask me for more information about their "problem." Their problem was being so painfully shy that they arranged much of their lives around avoiding situations where they might be put on the spot. We wondered together how unusual their reactions were and how prevalent such shyness was among young people. I could offer them a sympathetic ear, but not much wisdom about the causes, consequences, or "cure" of shyness. In best academic tradition, I recommended they go to the library to uncover what was known about shyness.

Meanwhile, word got out in the class that I was meeting informally to discuss shyness and soon there were a dozen students regularly attending a seminar on the psychology of shyness. At first, of course, it was not the most scintillating seminar I had ever led. Twelve shy strangers do not make for a lively discussion—except when the topic centers on the subject foremost in their minds, the subject they were experts on—their own shyness.

When we went beyond sharing our experiences with shyness to reviewing what was known "scientifically" about it, we discovered to our collective surprise that little research on shyness was available. There were some studies and speculations on shyness as a personality trait and on aspects of shyness, such as embarrassment, face-saving, stage fright, speaking difficulties, and so forth, but no systematic investigations directed specifically toward understanding the dynamics of shyness. What we needed was research on what shyness means to the shy person, to those he or she encounters, and to the society at large. With that goal in mind, our class prepared a questionnaire which asked people to decide for themselves whether or not they were shy. Other questions inquired into the thoughts, feelings, actions, and physical symptoms associated with shyness. We tried also to discover the kinds of people and situations that were likely to make those who answered the questionnaire shy. This first survey was administered to nearly 400 other students, then carefully revised to be more effective.

Now, nearly 5000 people have completed the shyness survey, and we have compiled a substantial amount of information from it. Our research team has also conducted hundreds of in-depth interviews and observations of shy and not-shy people in various settings. To study certain specific relationships of shyness to other reactions, we have also undertaken experimental research in controlled, laboratory situations. Discussions with parents and teachers are helping to fill in missing links in our knowledge of the complexities of shyness.

Although most of our information comes from American college students, we have also expanded our focus to include both noncollege populations and people from other cultures. Survey data have been collected from Navy recruits, business personnel, obesity-clinic clients, participants in encounter groups, and students from elementary, junior high, and senior high schools. Our foreign colleagues have provided us with valuable information on the nature of shyness in Japan, Taiwan, the People's Republic of China, Hawaii, Mexico, India, Germany, and Israel.

Many of those who answered the questionnaire wanted to know how to overcome their shyness. To develop successful techniques for doing this, we have established a Shyness Clinic at Stanford University where we are trying out various exercises that may help shy people. Through this clinic, we hope to help people overcome their shyness *and* learn more about the nature of this prevalent problem.

Although we now know quite a bit more than when we first began looking into the whys and wherefores of shyness, many questions remain unanswered. Our research program is very much an on-going inquiry into the many facets of this sometimes subtle and often puzzling phenomenon. Ordinarily researchers wait until they have more information in hand before writing a book such as this. However, this caution has given way to the urgency of appeals for advice, counsel, and information *now*. These requests have come in the form of hundreds of letters, calls, and personal appeals from people who are suffering daily under the intolerable burden imposed by their shyness. Hopefully this book will provide useful information and practical tools to help people begin to cope with their shyness.

The book is divided into two parts. In Part I, the emphasis is on understanding what shyness is all about. You'll learn what it means to experience different types of shyness, the unique problems faced by the shy person, the origins of shyness, and how it can be analyzed. You will also examine the role of the family, the school, and the society in programming a person to be shy, and you'll see how shyness makes intimate relations difficult and enjoyable sexual relations often impossible. Shyness may be a personal experience, but its effects are felt throughout society. Thus, Part I ends with a view of some of the ways in which shyness creates social problems through its less obvious relationship with violence, alcoholism, social movements, impersonal sex, and vandalism.

Part II focuses on the practical question of how to cope with the challenges posed by shyness. You'll find constructive ways to change how you think about shyness, and how you think about yourself. Often shyness is not caused simply by a lack of self-confidence or unfounded fears about social situations; it may be more a matter of not having or not practicing certain social skills. To help you develop these skills, you'll find simple tactics and strategies for enhancing your personal social effectiveness.

But even if there were a magic cure for every currently shy person, what is to prevent future generations from experiencing the anxieties brought on by shyness? The final chapter raises the most provocative issue of all: the therapy needed for a shyness-generating society. Retrospective therapy designed to help people after they are suffering is not enough. We must do all we can to redesign our society to prevent the suffering in the first place.

Shyness is an insidious personal problem that is reaching such epidemic proportions as to be justifiably called a social disease. Trends in our society suggest it will get worse in the coming years as social forces increase our isolation, competition, and loneliness. Unless we begin to do something soon, many of our children and grandchildren will become prisoners of their own shyness. To prevent this, we must begin to understand what shyness is, so that we can provide a supportive environment where shy people can shed the security of their private prisons and regain their lost freedoms of speech, of action, and of human associations.

Hawthorne may have been thinking of the shy person when he wrote: "What other dungeon is so dark/as one's heart? What jailer so inexorable/as one's self?" We can learn to make a heaven even from the hell of extreme shyness. It's not easy, but it's possible. Let's see how.

shyness

part I:
what it is

1
understanding
shyness

I remember as far back as 4 years old, some of the stuff I use to do to avoid seeing people that came to visit us. They were people I knew, like cousins, aunts, uncles, friends of the family, and even my brothers and sister. I hid in clothes baskets, hampers, closets, in sleeping bags, under beds and there's probably an endless list, all because I was scared of people.

As I grew up, things got worse.

Worse? It's hard not to chuckle at what sounds like the start of a Woody Allen routine. But our laughter is clearly a defense against empathizing too closely with this painful memory of a high-school student. We'd like to believe she's exaggerating; life just couldn't be that bad. But for many shy people, it clearly is.

My brother, who had to wear leg braces to correct the damage of infantile paralysis, developed this same morbid fear of people. Whenever there was a knock at the door, George would quickly count to see if all family members were present and accounted for. If they were, he would scurry to his post under the bed or to an even safer retreat behind the locked bathroom door. Only after much begging and pleading would he relent and come out to be greeted by a neighbor or visiting relative from out of town.

My mother, a compassionate woman gifted with insights into the workings of human nature, decided that she must help George before his shyness got completely out of hand. His agonies had persisted even after he no longer had to wear the leg braces. Convinced that he should be with other children his own age, she persuaded the public school to enroll George, although he was only four-and-a-half years old and it was already the middle of the term. As my mother relates:

> He cried and sobbed nonstop for nearly that whole first day, clinging to my dress in near terror. Whenever the teacher or another child looked his way, he'd bury his head in my lap or look at the ceiling. But when the

class was being told a story or playing musical toys, his curiosity got the better of him and he couldn't help but look and listen.

The idea came to me that George would not be so self-conscious if he could become invisible, if he could watch and join in the action but not be watched by the other children. Obviously he couldn't disappear; but he could do the next best thing—become a masked man like his hero on the radio, the Lone Ranger.

After dinner I encouraged George to help me make a hooded mask out of a brown paper shopping bag. We cut out eyes, a nose, and a mouth and colored it a little to make it attractive. He tried it on, liked it, and made me repeat over and over, "Who is that masked child?" Gleefully he'd reply, "The Lone Ranger," or "Mr. Nobody," or "None of your business," or he'd just roar like a lion. Sometimes he'd remove the hood to reassure me it was still him.

His teacher agreed to give my plan a try; in fact, she did more than that, she made it work. She told the other children that the new child would be wearing a special mask and they were not to try to remove it, but just to enjoy playing with this masked child. Surprisingly, this unusual approach worked. George could be part of the class, though set apart. He could imagine being unrecognized when he wanted to be without having to hide himself. Gradually he moved closer to the other children and eventually, in a few weeks, was lured into play.

He stayed on in kindergarten for another year, and his confidence grew as the classroom routine became more familiar. But still the mask—on every morning before class and off only when his brother arrived to take him home.

Then the big day came at the end of the year when the class circus was to be presented for the parents of the graduating kindergartners. Since George had been through it last year, he was an old hand at the festivities. "Would you like to be circus master?" the teacher asked him. He jumped up and down with joy. "George, you know that the circus master wears a top hat and a fancy costume, but not a mask," she wisely continued, "so, if you want to be the circus master, you'll have to exchange your mask for this outfit. Okay?"

And there George was, not only part of the group, but leading the circus. Shouting to look here and for everyone to notice that! No need for the mask any longer, he was on his way to becoming a happier, healthier child. Although he was never totally outgoing, he did develop close friendships with boys and girls, and was later elected to class office in junior and senior high school.

George's need to wear a paper bag over his head for a year and a half might seem bizarre. But this ingenious solution enabled him gradually to relate effectively to others and led to the day when he could take off the mask and be himself. The paper bag was a successful solution for an extremely shy child. Others aren't so lucky. They grow into adulthood without ever learning to deal with this agonizing problem.

Shyness can be a mental handicap as crippling as the most severe of physical handicaps, and its consequences can be devastating:

- Shyness makes it difficult to meet new people, make friends, or enjoy potentially good experiences.
- It prevents you from speaking up for your rights and expressing your own opinions and values.
- Shyness limits positive evaluations by others of your personal strengths.
- It encourages self-consciousness and an excessive preoccupation with your own reactions.
- Shyness makes it hard to think clearly and communicate effectively.
- Negative feelings like depression, anxiety, and loneliness typically accompany shyness.

To be shy is to be afraid of people, especially people who for some reason are emotionally threatening: strangers because of their novelty or uncertainty, authorities who wield power, members of the opposite sex who represent potential intimate encounters. George and the young girl whose comments opened the chapter both felt threatened by virtually everyone. They provide rather dramatic examples of shyness. But the everyday garden variety of this problem quietly intrudes itself into all of our lives.

Have you ever arrived at a party in full swing and discovered that the only person you know is the hostess—and she's not in sight? "Who are *you*?" someone asks and only invisible butterflies come out of your mouth. Or have you ever been in a group where the leader cheerily intones, "Let's get to know one another better by telling our names and something personal about ourselves." Immediately you're into full dress rehearsal: "My name is . . . (damn it, oh yes) . . . Phil Zimbardo. I am a . . . a . . . person (no that's not personal enough—why didn't I go to the movies?)." Once again, without gusto, "My name is, uh . . . ! !" Such common experiences make it possible for those people who are not shy to at least appreciate some of the agonies that shy people go through.[1]

Despite the negative consequences and the intensity of shyness, the problem can be overcome. But to do so, it's necessary to recognize the basis of the shyness and then tailor an appropriate program to alter its foundation.

What is shyness?

Shyness is a fuzzy concept; the closer we look, the more varieties of shyness we discover. So before we can even begin to consider what to do about it, we have to know more about what shyness is. The Oxford English dictionary tells us that the word's earliest recorded use was in an Anglo Saxon poem written around 1000 A.D., in which it meant "easily frightened." "To be shy" is to be "difficult of approach, owing to timidity, caution or distrust." The shy person is "cautiously averse in encountering or having to do with some specified person or thing." "Wary in speech or action, shrinking from self-assertion; sensitively timid," the shy individual may be "retiring or reserved from diffidence" or from a different mold, "of questionable character, disreputable, 'shady.'" Webster's defines shyness as being "uncomfortable in the presence of others."

But somehow such definitions don't seem to add much to common-sense knowledge. No single definition can be adequate, because shyness means different things to different people. It is a complex condition that has a whole range of effects—from mild discomfort to unreasonable fear of people to extreme neurosis. To begin to understand better this phenomenon, we gave the Stanford Shyness Survey to nearly 5000 people.

Do you presently consider yourself to be a shy person?

_____ yes _____ no

(Well, *do* you?)

If you answered "no," was there ever a period in your life during which you considered yourself to be a shy person?

_____ yes _____ no

In our survey, we sidestepped the issue of providing a specific definition of shyness. Instead, we allowed each person to adopt his or her own definition. First, we asked people to accept or reject the shy label. Then we wanted to know what went into that decision. We asked what kinds of people and situations make them feel shy, and what thoughts, feelings, actions, and physical symptoms were associated with their shyness. As you can see from a copy of the survey on page 135, we also tried to get at some other aspects of shyness.

It's a universal experience

The most basic finding of our research establishes that shyness is common, widespread, and universal. More than 80 percent of those questioned reported that they were *shy at some point in their lives,* either now, in the past, or always. Of these, over 40 percent considered themselves *presently shy*—that means four out of every ten people you meet, or 84 million Americans!

For some people, shyness has long been a regular intruder in their everyday lives. About a quarter reported themselves *chronically shy,* now and always. Of these, a lonely 4 percent—*true-blue shys*—told us that their self-definition of shyness was based on the fact that they were shy *all* of the time, in *all* situations, and with virtually *all* people.

The prevalence of shyness varies from culture to culture and with different types of people. However, we have never found a group of people where fewer than a quarter declared themselves presently shy, and, in fact, with some groups of people, like junior-high-school girls and students from some Oriental cultures, that statistic jumps to 60 percent. The percentage of true-blue shys is never less than 2 percent of any group we have studied, and may go as high as 10 percent in some groups, like the Japanese.

In deciding whether or not to call themselves shy, people who answered the survey used as one index how *often* they felt shy. About a third of the people had a sense of feeling shy at least half the time, in more situations than not. Over 60 percent reported being shy only occasionally, but they viewed these times as being sufficiently significant to label themselves shy. For example, you might be shy only in public speaking, but that could be enough to cause serious problems if you have to give reports in public, as many students and business people must do.

Fewer than 20 percent answering the survey reported that they do not label themselves as shy. Whatever shyness meant to each of them, they felt it didn't apply as a personal trait. But interestingly, most of these people acknowledged reacting with such symptoms of shyness as blushing, heart pounding, and "butterflies in the stomach" in certain social settings. In other words, some people and some situations made them react with the kind of thoughts, feelings, and actions that characterize the shy person. These *situationally* shy people do not see themselves as shy, but rather see certain external events, such as walking into a room of strangers, as causing temporary discomfort. This distinction between those who are ready to label *themselves* as shy and those who label only their *reactions to some situations* as shy is an important one, which we will explore more in a subsequent chapter.

To say shyness is a universal experience is a rather broad generalization, but one with a solid basis. Only about 7 percent of all Americans sampled reported that they have never, ever experienced feelings of shyness. Similarly, in other cultures, only a small minority of people claim to have never personally experienced shyness.

Who is shy?

Shyness is more prevalent among schoolchildren than adults, for many currently not-shy adults have managed to overcome their childhood shyness. Nevertheless, our research emphatically rejects the myth that shyness is only a childhood affliction. It may be more obvious to us in children, because they generally are under closer daily scrutiny than are adults. But a substantial portion of the adult population continues to be shy. Robert Young, TV's beloved Dr. Marcus Welby, is among those.

> I've always been shy. As a kid, I was even afraid of the teacher. Later I grew to be one of those tall, skinny youngsters who don't have the looks or the weight for football and thus weren't automatic high-school heroes. In my teens, that was important.[2]

Some provocative evidence suggests that adolescence may generate more shyness among girls than boys. In a sample of elementary-school youngsters from the fourth, fifth, and sixth grades, the average prevalence of those who were presently shy was 42 percent—like the original survey. These boys and girls were equally likely to label themselves as shy. But, when we look at seventh and eighth graders, not only does the average level of shyness escalate to 54 percent, but it is the teenage girls who account for this increase. It may be that the need to be popular in school and to be considered physically (sexually) attractive by the opposite sex is programmed more forcefully into our teenage girls than boys. A fourteen-year-old girl writes of her self-conscious anguish:

> I get very nervous and my head starts to itch very badly and I just keep scratching it like a fool. I don't know how to act around people. I act differently at home than I do at school. I don't even dress the way I want to.

And, from a letter to Ann Landers, we see the plight of the "mixed-up" teenage girl who feels "different" from her peers and longs to become just like them—yet maybe a little more special.

> Dear Ann Landers: I hope you won't throw my letter away just because it's from a mixed-up teenager. I really feel yucky and need help. My main problem is I don't like my personality—I try to be overly friendly to cover up my shyness and then I act loud. I'm jealous of certain girls and wish I was like them but when I try to be, it doesn't come off.
>
> Some days I feel popular just because a certain guy says hello or smiles at me. The next day I'm miserable because a group of girls are huddled in

a corner and I think they are laughing at me behind my back. My grades are O.K. but they could be better. Mom says I'm disorganized. She yells because I pay so much attention to my hair instead of my homework. This is my fourth letter to you. I've thrown all the others away, but this one is going into the mail no matter what. Signed, Different.[3]

More women are shy than men, right? Wrong! Another false generalization, probably based on observations that men tend to be more assertive, aggressive, and obvious in social encounters. Our information indicates no difference between the sexes in prevalence of shyness. In fact, a slightly higher percentage of college men than college women report being shy, but this slight sex difference is in the other direction for some noncollege groups, and varies according to the culture investigated (see summary table in "Notes" section, p. 233).

Shyness moves in mysterious ways, afflicting even those who have never been shy before. Newcomers to shyness make up slightly less than half of all those who are presently shy. Many of these are young adults who have not been shy as children, but for some reason have recently turned shy.

Still, shyness can be conquered, set aside, or outgrown. Some 40 percent reported that they used to be shy but are no longer so, a reassuring indication. Based in part on the experience of these shyness "has beens," we may be able to offer useful advice to the chronically and presently shy.

How does shyness affect people?

We are slowly beginning to gain some understanding of shyness. Although we can't define exactly what it is, we do know that it is prevalent. Another clue to this complex condition may be uncovered by examining how shyness affects different people. Shyness spans a wide psychological continuum: it can vary from occasional feelings of awkwardness in the presence of others all the way to traumatic episodes of anxiety that totally disrupt a person's life. For some people, shyness seems to be a chosen, preferred style of life; for others, it is an imposed life sentence without possibility of parole.

At one end of the continuum are those who feel more comfortable with books, ideas, objects, or nature than with other people. Writers, scientists, inventors, forest rangers, and explorers might well have chosen a life's work that enables them to spend much of their time in a world only sparsely populated with humans. They are largely introverts, and association with others holds limited appeal compared to their needs for privacy and solitude. Like Greta Garbo, they would rather be alone.

Indeed, many people today are rediscovering the attractive quality of Thoreau's solitary life at Walden Pond. But even within this narrow slice of the shyness continuum, there are gradations from those who can easily relate to people when necessary, to others who find interaction difficult, because they don't know how to make small talk, address a group of people, dance, or handle a formal dinner with ease.

The middle range of shyness includes the bulk of shy people, those who feel intimidated and awkward in certain situations with certain types of people. Their discomfort is strong enough to disturb their social lives and inhibit their functioning, making it difficult or impossible to say what they think or do what they'd like to do.

This type of anxiety may take the form of blushing and obvious embarrassment, as a young business executive describes:

> Throughout my thirty-three years I have been subject to excessive blushing as an especially incapacitating symptom of shyness. Although my drive and persistence has resulted in a Masters in Business Administration and a position as Assistant Vice President of a large, multibank holding company, the energy diverted by the shyness/blushing syndrome has undoubtedly prevented my movement into still higher responsibility.

Or this discomfort may be concealed behind an offensive attack that puts people off, as a writer reports:

> I barge in, hog conversations, rattle on endlessly making an ass and nuisance of myself, appearing to be insensitive to others, all for the same reasons others attempt to fade into the woodwork. My underlying terror of being in public is no less, and my problems are no less serious than those of wall flowers.

Even San Francisco lawyer Melvin Belli, who is noted for his dramatic courtroom tactics, admits that not only has he "often been shy," but that he "became flamboyant to hide shyness."[4]

Since the same source of shyness—a fear of people—produces such different reactions, a person's outward behavior is not always a reliable indicator of how shy he or she really feels. Shyness often has an impact on the way we act, but not necessarily in obvious or direct ways. Ultimately, you are shy if you *think* you are, regardless of how you act in public.

People in the middle range of the shyness continuum generally are shy because they lack social skills, and/or they lack confidence in themselves. Some don't have the social skills essential for keeping the machinery of human relationships functioning smoothly. They don't know how to start a conversation or ask for a raise or speak up in class. Others don't have the confidence to do what they know is right. What this lack of self-confidence can do even to a very intelligent person is illustrated by the account of a young woman whose shyness forced her to drop out of law school:

> I started law school in September, after scoring highly on the law board exams and maintaining a 3.94 [near straight A] grade-point average in college and being accepted to three law schools with no difficulty. But I withdrew before the first quarter was over. I didn't quit because I was afraid of putting in the many study hours, but because I am so shy that I could not take sitting in class and hoping (praying) that I would not be called on. This is true despite the fact that I prepared the work and knew the answers!

At the far end of the shyness continuum are those individuals whose fear of people knows no bounds—the chronically shy. They experience extreme dread whenever called on to do something in front of people, and are rendered so helpless by their overwhelming anxiety that their only alternative is to flee and hide. These incapacitating consequences of extreme shyness are not limited to the young or to students. Nor do they dissipate over time. A sixty-four-year-old woman writes:

> I have lived a whole lifetime of shyness. It was years before I could accept myself enough to believe that some person would think I was worthy of being his wife. I felt inadequate. I felt I wasn't good enough. I was considered antisocial. I couldn't relax with people. I never entertained my husband's friends. I was afraid of being no good, poor sport, anything. So if I didn't entertain them, I wouldn't be known. Finally, I was a cast-off, nobody liked me, including my husband. He divorced me and that was the end.

At its worst, shyness may become a severe form of neurosis, a mind paralysis that can result in depression and may eventually be a significant influence in suicide. A businesswoman who describes herself as an attractive, young-looking fifty-year-old responded to a radio talk-show discussion on shyness[5] with this shattering glimpse into her psyche:

> I am lonely beyond belief. I live in complete solitude without a friend in the world, neither male nor female. I have been betrayed many times over and my experiences in life have left me very unhappy and bitter. I spend the holidays in complete solitude. It is a period of great sadness and depression for me and I dread each approaching holiday more and more, because of the intensifications of my loneliness at a time when most people are in the company of friends and relatives. I often think of ending my life, but I lack the guts to go through with it.

For these people and for people in every segment of the continuum, shyness is a personal problem. Not a little irritation, not a minor perturbation, but a real problem.

The positive side of shyness

Although many of these stories and statistics are distressing, we need to remember that shyness has many favorable aspects, too. Between 10 and 20 percent of all those who are shy *like* it. They prefer shyness because they have discovered its positive side.

"Reserved," "retiring," "unassuming," "modest" are all descriptions of shy people which carry a favorable connotation. Moreover, when polished, such a demeanor is often considered "sophisticated" or "high class." David Niven, Prince Charles, Katherine Hepburn, and Jacqueline Onassis come to mind as typical of this "I'd rather be somewhat shy" type.

A British psychologist writing in 1927 offers us a most delightful view on the virtues of shyness:

> Shyness is so common, at least in this country, that we tend to accept it as something inborn, as a characteristic part of the charm of youth, and as evidence, when it persists into later years, of a certain fineness of character; it seems even to be a trait, perhaps not wholly to be deplored, in the national temperament.[6]

Shyness makes one appear discreet and seriously introspective. It also increases one's personal privacy and offers pleasures that only solitude can bring. Shy people do not intimidate or hurt others as overbearing, more forceful people may do. Isaac Bashevis Singer, the author, puts it eloquently:

> I don't think that people should get over being shy. It is a blessing in disguise. The shy person is the opposite of the aggressive person. Shy people are seldom the great sinners. They allow society to remain in peace.[7]

Another advantage of shyness is that one can be more selective in relating to others. Shyness offers an opportunity to stand back, observe, and then act cautiously and deliberately. Shy people can also feel secure in the knowledge that they will never be considered obnoxious, overaggressive, or pretentious. Similarly, the shy person can easily avoid interpersonal conflicts and, in some cases, may be valued as a good listener.

A particularly interesting positive outcome of being shy is the anonymity and protection it provides. Shyness itself can serve as a mask to keep a person from being noticed, from standing out in the crowd. Under conditions of anonymity, people often feel liberated from the restraints of what they "ought" and "should" do. Behavior is freed from the limitations usually imposed by social convention. The Mardi Gras and Halloween offer vivid examples of the marked changes in personality that the anonymity of masks and costumes encourages.[8]

In putting my shy brother behind a mask, my mother intuitively knew that he, too, would feel freer to act. Of course, to the other children he was anything but anonymous. But their perspective was not his. And it is the subjective view that is most important in understanding shyness.

In questioning people about shyness, we have let them do the defining—telling it as they see it. We now know that shyness is prevalent, often a problem full of anxiety and grief, but for some a sought-after state of being. The decision to call yourself shy is determined in part by how often you feel shy, and how long you have harbored such anxieties. But what is the personal experience behind that label? What is the psychology of shyness? Let us turn to the next chapter and find out.

2
the personal world
of the shy

S hyness, it seems, touches all our lives in some way. What we each thought was our own secret hang-up is actually shared by an incredibly large number of people. And we can take great comfort in knowing that we are not alone in our suffering.

But what, exactly, is this suffering? What does it *feel* like to be shy? Shirley Radl, a successful journalist and free-lance writer, describes the inner turmoil she experiences:

> Having personally suffered from shyness in varying degrees nearly all of my life, I know full well how it got started—skinny, homely little kid, skinnier and homlier teenager—and know all too well that neither the shyness researchers or those I've interviewed exaggerated how really awful and crazy it feels. I have known what it is to, no matter what the circumstance, feel self-conscious of my every gesture, have trouble swallowing and talking, see my hands tremble for no apparent reasons, feel as if I were freezing to death while perspiring profusely, be confused about issues I am thoroughly familiar with, and imagine all sorts of terrible things that might happen to me—the least of which being that I would lose my job for being a public disgrace.
>
> I have experienced dizzy spells and twitching when in the company of absolutely nonthreatening men, women, and children. I've known what it is to avoid going to the grocery store because I couldn't face the checker, to become excessively nervous while chatting with the man who delivers the milk, or be unable to tolerate the watchful gaze of my children's friends while making popcorn for them. I have known what it is to have the feeling that I was stumbling naked through life with the whole thing being broadcast internationally via Telstar.[1]

When shy people talk about their reactions to shyness, they mention three general areas of concern. First, there are the outward behavior signs that say to others, "I'm shy." Then, there are the physiological symptoms of anxiety, like blushing. And finally, there is an overpowering feeling of embarrassment and self-consciousness. Looking closely at these characteristics of shyness, we can catch a glimpse into the personal world of someone who is shy.

When silence is not golden

A shy person reveals his or her shyness in several ways. Fully 80 percent report that their reluctance to talk is the tip-off to them and to others that something is wrong. About half of the shy people report that they find it difficult or impossible to make eye contact. "If I can't say anything, at least I can say it quietly" seems to be a typical reaction in 40 percent of the shys. They judge themselves to have a too soft speaking voice (the bane of speech teachers—who, in turn, are the bane of shy people). Another seg-

ment of shy people simply avoid other people or fail to take the initiative to act when action is called for.

Phyllis Diller, for all her apparent outspoken zaniness, was one of the shy silent-avoiders:

Teachers who knew me as a child told my parents I was the most painfully shy youngster they'd ever seen. I was so shy at school dances that I'd stay in the room with the coats. I was so afraid of making a noise at ball games, I'd hum the yells.[2]

It is not only shy people who clam up. Research indicates that silence is a likely reaction to the anxiety we all feel in particular situations.[3] But because shy people repeatedly fail to express themselves, they are less effective in shaping their world. People relate to others by bargaining and negotiating—for services, commitments, time, security, love, and so on. As country singer Loretta Lynn writes, "Life is like going into a bargain store." Without the free exchange of ideas and feelings with others, this important bargaining doesn't happen.

"Reticence" is the term that best describes a shy person's reluctance to relate to others. Reticence is an unwillingness to speak unless prodded, a disposition to remain silent, an inclination not to speak freely.

Professor Gerald Phillips and his associates have been studying this reticence syndrome for the past ten years.[4] Phillips believes reticence is *not* just a specific avoidance of public speaking, it is a more general, deeper problem. Even when reticent students are taught specific techniques in public speaking, some are still generally inept at communicating. In fact, he reports that about a third of the students became even *more* anxious after they had mastered some speaking skills! Perhaps they no longer had an obvious excuse for not being more sociable, but still felt uncomfortable relating to others at a personal level. They had learned the "how" of communication, but still needed work on the "what" and "why."

The problem of reticence is not one of merely lacking communication skills, but involves, more fundamentally, a distorted perception of what human relationships are all about. The reticent person acts like a very conservative investor in a risky, volatile economic market. Expectation of what might be gained is outweighed by anticipation of what could be lost by getting involved. So why *bother*?

Blushing and butterflies

At a physiological level, shy people report the following symptoms: their pulses race, their hearts pound, they perspire noticeably and, down below, "butterflies" do their thing. Interestingly, we all experience these physical reactions with *any* strong emotion, regardless of whether we are sexually aroused, frightened, euphoric, or angry. Our bodies don't tell us much to help distinguish among these qualitatively different feelings. If we had to rely solely on physiological cues, we would never know when to say "I do" or "damn you," whether to make love or war.

However, one physical symptom is *not* part of general arousal. It's the one that shy people can't hide—blushing. A middle-aged salesman explains its effects on his life:

> I find myself developing a habit of turning red in the face when in certain situations. This is *most* distressing to me as it hinders my involvement in many activities that my line of work leads me toward. Public speaking is out of the realm of possibility, small group discussions are rarely handled well, and occasionally, even face-to-face communication is difficult without showing signs of embarrassment. The situation is progressively getting worse.

Most of us have occasion to blush, feel our hearts pounding, or find "butterflies" in our stomachs. Not-shy people accept these reactions as mild discomfort and look to the positive aspects of what might happen later—having a good conversation with the minister at the church social, getting the right directions from a French gendarme, learning the latest dance step. Shy people, however, tend to *concentrate* on these physical symptoms. In fact, sometimes they don't even wait to get into a situation that might make them feel shy. They experience the symptoms in advance and, thinking only of disaster, decide to avoid the church social or the tour to Paris or the dance.

Playwright Tennessee Williams relates how this self-fulfilling prophecy worked in his life:

> I remember the occasion on which this constant blushing had its beginning. I believe it was in a class in plane geometry. I happened to look across the aisle and a dark and attractive girl was looking directly into my eyes and at once I felt my face burning. It burned more and more intensely after I had faced front again. My God, I thought, I'm blushing because she looked into my eyes or I into hers and suppose this happens whenever my eyes look into the eyes of another?

> As soon as I had entertained that nightmarish speculation, it was immediately turned into a reality.

> Literally, from that incident on, and almost without remission for the next four or five years, I would blush whenever a pair of human eyes, male or female, would meet mine.[5]

Embarrassment

Blushing often accompanies feelings of embarrassment, a short-lived, acute loss of self-esteem which we all experience from time to time. We are embarrassed when the public spotlight is suddenly shining on a private event. Sometimes this happens when someone reveals something about us to other people. "John was just fired for incompetence," or, "Alice just spent an hour putting on her make-up—you should see her without it!" would probably be enough to embarrass any of us. On the other hand, unexpected praise often embarrasses those of us who are modest people. Other times we become embarrassed when we're caught in a private action —necking in a parked car, picking our noses, adjusting our pantyhose.

We also become embarrassed, when we realize that our ineptness is, or will soon be, observed by others, and they won't approve of it. Cornell MacNeil, baritone star of the San Francisco opera, recalls:

> As a young boy coming from Minnesota, I can remember being shy at parties. For example, in 1966, a dinner party in San Francisco was held following the opening of the opera. You know how elegant San Francisco is and how full of the beautiful people. At the dinner they served Rock Cornish Hens. They were slippery from having been held over too long. I was afraid if I ate mine that it would slip off the plate and down the decollete dress of one of the ladies opposite. So I only ate the rice.[6]

This notion of embarrassment-about-ineptness was tested in an interesting experiment by Andre Modigliani.[7] In a competitive "team" situation, Dr. Modigliani prearranged for some subjects to do so poorly on a task that their performance would cause the entire team to fail. Those who experienced this failure in public reported being quite embarrassed, more so than others who were allowed to "fail" the task in private. Those who failed in private became mildly embarrassed when they thought that their ineptness might soon be exposed publicly.

Those who felt the most embarrassed made the greatest effort to recover their lost esteem through "facework." Facework involves attempts to maintain one's poise, competence, and identity in social gatherings. This research identified six facework tactics:

- Defensively changing the subject: "How much longer will this take? I have an appointment."
- Excusing the performance: "Fluorescent lights mess up my concentration."
- Showing off other good qualities: "Tennis isn't my thing; I'm into chess."

- Putting down the failed task: "Eating with chopsticks is a waste of time when forks are available."
- Denial of failure: "Nobody else could please her either."
- Fishing for reassurance: "I hope I didn't mess you guys up too badly, did I?"

Since most shy people have a low sense of self-esteem, they may not attempt these diversionary tactics of facework. Rather, they learn to avoid any situation that may be potentially embarrassing, thereby further isolating themselves from other people and instead concentrating on their own shortcomings.

Some people report feeling shy even when they are alone. They blush and become embarrassed while vividly imagining a previous *faux pas*. Or they become anxious by anticipating an upcoming social encounter. With these retrospective and prospective attacks, shyness intrudes itself even into our solitary moments.

Self-consciousness

Since a general operating principle of shyness is obviously to keep a low profile, the shy person suppresses a multitude of thoughts, feelings, and actions that continually threaten to surface. It is in this inner mental world where shy people really live out their lives. While publicly the shy person seems to be going nowhere quietly, inside is a maze of thought highways cluttered with head-on collisions of sensations and noisy traffic jams of frustrated desires.

The most characteristic feature of the shy person's makeup is an extreme self-consciousness. Self-awareness, "getting in touch with yourself," and self-insight are central to many theories of healthy personality and are goals of a variety of current therapies. However, this same tendency toward self-analysis and appraisal of one's thoughts and feelings signals psychological disturbance when it becomes obsessive. Shy people often carry it that far.

More than 85 percent of all those who report being shy tell us they are excessively preoccupied with themselves. This self-consciousness has both a public and a private dimension (as revealed in the research by Arnold Buss and his associates).[8]

Public self-consciousness is reflected in a person's concern about his or her effect on others: "What do they think about me?" "What kind of impression am I making?" "Do they like me?" "How can I make sure they like me?" If you are a publicly self-conscious type, you would respond with a resounding "yes" to most of these items:

- I'm concerned about my style of doing things.
- I'm concerned about the way I present myself.
- I'm self-conscious about the way I look.
- I usually worry about making a good impression.
- One of the last things I do before I leave my house is look in the mirror.
- I'm concerned about what other people think of me.
- I'm usually aware of my appearance.

Private self-consciousness is the mind turned in on itself. It's not just the process of turning one's attention inward, but the negative content of that egocentric focus: "I am inadequate." "I'm inferior." "I am stupid." "I am ugly." "I am worthless." Each thought is a candidate for investigation under a powerful analytical microscope.

This psyche-analysis is comparable to that practiced by the world's greatest egoist, Sigmund Freud—with one exception. Freud's purpose was to understand where those thoughts and desires came from and to decipher meaning out of confusion. The goal of such self-searching was to free the person from unreasonable barriers to action, and to help him or her be more in tune with both tender and terrifying impulses. In contrast, a shy person's obsessive analysis becomes an end in itself, stifling action by transferring the energy needed for the deed to the thought.

If you are privately self-conscious, you will answer "yes" to all or most of these items:

- I'm always trying to figure myself out.
- Generally, I'm very aware of myself.
- I reflect about myself a lot.
- I'm often the subject of my own fantasies.
- I always scrutinize myself.
- I'm generally attentive to my inner feelings.
- I'm constantly examining my motives.
- I sometimes have the feeling that I'm off somewhere watching myself.
- I'm alert to changes in my mood.
- I'm aware of the way my mind works when I work through a problem.

This distinction between the two kinds of self-consciousness can be extended to shyness. The research of Paul Pilkonis has identified two basic types of shy people: those who are publicly shy and those who are privately shy.[9] One is more concerned about *behaving* badly, the other, about *feeling* badly.

The publicly shy are more distressed by their awkward behavior and their failure to respond appropiately in social situations. Concern with their possible inept performance is mirrored by their high scores on the measures of public self-consciousness scale. For the privately shy, what one *does* takes a back seat to one's subjective *feelings* of discomfort and fear of being found wanting. As you might expect, these members of the private club scored higher on overall self-consciousness as well as on private self-consciousness.

The publicly shy person

Of these two types of shy people, which do you suppose feels their shyness as a greater "problem"? The burden of shyness appears to be greater for public than for private shy persons. Their feelings affect their performance, which affects how others evaluate them, which affects how they come to think of themselves. Bad feelings, inadequate performance, poor show-and-tell ratings, low self-esteem. Next time around, lay low, shut up, stand short, and if they don't go away, at least they won't notice you.

Former football star Roosevelt Grier, a massive hulk of a man, took this low-road route to hide his childhood feelings of inadequacy.

> When I was a kid, my family moved North from Georgia to New Jersey. I was thrust into an area where people talked with different accents, different intonations, used different phrases, and—worse—I talked differently from anyone they ever heard. Therefore I became an instant target, particularly in school. In spite of my size, I was mimicked and laughed at. And I was so thrown by this ridicule that, instead of laughing in return, I went almost mute. I didn't talk unless I was forced to.[10]

The publicly shy cannot readily communicate their fears, uncertainties, good qualities, and desires to the appropriate others. Putting themselves in these nonreturnable self-containers, they don't get the help, advice, recognition and love everyone needs at one time or another.

I've had shy students who would never enroll in seminars or take the opportunity to work closely with a professor. Instead, they would hide out in the back seats of large lecture halls. When senior year comes, many are ready to go on to become doctors, lawyers, engineers, or whatever. But no matter how high their grade-point averages, they still need solid letters of recommendation to move up the next rung on the ladder of achievement. And no one knows who they are, because they were so effective in hiding out for the past four years. They almost "beat the system."

Not being able to ask for help for a personal problem also means a person can't benefit from the expertise, wisdom, and chicken soup that is available. In one study we did with nearly 500 naval personnel from the San Diego Navy Training Base, shy sailors reported that they were less willing to seek the counsel of their superior officer for a personal problem (such as alcoholism) than did their not-shy mates.

It is also reasonable to assume that the awkwardness or inability to perform effectively caused by shyness will be an impediment to job advancement. Being publicly shy can keep an otherwise good person down.

Finally, we can speculate that publicly shy people are just not going to become leaders. In most group settings, chosen leaders tend to come from the ranks of the big talkers. They don't necessarily have the most or the best ideas, but they are judged to be more in control of the situation simply because they fill up more of it. Research has shown that when a formerly quiet person in a group setting is made to talk a lot (by responding to a hidden "talk now" light), the other group members respond more positively and that person is ticketed for a leadership position.[11] However, it is not enough to simply give the publicly shy person on-the-job skills training. Their self-confidence and sense of worth must also be enhanced.

The privately shy person

Compared to the publicly shy introverts, the shy extroverts are obviously better off. Knowing what must be done to please others, to be accepted, to get ahead, the privately shy person who is competent can be successful.

Such people may rise rapidly in their chosen professions if they are gifted, and even may turn out to be celebrities. But nobody else knows how much it takes to pull off that confidence game. Too much nervous energy is expended in anticipation of the event and wasted on minor details of its execution. Such people may come to be seen by others as overbearing, slave drivers, or on an ego trip. Sadly, even success does not always bring satisfaction. The shy extrovert, all too aware of this tremendous emotional investment, expects perfection as the natural outcome, and is satisfied by nothing less.

Shy extroverts typically surprise their friends or the public when they come out of the closet to declare, "I'm shy." "No, not you! I mean you're so successful. You perform in public. You've got friends. You tell jokes, sing, dance, go on dates." Privately shy performers often escape detection.

They keep their anxiety to themselves, concealing it by well-learned social skills, sometimes drowning it with alcohol, or by avoiding situations where they are not in control. The mighty orator may become tongue-tied if asked to sing along at a party. The captivating actress can't believe anyone could ever love the "real" her. The "with it" talk-show host may freeze in his tracks when invited to dance.

Johnny Mathis talks about the relationship between his shyness and performing:

> I was really shy at the beginning of my career. I have spent half of my career learning how to do things in public. For a while I thought there was no way I could get over the hangups and be able to be at ease on stage and look like I belong here. It was hell at times. I used to be genuinely petrified. But I'm still not sure what to do and how to act between songs. I feel more at ease than I used to, but shyness on stage is still a problem.[12]

Funny lady Nancy Walker characterizes herself as "probably one of the shyest, most introverted ladies that ever walked. But the part of me that works is like the women I play!"[13]

That fame and fortune are not enough to dispel the self-doubting shyness of even the superstar is obvious in the description Elizabeth Taylor gave of herself during a newspaper interview. "I'm unpredictable, I'm unpunctual. I'm basically shy. I have quite a temper. When I look in the mirror, all I see is an unmade-up face or a made-up face."[14]

Barbara Walters, who makes as much news as she reports, was called "rude," "inhospitable," "aloof, very cold, very aggressive" by at least one other newsperson on *The Today Show*. Does that square with your view of this self-assured, always-in-control-of-the-situation person?

In recent interviews, Ms. Walters offers a very different view of the private side of her public image:

> I have a slight inferiority complex still. I go into a room and have to talk myself into going up to people. . . . I can't take a vacation alone, eat in a restaurant alone, have cocktails alone. . . . I'm always hurt if someone says, "She's aggressive."[15]

Her shyness created inhibitions that made her miss many opportunities during her sixteen years on *The Today Show:*

> My professional life used to be full of opportunities. I didn't get them because I didn't ask for them. I had never hosted a news special of my own. I have always co-hosted. But I've always been afraid I'd be thought too aggressive if I spoke up.

She cautions of false conclusions about the self-confidence of the publicly competent celebrity:

> But I still sometimes walk around saying, "Is that me?" If *I'm* the epitome of a woman who is always confident and in control, don't ever believe it of anyone.[16]

International opera star Joan Sutherland, certainly a commanding presence on stage, made these comments:

> I have felt so terrified that I didn't want to go on stage. But at the same time, I always knew it was impossible to run away. It's a case of sink or swim. No one can do it for you. If you are going to perform you must get out there.[17]

Finally, dynamic entertainer Carol Burnett raises an interesting point about the complex motives of the shy performer:

> I discovered long ago that shyness is often intertwined with a sort of off-beat selfishness. It's hard to explain, but while you are honestly timid about facing people on the one hand, on the other you are demanding recognition for yourself. You are (fearfully, yes!) saying, "Look at *me!* Accept *me!*"[18]

In Chapter 4, we will consider in more detail Carol Burnett's fascinating and articulate analysis of the origins of her shyness. In a telephone interview she described for us the shy performer's mask and what she tells her three daughters to help them overcome feelings of shyness.

Detecting shyness

Now let's get the glitter out of our eyes and look more closely at the people we see every day—at work, around the house, in school, or among our acquaintances. First, make a shyness judgment on each of your family members. Then, ask them to answer the question: "Do you consider yourself to be a shy person?" You might also have them guess what answer you would give. Do the same for other people you know reasonably well. It might be valuable to jot down the basis for your predictions.

Determine your accuracy and evaluate your sensitivity to shyness in different types of people and settings. You might find this exercise to be worth sharing with family and friends. It could trigger a lively discussion, enabling the shyer ones to open up and disclose what they have been feeling.

Shy people we've surveyed usually overestimate the prevalence of shyness in the general population. Perhaps projecting, they see the world as more populated with shy people than do our not-shy individuals. In addition, among those who report themselves to be presently shy, about half assume their acquaintances and friends do not consider them shy.

Observers are better at picking out who is *not shy* than distinguishing who in a group is shy. The privately shy are obviously going to "pass" some of the time and those whose shyness is limited to only certain situations, like public speaking, won't be detected as such in other situations.

A group of forty-eight students who were all living in the same dormitory were asked to estimate whether each of the others was shy or not. Those who considered themselves "shy" were seen as shy by only 45 percent of their dormitory mates. But a third of the other students saw them as a not-shy person instead. (Twenty percent didn't know them, or were uncertain.) The not-shy students were accurately judged so by nearly three-quarters of the others. However, they came off as being shy in the eyes of 16 percent of the other students. (Eleven percent were uncertain.) There were some shy students who were judged to be not shy by as many as 85 percent of the people who knew them, and on the other side, there were several who were rated as shy by more than half of their friends, although they considered themselves not to be.

What makes others see you so differently than you see yourself? The impression you create of course involves more than just the shy or not-shy cues you give off. But we can learn much about ourselves from the errors in perception other people make about our shyness.

In the dormitory study, some of the reasons for judging another person shy were: that person speaks softly, doesn't initiate conversations or keep them going, is afraid to voice opinions or say "no," is uneasy with the opposite sex, does not look you in the eye, and associates only with a small group of friends who also tend to be quiet.

Those who were thought to be not shy: talked a lot and loudly, were enthusiastic, joked and smiled, expressed ideas, attracted attention, made eye contact, and were "natural leaders."

Frequently, not-shy people will be mistaken for being shy if they are judged to be uncomfortable with the opposite sex. But those judgments might conceal the possibility that it is actually members of the opposite sex who feel uncomfortable around those not-shy people.

Shy people who are unusually attractive are distressed at how often other people react to them as being "aloof," "condescending," or "rejecting." With good looks going for you, it is assumed you ought to be on top of every situation, in the limelight. When you are not, the interpretation is that you have *chosen* not to because you are "bored," "above it all," or "too good for the company." Tennyson says, perhaps of such a beautiful woman, "Shy she was and I thought her cold."

We talked earlier about the fuzziness of the concept of shyness. Much of that fuzz comes about because people are not always consistent, nor do they react similarly to different people. In addition, we are faced with individual differences among "judges" in their sensitivity to shyness and readiness to apply the shyness label. Some teachers have told me they have no shy students in their class, while other teachers who work with the same children label every third one as shy. In the dormitory survey, differences among judges were great: one diagnosed 65 percent of all the other students as shy, while another rated over 80 percent of these same people as not shy.

What makes us shy?

Now that we have a sense of what shyness means to the shy person, let's examine what switches on the shyness circuit. A summary of the types of people and situations that make us feel shy is given in the accompanying table. Strangers (especially those of the other sex) and authorities lead the list. But your relatives can do it, too. Curiously, people of a different age—older or younger—can press the S-button. And, surprisingly, even one's friends and parents can be shyness elicitors.

The list of situations that can bring a blush to the cheek or start the heart pounding is considerable. The worse situation imaginable on this score would be having to give an assertive speech to a large group of higher-status people who were evaluating you.

It is important to emphasize here that for many shy people shyness is limited to certain kinds of situations and types of people. Robert Motherwell, the artist, claims, "A group of businessmen or small children can still make me shy, whereas I can easily identify with graduate students and aspiring artists."

A woman journalist talks about the specific situations that make her feel shy:

> Journalism has been my career, and I don't feel a bit awkward interviewing people, or even groups of people. But during my ten years on a local newspaper I was asked a number of times to speak to professional groups on my specialty, and always had to beg off. Each month when the newsroom staff had a meeting, I was acutely uncomfortable, hoping that I wouldn't be called on to make a comment before the group.

As the shyness becomes more narrowly focused, our suggestions for overcoming the shyness can be more specific and more readily tried and

What makes you shy?

Other People	Percentage of shy students
Strangers	70%
Opposite sex	64%
Authorities by virtue of their knowledge	55%
Authorities by virtue of their role	40%
Relatives	21%
Elderly people	12%
Friends	11%
Children	10%
Parents	8%

Situations	
Where I am focus of attention—large group (as when giving a speech)	73%
Large groups	68%
Of lower status	56%
Social situations in general	55%
New situations in general	55%
Requiring assertiveness	54%
Where I am being evaluated	53%
Where I am focus of attention—small group	52%
Small social groups	48%
One-to-one different sex interactions	48%
Of vulnerability (need help)	48%
Small task-oriented groups	28%
One-to-one same sex interactions	14%

tested. On the other hand, when any and everything starts the shyness juices flowing, a more major overhaul might be in order.

The answers to "what makes you shy?" are essentially the same for shys and not shys. The difference is quantitative not qualitative. There is a clear tendency for the shy to report experiencing *more* of everything, but not different *kinds* of things. More types of situations and a wider variety of people are capable of generating shyness, and there are more manifestations of shyness among those who label themselves shy.

Knowing something about the "what," "when," and "how" of shyness still leaves unanswered the "why." "But *why* am I shy, doctor?" That question takes us out of the realm of surveys and statistics and leads us beyond data to theory.

In the next chapter, we'll analyze just how shyness fits into a person's total psychological makeup. We'll also examine different ideas about the underlying dynamics of shyness, and question whether shyness might not start out modestly as a label in search of some symptoms.

3
why shy?

A large number of psychologists, psychiatrists, sociologists, and other researchers have attempted to make sense out of the complex experience of shyness. Their very different answers to the question, "Why shy?" offer a wide range of possibilities:

Personality-trait researchers are convinced that shyness is an inherited trait, much like intelligence or height.

Behaviorists think that people who are shy just didn't learn the social skills necessary for relating effectively to others.

Psychoanalytic types say that shyness is merely a symptom, a conscious manifestation of unconscious conflicts raging deep within the psyche.

Sociologists and some child psychologists believe that shyness must be understood in terms of social programming—the conditions of society make many of us shy.

The social psychologists suggest that shyness starts out in life with nothing more than a humble label, "shy." "I am shy because I call myself 'shy,' or other people label me that way."

To be sure, these five perspectives do not exhaust all the possibilities —for example, one writer has an unusual theory that people are shy because they have limitless aspirations to be wealthy. But, each of these explanations can add considerably to our understanding of shyness. As you will quickly see, just as there is no single definition of shyness, there is also no single answer to "why shy?"

Born shy

All morbidly shy persons are nervous in temperament. They come of a stock in which insanity, epilepsy, migraine, angina, hypochondria, eccentricity, are common. We are frequently able to trace the direct influence of heredity in its causation: *No fact is more certain than that shyness runs in families.* (Italics added) [1]

This confidently pessimistic view of a London physician around the turn of the century puts the "blame" on the genes shy parents pass on to their unsuspecting offspring.

A modern version of this born-to-be-shy theory is presented by psychologist Raymond Cattell.[2] He believes that an individual's personality is made up of a collection of basic traits which can be discovered by mathematically analyzing the person's answers to a questionnaire. People are given scores for each trait the questionnaire measures. The scores are correlated to establish patterns or "syndromes" of traits. Then, they are compared for parents and children to see whether the trait is "inherited."

In this approach, Cattell determines personality traits, not by observation, but by a pencil-and-paper test:

- When coming to a new place, are you painfully slow at making new friendships? *Yes* or *No*
- Are you a talkative person who enjoys any opportunity for verbal expression? *Yes* or *No*

People who answer "No" to the first and "Yes" to the second item (and respond similarly to comparable other items) are rated as high on what is called the H factor. The H factor is composed of two traits: H^+ (Boldness) versus H^- (Susceptibility to threat). The H^+ types are tough, thick-skinned, and stout-hearted in response to the shocks of life. Teddy Roosevelt and Winston Churchill are given as paragons of this H^+ trait.

In contrast, H^- people reveal a high susceptibility to threat. The trade name for the H^- trait is thus *threctia*—we know it as shyness. The physical and social shocks which an H^+ is able to endure or even be insensitive to "reduce the threctic person to exhaustion and inhibition." Emily Dickinson and inventor Henry Cavendish are instances of this type, as are, according to Cattell, "ministers and priests, editorial workers, farmers and those seeking vocational rehabilitation."

Of interest to us is the theory behind the types. The shy H^- type is born with a more sensitive, easily aroused nervous system than the fearless H^+ type—so the theory goes. This high sensitivity leads to shyness and withdrawal from conflict and threatening events. Cattell argues that since this H trait is largely inherited, it does not change with events in one's lifetime. However, he does state that "shyness of an excessive kind tends naturally to cure itself." As to how or why, we are given no clue, except that it is *not* through "education directly trying to obliterate shyness." So forget about attempting to treat shyness, according to this pessimistic view.

Clearly there are a great many individual differences in the constitution and behavior of newborns. They have different sensitivities to noise, light, pain, temperature; some cry a lot, while others sleep most of the time. But no one, including Cattell, has ever shown that these differences predict which baby will become a Wilma Wallflower and which will become Teddy Tough Guy.

Personality-trait researchers only *assume* that the psychological differences between H^+ and H^- would be evident in newborns if they could be tested. Based on this assumption, they declare that a sensitive-shy nervous system is inherited. Not only is this type of reasoning backward, it also has dissuaded many shys from trying systematic treatment programs.

Born shy, these hypersensitive people are condemned to go through life waiting for excessive shyness to "cure itself." Better to wait for Godot or for the Long Island Railroad to be on time.

Learning to be shy

The view of personality-trait researchers that shyness is an inevitable consequence of inheriting a soft-in-the-guts constitution runs contrary to the basic tenets of behavior theorists. Behaviorists believe that, for better or worse, we are what we have learned. We learn to act in ways that are positively rewarded and we stop or suppress actions that have negative consequences for us. By arranging a world in which only "desirable" behavior is rewarded, the behaviorist claims to be able to make a fair lady of a gutter snipe, or maybe even transform a shy H^- into a bold H^+.

John B. Watson, the popularizer of behaviorism in America, proclaimed the limitless power of positive reinforcement to modify personality traits and temperament with his immodest boast:

> Give me a dozen healthy infants, well-formed, and my own specified world to bring them up in and I'll guarantee to take any one at random and train him to become any type of specialist I might select—doctor, lawyer, artist, merchant-chief, and, yes, even beggar-man and thief, regardless of his talents, penchants, tendencies, vocations, and race of his ancestors.[3]

Modern behaviorists say that shyness is a learned phobic reaction to social events. This learning may be the product of:

- a prior history of negative experiences with people in certain situations, either by direct contact or by watching others getting "burned";
- not learning the "right" social skills;
- expecting to perform inadequately and therefore becoming constantly anxious about your performance;
- learning to put yourself down for your own "inadequacy"—"I am shy," "I am unworthy," "I can't do it," "I need my Mommy!"

According to behaviorists, a child can learn to become shy by trying to be effective in a world dominated by adults. A forty-nine-year-old teacher relates her story:

> When I was four, I suffered what to me was a very traumatic experience in the art of communication. I remember the kind of day it was, the prep-

arations for going out with my mother, the light in the room, I confess to forgetting what exactly I was trying to communicate and naturally my mother doesn't remember the situation at all. Whatever it was, it was important to me at the time. I was trying desperately to tell my mother something—it was not concrete, but something of an abstract nature, and I simply lacked the vocabulary to make it understandable to my mother. She was straining to understand as I tried one way and then another. Finally, after about five minutes of mutual frustration, she burst out laughing. I cried and could not be comforted. My ideas were lost forever, but my feelings about her, about adults, and about myself were frozen in that moment for many years.

I felt I was a failure. I was ridiculous, incompetent, and stupid. This was reinforced by the general attitude of most adults I grew up among that "children should be seen and not heard," and "things are more important than people." The message was loud and clear that I couldn't do anything right. I learned early to fear and mistrust.

It is also possible to learn to be incompetent—if incompetence gets you the attention you want. Take the class clown who gets into trouble with the teacher for always cutting up and disrupting the class. He may be laughed at by his classmates, scolded by his parents, and punished by the teacher, but he is *noticed* by everyone. Social recognition is one of the most powerful of human reinforcers, and people will often go to great lengths to get a little. Some of us learn to talk too loud, others learn to whine; some get attention by going the wrong way on a football field, getting "sick" and having to be taken care of, or by stumbling while climbing out of the presidential airplane.

The Jewish tradition is rich in its comic derision of such incompetence. The *schlemiel* gets noticed for spilling the soup, taking the wrong plane, locking the car keys in the trunk. The *schlemazel* is the hapless victim of this bumbling incompetence—getting the soup in his lap, being bumped from that plane, having to bring the extra set of keys at 2 A.M.

Curiously, the passive nature of the shy person may be a learned pattern of responding to a televised world. Where there is no other way to relate to the electronic images except by changing channels or tuning out the commercials, our TV-reared generation is learning to let Kojak be tough for them, Rhoda do the talking for them, and Mary Hartmann get in and out of trouble for them. A young man relates his experience with TV:

Perhaps the single greatest factor in my life was television. I was taught manners by my mother and not much by my father, but I was taught almost everything by television. I would estimate an average of at least three hours of TV a day, all my life. The largest factor that TV played in my life is that no feedback is required. When you watch TV, you are *passive.* I have always been good at listening and learning but poor at speaking to others. I would learn in school but not participate. In college I would always sit in the back of the room. Since class participation was usually 10 percent of the grade, my grades suffered from my shyness.

If shyness comes from learning the "wrong" ways to react in the presence of people, it should go away if one is reinforced for practicing the "right" ones. In this view, it is the behavior of the shy person that causes the experience of shyness. Since it is learned, it can be unlearned just as any bad habit or specific phobia, like fear of snakes, for example. In Part II, the social skills that we outline—assertiveness training—are based on this behaviorist approach.

The optimism of the behaviorists is a welcome change from the fatalism of the trait theorists and their "born to be a loser" outlook. However, remember what we already know about the different types of shyness. Some shy people *have* the appropriate social skills already, but a lack of self-confidence prevents them from being socially successful. Teaching the reticent people described in Chapter 2 the proper speaking skills didn't necessarily "cure" their reticence. Sometimes it did, but sometimes it made their shyness worse. Along with supervised, successful practice of social skills must go training to reduce social anxiety, exercises to promote self-esteem, and better insight into some of the irrational bases of one's shyness.

For some of the more extremely shy people—the true blues—particular events may be threatening in a *symbolic* rather than literal way. Their shyness doesn't depend on a distressing personal experience with specific people or situations. Rather, they feel anxious because these people and situations represent unresolved, suppressed conflicts that started early in life. You have, no doubt, recognized a Freudian flavor to this recipe for shyness, as we now move the behaviorists to a back burner.

Over-ego, ergo shyness

Psychoanalytic approaches to shyness are wonderful at explaining everything—but proving nothing. They are filled with scenarios of battles between inner forces, defenses erected, assaults, disintegration, regrouping, guerrilla warfare, double agents, and secret symptom codes waiting to be decoded. But because much of the theory is stated in general terms and replete with abstract, vague concepts, it cannot be scientifically disproven. It is "right" because it doesn't allow itself to be shown "wrong."

Freud, the founder of psychoanalysis, developed this theory from his experiences and insights as a therapist treating neurotic Victorian patients.

Psychological disturbance was viewed by Freud as the outcome of a disharmony between id, ego, and superego, the three basic aspects of personality. Id refers to the instinctual, passionate side of human nature. Ego is that part of the self that perceives reality, that learns what is possible and controls what is practical to do. The superego is the voice of a stern conscience, the monitor of morals, ideals, and social taboos.

The task of the ego is to moderate between the lust of the id and the laws of the superego. When the ego is functioning well, it arranges things so that courses of action are chosen for the self which gratify the needs of the id without violating moral sanctions or social codes of the superego. But that negotiation, like most labor-management arbitration, is neither easy nor ever completely finished. The instinctual urges of the id press for gratification here and now. Powerful among these needs are sexuality and aggression—and there is no way the superego is going to allow those troublemakers of the id to do their thing. Thus, the basic conflict between desire and deprivation rages.

In these terms, shyness is a symptom. It represents a reaction to the unfulfilled primal wishes of the id. Among these wishes is the oedipal desire of the child for mother's total affection to the exclusion of all others, including father.

In various psychoanalytic writings, shyness is traced to different disturbances in the normal development of the personality where id, ego, and superego live in integrated harmony. A sampling of these views provides us with a sense of the psychoanalytically derived origins of shyness.

John, a shy male turned flasher, is understood through the following psychoanalytic explanation of his exhibitionism:

> His unfulfilled longing for his mother's affection and oedipal strivings led to castration fear, aggravated by the fact that his father was realistically a threatening figure. With the stimulation of sexual drive at puberty, John's wishes assumed frankly incestuous implications. All sexual interests consequently became taboo, and shyness ensued, the result of repression. John's exhibitionistic acts represented a "return of the repressed." He expressed perverse sexuality aimed at a substitute figure (a nonincestuous, strange female) as a defense against the more forbidden sexual impulses [toward mother].[4]

Shyness is viewed in part by New York psychoanalyst Donald Kaplan as originating in the preoccupation of the ego with its self—i.e., narcissism. Paradoxically, the shy, unassuming, modest patients he treats appear to be full of grandiose fantasies and hostility. These affects become distorted and displaced because they are not allowed direct expression.

> . . . [I]n shyness the traumatic force of the social event *begins* with a displacement of a "dangerous grandiosity" from elsewhere in the patient's

life where it is active in a subjectively more benign form. The torment embodied in the symptom of shyness—the dread of being overlooked, ignored, rejected—is also displaced on to the social event from subjectively more benign expressions of derogation and disdain elsewhere in the patient's life. . . .

I have also found it clinically remarkable that in solitude morbidly shy persons are inordinately preoccupied with grandiose fantasies that afford enormous pleasure. Indeed, prolonged, vivid daydreaming is an important characteristic of the existence of clinically shy patients. . . .[5]

Other writers lay stress on the process by which the child separates psychologically from the mother and develops its own sense of individuality. If this separation occurs prematurely, if the mother does not fulfill her protective role, trauma results. It is as if the ego were set adrift in a paper boat, aware that a storm is brewing just over the horizon. Psychoanalysts say that this abandoned ego later produces a dread of not being able to cope with the uncertainties of life. This dread is a hallmark of the extremely shy.[6]

We must remember that many psychoanalytic accounts of what makes a person shy come from the more extreme varieties of shyness, the "clinically shy," the "morbidly shy." Therefore, such theories are based on the histories of patients who are severely disturbed or incapacitated by shyness. In some reported cases, the shyness is so great that it prevents the patients from ever leaving their own homes. For some of these patients shyness may indeed be a symptom of deeper mental problems, a smoke screen that hides a psychopathological condition. For such shy people, professional care is clearly necessary. The recommendations in Part II of this book may do little more than scratch the surface of their problem.

However, the psychoanalytic orientation is of value in making us aware of some irrational features in the makeup of normally shy people. It suggests provocative links to needs for power, superiority, hostility, and sex. And it invites us to peek behind the somber curtains into the fantasy world of some shy people.

Actor Michael York describes a driving force in his shy life:

I was shy and yet I had a terrible kind of ambition too. I remember at infants' school—that's what we call it—they were putting on "Little Red Riding Hood." I was just working behind the scenes, and I used to stand there and stare at the kid who was playing the Wolf. I was so envious that I hated him. I just stared and stared. And you know what? He got sick, and I got the part.[7]

A twenty-six-year-old, middle-class male begins to discover his underlying fears and hostility as his shyness lessens:

> The more I discover my own self worth, the more I lose respect for others. Instead of being afraid of people, I have come to regard most people as being irrational. I have a close group of friends, mostly from school, and I find I can no longer relate to them and their goals. They work where they can make the most money and spend their spare time at bars trying to pick up girls for the evening. They like "dope, sex, and cheap thrills."

A young woman from my shyness seminar confides:

> The bathroom was my fantasy land. I'd sit in there and look at the mirror and live thousands of different roles. I could spend hours doing this at a stretch. It occurred to me that this was not a good thing and that I was probably incredibly vain (I'd tell my brother that I was vain in vain) and this bothered me. My solution was to pretend that there was a hidden camera behind the mirror and that Jimmy (the boy I liked) could watch whenever he felt like it. He might not be watching, but there was always that possibility that he was. I would ask myself how I'd feel if he was watching—would he like what he saw, so that even if I wasn't able to tear myself away from the mirror, I would alter my behavior for Jimmy. I now don't feel so guilty doing this and still visit this kind of separate world at times when I'm home.

This egocentric predicament of shyness is also apparent in a woman I have worked with who shrinks from the spotlight she would like to have shining on her at all times:

> I am very shy about dancing. However, there is a real threshold of self-consciousness there, and once I jump that hurdle by getting stoned and by actually dancing, I usually have a wonderful time. In fact, whereas I start out feeling wooden and ill at ease with the music and with my body, and an appropriate object for everyone's amused attention, once I get into it I have the perception that I am the best dancer in the room, and that now I am rightly the object of admiration and awe. My psychiatrist tells me that, rather than feeling hopelessly inferior to everyone, as I always thought I did, I really want to surpass everyone else.

Social programming

Recently the director of a major college's student health service told me that about 500 students a year (5 percent of the student body) came to the center saying they had a special problem. They were lonely. Each student is given a personalized treatment according to what the therapist believes the loneliness reflects. Hardly any of these cases would benefit from traditional Freudian analysis, according to the director. Rather, they represent more conscious on-going problems the ego must cope with in its day-to-day existence.

"Suppose all 500 came to the clinic at the same time to complain of their loneliness?" I asked. "What would the diagnosis be and where would the therapist look for its causes?"

"We'd call the dean or the director of the dormitory and ask what's happening in this campus to create such a mass reaction," he replied.

"But when they dribble in single file, then you ask each one what's wrong with *you,* instead of what's wrong *out there?*"

"Generally."

It's obvious from this exchange that we need also to search for the roots of shyness in the ecology of the social self. The director's bias is similar to that of psychiatrists, psychologists, medical doctors, and those in criminal justice who analyze, investigate, treat, cure, judge, and pass sentence on *individuals* while overlooking and minimizing the power of *situations.* In this section we will review some of the situational forces beyond the individual's control that may help to shape a shy person's pattern of relating to others.

Mobility and loneliness

Vance Packard's *A Nation of Strangers* documents the geographical mobility that has come to be a common experience for the American family. "The average American moves about 14 times in his life time," writes Packard. "About 40 million Americans change their home addresses at least once each year." More than half the 32 million people living on farms in 1940 have migrated in two decades. In many places and for many occupations, transience is a permanent nomadic state. College towns, company towns, travelling sales representatives, pilots, stewardesses, and migrant farm workers are obvious examples of this principle in practice.

The consequence of this new restlessness, according to Packard, "is a substantial increase of inhabitants suffering a loss of community, identity, and continuity. These losses all contribute to a deteriorating sense of well being, both for individuals and for society."[8] And what about the children? What is the impact on the millions of youngsters who are moved about with no voice in the decision? What emotional price do they pay for severed friendships, and the exchange of familiar places and faces for the uncertainty of novelty? And who will replace grandma?

The excruciatingly shy high-school girl who introduced Chapter 1, the one who hid everywhere to avoid people, is a casualty of this mobility factor.

> . . . As I grew up, things got worse. Every year I went to a different school as the year before. We were poor and it reflected on me, so a lot of kids just didn't want to except [sic] me until they needed me and then after they used me, I just waited until they would need me again. I felt like a football during basketball season. I was crawling into a shell and every new school made the lid close more until in ninth grade it closed all the way.

Researcher Robert Ziller has studied, with dramatic results, the psychological effects of geographic mobility.[9] He compared three groups of eighth-grade schoolchildren all living in the state of Delaware. The group with the highest mobility consisted of eighty-three children of U.S. Air Force personnel who had already lived in about seven different communities in their short lifetime. A second, civilian group of sixty children had lived in three or more communities during their lives. And the third group of seventy-six students had lived in one community all their lives.

Various tests were administered to assess each child's sense of identification with children or adults, social isolation, and self-esteem. As you may have guessed, the children who moved a lot were more socially isolated. The Air Force children showed the most extreme results. For them, the self rather than others emerged as the major point of reference. While this self-centered orientation is understandable in response to a constantly changing environment, nevertheless, it fosters a sense of alienation in the mobile child. These children in general tended to describe themselves as "different," "unusual," "strange," and "lonely." Also, they identified more with adults than with other children.

Loneliness—as experienced by the child, the adult, and the older person—is becoming increasingly prevalent, as more and more people are living alone or in ever-smaller families. Americans are marrying later, having fewer children, divorcing more often, and moving greater distances away from "home."

Today the average number of people living in a single household is less than three. We are fast becoming not only a nation of strangers, but a nation of lonely strangers at that.

The individual caught up in these social forces may become shy simply because ready access to other people is difficult. There are fewer occasions to observe warm, giving, sharing relationships among family members or neighborhood friends. Similarly, opportunities to practice conversation, to learn to monitor feedback from others, to negotiate, and to accept and give compliments are few and far between for the isolated person.

One of the saddest sights I have witnessed is the Saturday shopping-mall gangs of lonely children. Driven together for a few hours while mothers do the weekly shopping, they sit bored and expressionless around a center fountain eating slices of pizza or a Big Mac while Muzak fills the void around them. Then, home again to the suburban privacy that affluence has purchased—a privacy that isolates each landowner from the next.

Meanwhile, in the city they fled, fear of crime has turned apartment dwellers into frightened victims under siege. The castle becomes a prison when it is surrounded with iron window fences and triple-locked and bolted doors. Some older women never go out until their husbands come home from work to take them to the supermarket. And for the single elderly, the very real terrors of city life continue to multiply.

Less obvious social forces are also at work to make ours a shyness-generating society. As chain stores replace the less efficient and less economical mom-and-pop stores, we are forced to pay some hidden costs. No longer does one see the "Credit Given Here" sign. Not only do you no longer have credit, you have lost your identity as well if you can't produce three pieces of identification to verify your existence. The friendly small talk with Mr. Bower or Druggist Goldberg is a thing of the past. A small breakdown in the quality of social interaction, a sacrifice for "progress," and a loss, nevertheless, in what we perceive we mean to others and they to us.

When I was growing up in the Bronx, few people owned phones. The neighborhood candy store was the phone center of the block. When Uncle Norman wanted to reach his girlfriend Sylvia, he would first call Charlie's candy store. Charlie would take the call and ask which of us kids wanted to make a few pennies by going to Sylvia's house to tell her of the waiting call. Sylvia, satisfied with her call, would pay the intermediary two or three cents, and the intermediary would in turn spend these earnings on candy or a "2¢ plain" glass of seltzer—in Charlie's candy store, of course. The social link was thus completed. To put two people in contact required the coordinated efforts of at least two other people. The process was clearly slow and inefficient compared to how easy it is now for Norm to dial Syl—if only he'd remember her number and not have to bother the information operator.

But something has been lost. There's no need to rely on or trust others if you can direct dial, no need to even ask for a favor. Sylvia doesn't need to talk to the kids, nor Norman to Charlie the candy-store man. Anyway, they couldn't, because the candy store is not there any more and the kids are in the Smithtown Shopping Mall—if it's Saturday, that is.

The number one syndrome

American values—especially the overemphasis on competition and individual achievement—may also be responsible for the prevalence of shyness. In our culture where, as James Dobson says, beauty is the gold coin of human worth and intelligence its silver coin, shyness may be the debit statement. An eighty-four-year-old great grandmother recalled this source of her lifetime of shyness:

> Another reason that contributed to my lack of self-assurance was, I think, I had two beautiful sisters, one a year and a half older than I with lovely come-hither brown eyes and another sister three years my junior with lovely violet blue eyes, golden hair, and pink and white complexion; and my eyes were plain. As I grew up I felt an ugly duckling between two swans. Neither of those sisters were shy.

The failure of so many to live up to their ideals is often the fault of the ideals and not necessarily a reflection on the person's competence or worth. When will you know you are a success in life? Is it enough to be "average" in looks, intelligence, height, weight, income? Better to be above average. Best to be—the best! Business, the educational system, and sports all stress the need to achieve, to be number one.

After Nolan Ryan, star pitcher with the California Angels, pitched a no-hit game, his mother told inquiring reporters that she was only semi-pleased. After all, it wasn't "a perfect game" (where no one gets to base on balls or errors). Where success is defined as being "the best," isn't "failure" what's left over for everyone else?

The national emphasis on individual achievement, be it Hertz, Little League, Miss America, Ohio State football, or the baton-twirling championship, pits individuals in competition against all comers. Our society has been willing to profit from the achievements of the outstanding few who excel, and take a tax write-off on the failure of the losers.

The importance placed on proving one's worth, on material success, on status, on measurable achievement is acutely felt by children. To be loved, accepted, and valued, they must produce the desirable responses. Recognition of individual worth is contingent on what people have produced—not on what they are. When our relationship to our fellows is purely utilitarian, it is only natural to be anxious about whether what we have to offer is good enough or if we'll be cast off when we are no longer useful to them.

Attributions and labels

Thus far we have talked about shyness as if we were examining a tooth-ache. It has been described as an unpleasant experience, caused by the faulty functioning of our genes, mind, body, or society. Let's turn the analysis around and argue that maybe the shyness *label* comes before the shyness. A fifty-seven-year-old woman writes in support of such a view:

> I consider myself to be shy. I wasn't until I was in the seventh grade
> when a teacher said I was "quiet." From that time on, I have felt I am
> below average in my conversational ability. I now have a fear of rejection.

We are constantly putting labels on other people, on our feelings, and on ourselves. Labels are convenient, simplified summaries of complex experiences: "He's Norwegian," "She's a swinger," "They are boring," "We are honest," "I am a bad boy." However, labels often reveal the values of the labeller as well as communicate objective information. To be labelled "communist" by Senator Joseph McCarthy in the 1950s was to be condemned as an evil tool of Russian totalitarian forces of oppression. It's the other way around for "bourgeois capitalists" in Moscow.

It is important to realize that many times a label is based on little or no concrete information, but is prompted by some personal prejudice. Furthermore, what information there is often is filtered through the sub-jectively tinted glasses of the labeller.

"Mental illness" is a label that is elaborately defined in textbooks on psychiatry. But what is mental illness? Someone *is* mentally ill when an-other person with more power and authority says he or she is. There are no conclusive blood tests, X-rays, or other objective measures that don't rely on the subjective interpretation of the person doing the judging.[10]

To illustrate this point, my colleague David Rosenhan had himself committed to a number of mental hospitals in different parts of the coun-try.[11] A group of his students did likewise. Each one went to the admissions office complaining of hearing voices and ominous sounds. Nothing more. It was enough to get them put behind locked doors. After that, each of these mock patients began to act perfectly normal. The question being studied was how long it would take before they were detected as "normal" and discharged. The answer was "never." The original label of "psychotic" was never replaced by "normal." Getting out required assistance from wives, friends, or lawyers.

Other research also documents the power of labels. Negative reactions to the same target person are greater if the subjects are told in advance that the person is a former mental patient rather than an unemployed person seeking work. If students are told that a member of their group

whom they can't see is "old," they tend to ignore him, pass over his recommendations, and speak slower and louder to him—even though he is their same age.[12]

It is possible, then, for people to adopt and accept a label without concrete evidence to support it—and, subsequently, to make the label stick regardless of what the person labelled does or really is.

Even worse, we are also too ready to pin labels on ourselves without real justification. A typical scenario: I notice I'm perspiring while lecturing. From that I infer, I am feeling nervous. If it occurs often, I might even label myself a "nervous person." Once I have the label, the next question I must answer is, "Why am I nervous?" Then I start to search for an appropriate explanation. I might notice some students leaving the room, or being inattentive. I am nervous because I'm not giving a good lecture. That makes me more nervous. How do I know it's not good? Because I'm boring my audience. I am nervous because I am a boring lecturer and I want to be a good lecturer. I feel inadequate. Maybe I should open a delicatessen instead. Just then a student says, "It's hot in here, I'm perspiring and it makes it tough to concentrate on your lecture." Instantly, I'm no longer "nervous" or "boring." But suppose everyone in the class were shy and no one talked up? Then what would I still be?

Often we leap to labels on the flimsiest of observed evidence. Once labelled is twice proved. Our search for explanations is thereafter *biased*; we accept anything that confirms the label and ignore any disconfirmations.

The label may be all wrong to begin with, as in my overheated lecturer example. It then diverts attention away from the true external cause to a preoccupation with one's own inadequacy. Misattributions developed in this way are also common when it comes to the label "shy," as actress Angie Dickinson describes:

> I believe that people who call you "shy" often don't realize that shyness may be another word for sensitivity. And they don't understand, or don't try to understand your sensitivity. I developed my own trust in myself when I learned to ignore those who were insensitive to me. Being sensitive, as many children and even adults are, can be a nice quality. So I don't allow myself to be shoved into a corner by those people who tend to mistake sensitivity for shyness.[13]

Turning back to the data presented in Chapter 2 on personal reactions to shyness, we can see this labelling process operating. Those who said they were shy did *not* differ from those who said they were not shy in the kinds of people or situations that created *feelings* of shyness in them. Nor did they report different reactions to such feelings. The causes and the effects are comparable, but only one set of people believed they had a shyness problem. Why?

Objectively the situations and experiences are not different; the difference lies in whether or not a person chooses to use the label "shy." Shy people blame themselves; the not-shy blame the situation. "Who likes to make public speeches or go on blind dates? They're a drag," says the not-shy person to account for feelings of discomfort in these situations. In contrast, the shy person says, "I am reacting negatively because I am shy, it's something I am, something I carry around wherever I go." The former focuses outward to external causes that might reasonably produce reactions similar to those caused by shyness: "It's normal, right?" They can then work to change the situation—like turning down the thermostat in an overheated room.

Other views

Other perspectives on human nature—from philosophy, literature, and psychology—could also be applied to an understanding of shyness.

For example, we have not mentioned the conflict between the forces of individuation and deindividuation that is at the foundation of Greek tragedy. The person desires to be singular, unique, recognized as special (individuated). Yet security and immortality are found only in the anonymity of being part of the cycle of nature, being one of the chorus, not standing out as the tragic hero.[14] We have seen this conflict at a psychological level in the shy person shrinking from notice while desiring to stand out, or being noticed because he or she is acting shyly.

Existential views such as those of radical psychiatrist R. D. Laing are relevant to the sense of insecurity that plagues the shy.[15] If we accept that our sense of identity depends on the recognition of others, it then follows that our very existence could be obliterated by them—if they knew the "real" us, or if they chose not to know us at all.

Theories are like enormous vacuum cleaners, sucking up everything in their paths. Each of the theories outlined here has vigorous backers, hawkers of the best vaccum cleaner on the market. We shall borrow freely from any and all of them when we come to design programs for coping with shyness. From attributional notions, we stress changing how you label, observe, and think about shyness. From the behaviorists, we take ideas for changing nonassertive, ineffective, or disruptive behaviors. Psychoanalytic theory sensitizes us to the need for insight into deeper conflicts, of which shyness may be a symptom. The temperament theories are of limited value except in alerting us to individual differences in sensitivity of infants and children, so that we may try to devise ways to provide them with more ideal environments. And, after all is said and done, we challenge the prevailing social and cultural values that have made shyness a national epidemic.

But for now, let's visit shy children at home and in school to investigate how some parents and teachers contribute to the shyness of their children, while others help them to overcome it.

4
parents, teachers, and shy children

B irds don't do it, bees don't do it; but parents and educated teachers do it. They lay shyness trips on their children and students. They do so by tossing around the shy label when it is not deserved, by being insensitive to shyness when it is there, and by creating or perpetuating environments that breed shyness. Sometimes the effect is unintentional:

> I was a very sensitive, highly nervous, self-conscious child, so much so that my parents, with a well-meant but mistaken idea, decided to keep me home to protect me. I was denied formal education, only one-room country school part time until I was sixteen. I knew I was different from my sisters and brothers and tried to hide it, which didn't help. When I was five an aunt (who painted beautifully without any lessons) stood behind me one day and said, "Huh! She's going to be an artist and they are all queer." I never forgot that.

Sometimes shyness is triggered by the personality of the parent:

> My shyness was prompted by my ungrateful sober father whose disposition can be likened only to Sir Walter Scott's description of his father: "A man with a temper constantly unstrung who disapproved of anything and everything we tried to do to please him; who spoke with a forcefulness that no one dared or could ignore." So, shy I was for many years out of sheer frustration!

Or, as another older woman informs us, it can be in the character of the system:

> My mother died when I was five years old and I was reared in a Catholic school. In school the nuns were wonderful and I loved them as my own parents, but they had the habit of insulting you in front of the other children. It made me feel very shy.

One bright undergraduate in the shyness seminar sent shock waves through the class when he revealed that his mother, in town for Saturday's football game, told him that "he was boring." "She asked me if I knew I bored her or was it unintentional, and why couldn't I be more fun like my roommate was." Who would have thought a mother could make such an evaluation of her child? For the extremely shy in the class, this was a confirmation of their worst fears: *everyone* out there is a potential Grand Inquisitor, even mothers.

To get a better sense of the effect of the school and home environments on shyness in children, we observed every grade from nursery school through junior high in several Palo Alto, California schools, and we interviewed and surveyed the parents of the children in these schools.

There's no place like home

Be it ever so humble, it can still make you shy. While it is easy to say "shyness begins at home," it is not obvious which factors in the home environment contribute the most to shyness. Since shyness takes many forms in its expression, intensity, and dynamics, it is safe to assume that its origins will also be varied. While a certain event or family experience may be significant in the early life of the child who becomes shy, a brother or sister in the same family will be unaffected by the same kind of incident. We need more research before we can definitely predict the influence of the family or schools on the development of shyness. However, we have found interesting patterns of shyness in four areas: the self-image of the shy child, the child's birth order, how well parents and children predict each other's shyness, and the extent to which shy parents have shy offspring. Let's look at a group of ninety children, ages twelve and thirteen, and some of their parents.

Self-image of the shy child

A sad picture emerges from the self descriptions of shy boys and girls. The boys feel they are too tall, too fat, too weak, too ugly, less strong, and generally less attractive compared to their not-shy classmates. Similarly, the shy girls are more likely to describe themselves as thin, unattractive, and less intelligent than their peers. All this adds up to the most important aspect of self-image for these young children: they see themselves as "less popular" than the not-shy students. This is staggering, especially for the shy boys. None of them feels he is "popular" and three-fourths say they are downright "unpopular." Yet, paradoxically, not-shy kids say they like being alone more than shy students.

Are shy children really less attractive, or do they only feel that way because they generally sell themselves short? Is their lower self-esteem the consequence of their less attractive physical attributes, or the other way around? Or, as we hinted in the last chapter, do they feel inadequate because their standards are unrealistically high? They are probably their own worst critics. This conclusion is supported by another study of elementary-school children which showed that the shys are more intolerant of others than the not shys and, at the same time, less self-confident.[1]

An important aspect of the shy child's self-image is also revealed in answers to the question: "Do you ever feel other children would not like you if they knew what you were thinking?" Shy children think so. The shy female's conception of her intelligence further illustrates this mind set. Among *both* junior-high-school and college women in our surveys, those who are shy rate themselves as less intelligent than do not-shy females or any males. These shy girls and women stigmatize themselves by saying, "I'm not as smart as the other students here." Research by other investigators[2] shows shy children are no less intelligent, nor do they do more poorly on achievement tests than the not shy.

But even when their school grades are just as good as those of everyone else, shys don't change their put-down label. They only change the evidence they use to confirm it: "I don't have as much to say as the other kids; I'm not as intelligent as them." They think they're not talking because they aren't very intelligent, while, in fact, they're just anxious about talking out in class. They equate their silence with lack of ability.

The birth-order factor

Considerable research indicates that a child's order of birth in a family has a host of psychological, social, and vocational consequences. For example, of the first twenty-three American astronauts, twenty were first borns or only children. Proportionately more first borns also go on to college. In an anxiety-provoking situation, however, first borns get more upset and need to affiliate with others more than do the more self-reliant later borns.[3]

Parents are more anxious and concerned about the health and future of first borns than they are of their later born children (they mellow out as they become old hands at being parents). They set higher ideals for first borns than they do for the younger children and, consequently, place more demands on them. If the first born has the stuff (competence, skills, intelligence), then this greater parental push will pay off in terms of social and vocational success. They are likely to try harder, go for more prizes, and succeed. But if they don't have the talent and still experience those same pressures, inadequacy and low self-esteem follow. Dr. Lucille Forer, a clinical psychologist, concludes that "firstborns (both male and female) followed by other children have more need for approval than later borns and only children. Therefore, firstborns, in general, have lower self-esteem than later children do."[4]

It is likely, then, that an awful lot of first borns feel they have not measured up to the goals set by Mom and Dad. In light of this, how might shyness and birth order be related? If feelings of inadequacy are common to each, then perhaps more first borns are also shy than are later borns.

Some support for this idea comes from our evidence that significantly more preteen first borns are shy, while a significantly greater percentage of later borns are not shy. By college age, shyness is not any more prevalent among first borns than later borns. It may be that shy first borns are less likely to make it to college, because their low self-esteem, feelings of inadequacy, and nonassertiveness prevent them from making the grade—even though they are equally intelligent.

Another way to look at the relationship between birth order and a child's popularity with peers is in terms of the power disadvantage of later-born siblings. Later-born children may learn to develop more effective interpersonal skills (negotiation, ingratiation, persuasion, compromise, for example) because they can't rely on the kinds of power their older siblings enjoy. If so, then later-born children should be both more popular and more liked by their age mates. Convincing support for this line of reasoning has just been put forth by a team of southern California researchers.[5] Among a large sample of 1,750 grade-school children, later borns were found to be more popular than their early-born peers on measures of friendship and playmate choices. Teachers' ratings further indicated that early borns were less effective in their use of social skills in the classroom and play situations.

These findings point to another possible explanation for the development of shyness in first-born children. They are less popular because they have not developed their social skills to the same extent as later borns. Later borns do so as a matter of social survival, having to interact with their siblings who are initially bigger, smarter, and tougher. They learn to use social finesse instead of raw power to achieve their ends. They act more like wily lightweight boxers than powerful heavyweight punchers in the contest for social control of their environment. In the process, however, the less popular early borns are more likely to label themselves as "shy," because they accurately perceive themselves as "unpopular." According to such a view, they become shy because they are not popular, rather than the reverse.

The most ambitious investigation relating shyness to birth order comes from the University of California Guidance Study of 252 children whose development has been observed from birth (back in 1928) to maturity.[6] At virtually every age (from 7 to 14) for which shyness information was gathered, girls are reported to be more shy than boys, and first-born girls are generally much more shy than later-born girls. First-born boys were more shy than later-born boys only until age 7; after that, birth order is not significantly related to shyness. By age 14, shyness totally disappeared in the sample of boys! The drop in shyness among boys with the onset of their teen years also occurred for instances of their physical timidity, oversensitiveness, and specific fears. This information comes from mothers' evaluations, not the self-ratings of the children. The mothers may have underreported these "negative" traits in their sons because they conflicted with the masculine ideal of the man they wanted their boys to become. Perhaps with the decline of the John Wayne he-man ideal we are witnessing in our day, modern mothers will be better able to tell it like it is—rather than as they would like it to be. We have evidence that this is so.

Sensitivity to shyness

Children are totally insensitive to their parent's shyness; it is the rare child who labels a parent shy. While nearly half of all parents of the junior-high-school children we studied were shy by their own admission, only 10 percent of the parents were judged so by the children. This is understandable, since parents are in positions of control and authority in their homes and may not reveal their shy side to their children. Also, since shyness is viewed as undesirable by many children, it may be threatening to think of their parents in these terms. At this young age, the parent is still idealized as all knowing and all powerful—not dumb, ugly, or weak. However, when asked to single out teachers who are shy, these same children can do so. It is not their inability to judge shyness in adults, only their unwillingness to see it in their parents.

How good are parents in detecting shyness in their children? At first glance, our information indicated modern mothers were quite sensitive to the nuances of feelings and actions of their shy children, while fathers were insensitive on that score. Not-shy fathers were not very accurate in detecting shyness either way. However, shy fathers accurately described their children as shy two-thirds of the time. But they were not nearly as accurate with their not-shy offspring. It is the shy mothers who have the most sensitive shyness radar systems operating. They know when a shy child is shy (80 percent on target) and when a not-shy child is not (75 percent accuracy). Such a high level of accuracy is rare in psychological studies of interpersonal judgments.

Shyness-generating parents

What kind of children do shy parents have? Of the children of shy fathers, three-fourths were also shy; a similar ratio appeared between not-shy fathers and their not-shy children. Not-shy mothers also had more not-shy children than ones who labeled themselves as shy. The same pattern holds for shy mothers, 20 of their 32 children (62%) were also shy. In general, then, about 70 percent of the time parents and children share the same shyness label; they tend to be shy together.

Although the high similarity of parent and child shyness tempts one to agree with the personality-trait theorists that shyness runs in families, a note of caution is in order. Shy children are not likely to be found in families where both parents themselves are not shy. Having at least one shy parent increases the chances a child will become shy, but families with two shy parents don't have any more shy children than those with only one shy parent.

In our study, the shyness of the parent was highly correlated to the shyness of the child. But, when we looked at the child's brothers and sisters, they tended not to be shy. One possible interpretation is that shy parents are likely to have at least one child who is similarly shy. That child probably is their first. Later children are less often shy because of the somewhat lower aspiration levels parents set for them. In addition, families subconsciously arrange roles for each member to play—for example, Jon is a talker and Harold is a passive listener. So, each child's self-definition is influenced in part by the expectations the others have toward him or her. Jon talks more at the dinner table to compensate for the nonresponsiveness of shy Harold. This role taking is not a conscious act. These expectations of the group may also work to suppress the *unusual* output of one of its members—e.g., to ignore the quiet Harold who suddenly "talks too much."

Once our parents, our siblings, our friends, and our enemies get a fixed notion about what we are all about, they work to prevent us from changing, for better or for worse. They will fill in for, or make excuses for, our deficiencies, suppress our excesses, and hold us on a steady course to ensure that "we act like ourselves." Their script and their navigation map too often define what that "self" is.

The operation of expectations about how we "should" behave are well illustrated in this letter to "Dear Abby" about Norton's problem.

> Dear Abby: My husband is almost perfect. We've been married for three years and get along fine, but there is one problem. When we are with people Norton is very quiet. I am forever making up excuses for him, like, "Oh, Norton is tired tonight," or, "Norton isn't feeling very well."
>
> When he and I are alone together he is fine, but when we're in company, he clams up. People keep asking me if he's mad.
>
> Have you any suggestions for him? Or for me?   *Norton's Wife*

> Dear Wife: Tell Norton that silence is sometimes mistaken for unfriendliness, so to please try to be more sociable. But don't nag him about it. He's probably shy, and too much pushing on your part will make him even more self-conscious.[7]

Everyone is disturbed by Norton. He's unsociable. He's unfriendly. He's mad. He's sick. He's exhausted. He's self-conscious and he's also "probably shy." He is all these things, and less. All we know for sure is that Norton does not talk as much in company as his wife would like him to. He is not fulfilling her expectations and that upsets her. But before advising her of what to do for Norton's problem, one should be certain it isn't "Norton's wife's problem" instead. How so?

- Maybe Norton is as quiet when alone with his wife as he is with company. He doesn't change in the two situations, only her expectations do.
- Maybe it is Ms. Norton who changes when she is in company—talks too much or acts in ways that embarrass her husband. That's why he clams up.
- Maybe Norton does not like her friends and is making a sacrifice just to accompany her, and he's too much of a gentleman to tell her.
- Maybe the company Ms. Norton keeps all talk a lot or talk about topics that Norton has no interest or expertise in. His silence then may be purposely chosen to save face (or not embarrass his social-climbing wife).
- Maybe Norton's silence conceals his anger at the typically bigotted conversation, or his moral outrage at the grossness of the table talk.

And anyway, why doesn't anyone tell Norton directly that they think he is a drag? Last but far from least of all the alternative scenarios we could make for "All Quiet on Norton's Front" centers on Norton's shyness. Why did Norton's wife have to wait for "Dear Abby" to supply the shyness diagnosis? Often, parents apply this same kind of social pressure to their children, "forcing" them to become shy, and then failing to notice the problem they have created.

Shyness and schools

A young child needs confidence in his (or her) environment and security in his (or her) relationships in order to grow and learn well. Confidence and security come from living in a world with some degree of order and predictability as well as with flexibility and freedom to experiment, explore, and cope with new and unfamiliar situations . . . warm and understanding teachers help the child learn to share with other children space, equipment, play materials, affection, and attention, and to get along happily and successfully in a group of children.

Catalog Description, Bing Nursery School,
Palo Alto, California

This description of the ideal home and school of the young child is a prescription for shyness prevention. All children need a sense of belonging. They need to feel that home and school are *safe* places, places where they are recognized for their personal worth, where their opinions are valued, and where their uniqueness is cherished. School and home should be places of refuge from anxiety, not sources from which self-doubt first springs. They should be "power spots" where a child learns intuitively the power of unconditional love and the strength of learning how to learn.

Schools are good hideouts for the shy if teachers are insensitive to the fact that they are fugitives from participation instead of pleasingly passive pupils. Visits to classrooms and talks with elementary school teachers confirmed what several previous studies had shown—teachers in general did not perceive shyness in their students.[8] Those studies showed no correlation between self-reports of the children and teachers' predictions. When I asked teachers to point out their shy students to me, some said there were none, while others could identify several of the shyness-crippled students. Teachers who themselves were shy reported having more shy pupils, that is, they were more aware of their presence.

Marilynne Robinson, a gifted second-grade teacher, is sensitive to the problem that shyness poses for her pupils and the role of schools in adding to the problem:

> Children who are shy in the classroom fear running and dancing to rhythm records. Their voices can barely be heard when asked a question, and will frequently answer, "I don't know." They are afraid to sing out, speak out, and in general, afraid to make mistakes. They sit back and wait for someone to ask them to play. If this doesn't happen, they may wander around the playground sometimes finding a "sore finger" so that they may see the nurse.
>
> As long as parents, the community, and the institutions place such strong emphasis on grades and reading level, our children will feel less confident and less able to feel joy in their lives. Due to the strong emphasis on being able to read in our institutions, those with a slower start are disadvantaged to begin with. They become real prisoners in our schools.
>
> Take the case of Jay Jay.
>
> Jay Jay was a loving eager child, entering second grade. He came from a low socioeconomic background and spoke pidgin English. He had slipped into the "low group" toward the middle of first grade. Our school at that time sent all their children out to top, middle, and low reading groups, much to my dismay. I was ineffectual in getting the "higher ups" to change this, so I offered to take the "low group." I had great visions of improving self-images, and starting these children on the road to becom-

ing great readers. The children soon got the picture that they were in the low group and that there was no way to move up. The middle and high classes were too full.

Jay Jay was teased about being in the low group, but continued to work hard. As the years went by, Jay continued to be in the low groups. There's rarely a way to move up, once one is labeled in the early years.

Jay Jay found he had some esteem by being an excellent athlete. This worked well for him until his friends grew in size, and he remained small. At the intermediate school there were no longer any recesses to play ball. Now it was real competition in sports. The big boys made the team. The small boys, like shy Jay Jay, didn't qualify for the "real" sports.

Jay Jay is now entering the eighth grade. If he can excel at the hi-jacking game ("You got quartah?—Search—Take"), or gambling in the bathrooms, he may make it in the underworld, and perhaps end up in another one of society's institutions—prison.[9]

"If only Jay Jay had more brains, then he wouldn't have the trouble with shyness and self-doubt!" This is not so, even for the intellectually outstanding students operating in an academic economy where brain power is the measure of one's worth, and every few years inflation sets in. Just when you are the hotshot of elementary school, it's time to move along to junior high, to high school, to college, to graduate or professional school, to the firm, etc. At each rite of passage only the best may move on; but half of them will be below the new average of the smaller, more "elite" group. When self-worth is based so much on social comparison and the stakes keep going up, it's hard not to fear that the others will discover you've been bluffing all along.

Friday in Mrs. Gainey's sixth-grade class at P.S. 25 in New York City was the weekly day of reckoning for us. The mornings were spent taking tests which she graded during lunch period (who ate?). When we reassembled after recess, all thirty of us cleared out our belongings from the "old" desks and stood at attention around the perimeter of the classroom. We waited to discover for whom the bells would toll and for whom the chimes would ring out. On the basis of a combined average of the test scores, each child was ranked from one to thirty and seated accordingly. The best and the brightest would be placed up front from left to right in the first row closest to the teacher's desk. There would always be a lot of tension between these ambitious little hotshots to determine if they would keep their exalted places or move even further toward Row 1, Seat 1. There was also the sex thing: would a boy beat out Joanie this week or would the girls continue their stranglehold on the top spot?

After the first ten names were sung out by the teacher and the pupils took their seats, the tension eased somewhat as the insignificant middle-level kids were put into their places. As Mrs. Gainey got down to the final ten kids already standing nervously at the back of the room, all forty eyes were riveted on them. Accompanying each name called was the math grade, spelling grade, history grade, and science grade. Smiles broke into snickers as these grades got lower and lower. Sometimes you'd have to bite the inside of your mouth not to laugh out loud as these unfortunates squirmed in agony. It didn't help to have the teacher remind us not to laugh at them because one day we might be in the same boat and then we'd be sorry. Unimaginable! As usual, "Baby" Gonzales brought up the rear. I was sure he did so on purpose as a status thing to hear the teacher say, "And last again this week, Mr. Gonzales." No one laughed or looked his way; "Baby" was the biggest kid in the class and did not "work and play well with others."

I can empathize with Baby Gonzales. Yet, until recently, I was a taskmaster to my own college students. I was part of the system that forced students to give public reports rather than privately discuss ideas. I was unconsciously encouraging competition for grades rather than learning for the sake of mastering a challenge. I changed when my prison research forced me to realize I had become a controlling guard, and my shyness research gave me some idea of what my prisoner-students were experiencing.

On the basis of our observations of schoolchildren in their classes and college students carefully observed in experimental situations, as well as in our shyness clinic, we can make the following conclusions about the shy students:

- They are reluctant to initiate conversation, activities, add new ideas, volunteer, or ask questions.

- They are reluctant to structure situations that are ambiguous.

- As expected, shy students talk less than not shys during most interactions with classmates. They allow more silent periods to develop and interrupt less than not shys.

- Unstructured permissive situations, such as a dance, create special problems for the shy that are not apparent when the guidelines for appropriate behavior are more spelled out, as in a lecture class.

- In situations where initiative must be taken in male-female encounters, shy males have a harder time initiating conversations than shy females. Men show decreased rates of talking and eye contact. Shy women react by smiling and nodding more when they are made more anxious.

- Shy students use fewer hand gestures during interviews than not-shy students.

- Shy children spend more time in their seats, wander around less, and talk to fewer other children. They obey orders and are rarely troublesome.

- Rarely are the shy chosen for special duties such as teacher's errand monitor.

- They get fewer social rewards and give fewer strokes in return than do the not shys.

Shyness in the classroom

"Teach, I need help. I can't figure it out."

"Okay, Robert, now what seems to be puzzling you with the math lesson?"

"I don't remember what you said about which of these numbers goes into which."

The teacher helps and Robert completes the rest of the math problems on his own. He then gets to play "space flight" with the other children who join the game in progress as they finish their mathematics problems.

Warren doesn't finish in time, although his head is buried deep in the math problems. He doesn't get to play in the game and he gets an "unsatisfactory" on the lesson. Double trouble for Warren.

This scenario was repeated in many of the classes we observed—only the names of the students and the content of the lesson changed. The brighter children who weren't shy readily asked for the help they needed, and got it every time from responsive teachers. Warren, like other shy not-so-brights, could neither handle the work on his own nor ask for assistance. Even with the model of Robert in the next seat getting the help so easily, Warren could not bring himself to raise his hand, to call for the personal attention he so desperately needed.

I remember one day way back when I was in second grade. The little girl seated in front of me was squirming in her seat long enough that it was obvious to us kids where she had to go. Her hand went up, but Mrs. Bachman did not notice it. The hand began waving more frantically until it caught the teacher's attention.

"Where are your manners, young lady? Don't you know any better than to wave your hand in someone's face when they are talking? You have to learn to be more polite; wait until I have completed the lesson and then you may ask whatever it is that is just so urgent. Do you all understand that?"

"Yeess, Mrs. Bachman," we all chorused back.

The little girl wet her pants—and then some. The teacher got furious at her, but for us it was the funniest thing imaginable. "She peed in her pants. She wet the floor. Teacher's mad, but we want more."

I don't recall what the little girl's name was, but I vividly remember the nickname we gave her of "Pissha." It stuck until at least the sixth grade when we moved on to different junior high schools and I never saw her again. I wonder if she also remembers it, after all these years? We can never know the lasting effect of such childhood traumas, but I'd wager they are not filed away in her memory under "humorous anecdotes."

This inability to ask for help is one of the most serious by-products of shyness. In this case, it affected both Warren's academic performance and his opportunity to interact with others in the space-flight game. This same reluctance to seek aid is typical of shy college students. When asked, "If you had a personal problem that was important to you, would you seek help from others for it?" Many more shys reply, "No way."

For their part, what do the shys contribute to the class and to the teacher? Well, they don't make trouble and they don't make noise, which adds up to they aren't a "problem." But what feedback do they give to our stroke-deprived teachers? Not much to be sure. They don't ask stimulating questions. They don't bring in interesting things for show and tell. They don't sing out loud; many of them don't sing period. And they certainly don't become teachers' pets.

In short, the shys don't engage the teacher on a personal level, do not allow her or him to offer the counsel and expertise they are ready to give, and offer little or no feedback for the efforts the teacher is making. No wonder teachers are insensitive to them. In a very negative way, they have beat the system, and the system will let them hide out in a nice warm schoolroom for the next twelve or twenty years, without intervention.

Teachers, too, can be shy, like most everyone else. And when they are, teaching is never just a casual job. Especially not that horrible first day of each new school year. Facing an audience of total strangers where you are expected to talk, lecture, enlighten, and even entertain can be paralyzing.[10] An elementary-school teacher sums up the feeling, "You're on stage every minute, and you're so conscious of the reaction of the children . . . they notice everything you wear—your clothes, your shoes, your rings. They even say something if I wear different color lipstick."

Another teacher remembers his first teaching assignment. "During the first hour, I thought I was never going to make it through the day, that I was going to be sick to my stomach, I was so nervous."

For some, the solution lies in trying to anticipate and plan activities down to the last second. But with so much attention to keeping the butter-flies from taking over, there's not much left. It becomes difficult to notice any but the most obvious students—the assertively bright talkers and, of course, the troublemakers. When a teacher loses control of the class, for whatever reason, troublemakers multiply and all of a sudden there is only time and energy for discipline.

Some shy college professors prefer large formal lecture courses to small informal seminars, despite the greater work required in the big class. They find security in structure. Lectures ensure a set format, an outline, rules for listening, and not much interruption. The professor can prepare a game plan and usually stick to it—a good offense to cover one's weak defense. To the not shy, the informalities of the seminar provide open-ended freedom to explore ideas; but to the shy, the seminar is a dreaded, torturous route through mind traps set by critical, brilliant, or incompre-hensible student questions. In addition, the emotional detachment possible from the lectern is challenged by the intimacy of the small class.

Shyness and memory

It's obvious by now that shyness has undesirable social consequences, but can it also have a negative effect on the thought processes required for affective academic performance?

> One of the key things about shyness as I have found is that the worse effects of shyness cause a person to be so self-preoccupied that, truly, he simply misses what is going on, doesn't hear, or see. For instance, I often find myself unable to follow what's going on in a conversation because I've been so nervously conscious of myself.

This middle-aged businessman puts his finger on an interesting issue: Does the anxiety associated with shyness interfere with your attention dur-ing a distressing experience, and thus impair memory?

To answer this question, an experiment was performed in our labora-tory in which male students were asked to evaluate a speech given by a female student.[11] Half the males described themselves as not shy, the others said they were basically shy, especially with women. Each subject was paired with the same attractive woman who worked with us. Each man listened to her informative speech and then was tested for how much of it he remembered. Each man was obviously observed from behind a two-way mirror.

A third of the men were alone in the laboratory room with the attractive woman and were allowed to ask questions and talk to her during and after her talk; another third were also alone with her, but were only allowed to listen, not to interact; and the last third were alone in the room with a TV monitor on which she was seen giving the same speech. We predicted that shy males would have a harder time remembering what she said the more anxious they felt. Which situation above do *you* think would cause the most anxiety?

The men felt the most discomfort in the TV-speech situation and the least in the direct interaction situation. Are you surprised? Well, let's think about it. Remember what we have recently learned: shys are concerned about being evaluated and about reacting in unstructured situations. When they are alone in the room with the TV-presented speech (and researchers watching from behind a two-way mirror), it is most evident that *they* are the subject of investigation, not the speech maker. When they are allowed to ask questions and interact, they have been given a public sanction by the researchers to take action in the course of evaluating *her*.

As anxiety goes up and the self-monitor is switched on, the shys pay less attention to all of the information that is coming at them. Then the agony of shyness impairs memory. Shy men in the TV-speech situation had the poorest recall of the speech—significantly more so than the not shys or the men in any of the other two situations.

We noted an interesting effect when all subjects were asked to rate the attractiveness of the woman speech maker. Shy males "saw" this beautiful woman as *less* attractive than the not shys did, and even as less attractive than the average woman on campus. It appears that shyness can cause a person to lose not only his tongue, but his memory and perception as well.

Invulnerable children

Psychologists have coined the term "invulnerables" to refer to those children who, though battered and buffeted by stressful, deprived childhood experiences, nevertheless rise above it and end up as normal, healthy adults. Research evidence is beginning to support such a conception and carry it further. Many eminent people in such diverse fields as politics, the arts, and science come from backgrounds that would be considered pathological. People like Eleanor Roosevelt, former President Gerald Ford, and Senator Daniel Patrick Moynihan somehow had the resiliency to bounce back from a calamitous beginning in life to be highly successful.[12]

One clinical study of 100 males, all of whom came from backgrounds filled with trauma and conflict, concludes, "Despite these childhood circumstances, it seems clear that in the present, as adults, these men must be regarded as [normal], or even in most instances superior."[18]

Such a "catastrophe theory" of child development runs contrary to traditional ideas that deprived, abusing environments breed madness and badness. Serene, benign, enriched environments were thought to be the cradles of sanity and adult success. The support for this view came largely from the observation that adults who were mentally ill or law breakers came from impoverished or high-stress backgrounds. The thinking behind this is faulty. Only a minority of all those who grew up under adverse circumstances are in our jails and mental hospitals. Those who bend instead of breaking may develop and utilize the self-reliance necessary to carve a significant place for themselves in society.

Perhaps the next generation will come through the shyness conditioning outlined in this book without the psychic numbing of chronic shyness. We hope so. But, in the meantime, it would be well for us to investigate further the children who are invulnerable to all that home, school, and society can do to make them incapacitatingly shy. The research is comforting, because it holds out hope for those of our children who must face not the best we can give at home or in school, but sometimes the worst.

Comedienne Carol Burnett is a person gifted with the special ability to make others laugh. In a candid telephone interview she confided how her childhood shyness made for many unhappy days at home and in school.[14] She describes how her comedy has helped her cope with her childhood anxiety and shame over not being fully accepted, appreciated, and admired.

Burnett	I think I was shy pretty much at the start, mainly around my mother. She was a very, very outgoing, beautiful woman. She had one big major problem, she was an alcoholic later on, and my Dad was too. They were both very attractive, beautiful people. He always reminded me of Jimmy Stewart and she was a little like a fire ball. I knew I was not an attractive child and so I think I was shy mostly because of my appearance. I tried to make up for it when I was little by being good in athletics and I would try to run fast and beat all the boys in school and think they might like me because I was a fast runner. And so I always kind of joked around with the kids—and clowned around more at school than I did at home—just to get over the fear of not being liked because I was poor and not very pretty.
Zimbardo	You weren't the class clown were you?
Burnett	No, but I was with some of my other girl friends at lunch time. I was very quiet in school and I was a good student—I did what

the teacher said—I respected the authority. And so consequently, I was pretty much a square in school, very much so. I was not really popular with the boys you would want to be popular with like the football players, but then I developed some very nice friendships with other boys in school who were kind of in the same boat I was.

Zimbardo   You mean they were also shy?

Burnett   Yes, they were kind of shy and also not attractive. But still, I would think to myself, "Oh gosh, I sure wish the captain of the football team would smile at me, or know my name." My mother wanted me to become a writer—she said no matter what you look like you can always write. So I said to her, "Okay I'll be a writer," and I became editor of the school paper at Hollywood High— and I was pretty good.

I took Theatre Arts English at UCLA on the pretext to major in playwriting, but I think deep down in my heart I wanted to get up on a stage, but I would never admit it. I remember one time when I was very small—I have a very beautiful cousin who is nine months older than I am—blonde, petite, and gorgeous. She took all kinds of singing and dancing and acting lessons. I remember one time I wanted to tap dance like her but I couldn't tap dance, so I went into the closet and started to tap dance. But I stopped the minute my mother opened the closet door.

I'm painting my mother as a kind of villainess, but she wasn't. I had good fun with her and I adored her and I know she loved me. It was just that I was never given a heck of a lot of support, so that when I did do a play at UCLA, I didn't want any of my family to know in case I fell flat on my face. I was surprised to discover that I didn't. Instead, I got laughs and all of a sudden people on campus started coming up to me and saying, "Say, I saw you in that play and you were funny." And I was asked to lunch with a couple of the senior bigwigs on campus and I as a lowly freshman was overwhelmed by it.

Then another boy stopped me on campus and said, "Can you carry a tune?" and I said, "Yeah, but I can't sing in public or anything." He said, "Well, it's a comedy song, 'Adelaide's Lament' from *Guys and Dolls*." As long as it's funny, but don't let me be serious, I can't be serious about it because I don't know what sort of a voice I have, and if you don't have a pretty voice you don't want to sing a pretty song. So I sang a comedy song and it went very well and my mother came to see me and she was stunned. And then I got hooked and knew I wanted to be a musical comedy performer. It upset my mother and my grandmother but I told them, "That's really where I feel loved by other people, where I'm making some kind of a mark for myself. It's not in my writing, and it's not in my drawing." (I was a pretty good little artist.) What I wanted from then on was the direct feeling of a response as I do something. And that's where performing came in. And as it is now, I'm not on when I'm off—you know what I mean by that? I'm not a stand-up comic. I still find it very difficult to sing a straight song.

Zimbardo Difficult in what sense?

Burnett I get scared. I think people expect me to be funny and I get a lot of mail saying, "Why don't you just quit clowning around sometime and sing a straight song?" And the people on the show try to get me to do it. I do it, but I'm not comfortable.

Zimbardo Why do you feel that way?

Burnett It's a hang-up from my youth. I feel that in comparison with people who really earn their living singing (like Edie Gormé or Helen Reddy), what right do I have to sing a straight song? I could do it in a book musical through a character—but not as Carol Burnett coming out in a pretty dress pretending to sing a straight song—it's a lot of medicine for me to swallow.

Zimbardo Is it being able to step out of yourself and into a role, a character behind a mask of anonymity that enables a basically shy person to perform in public?

Burnett Right—you're somebody else. You're not you. That's why if you become someone else it's a little easier. You see also, I have the best job in the world for somebody like me. When I was growing up I went to the movies with my grandmother—I saw about eight movies a week—and I was growing up in the era of Judy Garland, Betty Grable, Joan Crawford. I used to go home after the film, and I'd get my girl friends and we'd play acting out the movies we saw. Now I still can do that. I can be Betty Grable one week—and I can be Joan Crawford another week—I've got wigs, I've got costumes, I have an orchestra—I mean I'm a grown-up, but I'm still a kid.

Zimbardo Are there still situations you feel shy in when you are not performing and are the other Carol Burnett?

Burnett Yes. If I meet someone I'm in awe of, and I'm in awe of a lot of people. For example, the first time I met James Stewart I couldn't speak, because I've loved him all my life—since my father resembled him. You know what I did next, I turned right around and stepped into a bucket of whitewash—dragged it all the way out across the set, and never went back I was so humiliated. Two years ago I met Cary Grant and again I could hardly speak. What came out of my mouth, I wish I could have put right back in. I said to Cary Grant, "Oh you're a credit to your profession." I felt like a real ninny. He came up and said, "I'm a fan of yours," and he was just delightful, but I could hardly speak—I felt like I was ten years old again. So, I think some of those early feelings never leave. In a way, I'd rather be shy that way than to come on too strong. It would be nice to have a happy medium, as long as people could be secure within their own being.

Zimbardo   Yes, shyness becomes a problem when it is an inhibiting force that keeps you from doing things you want to do and could do.

Burnett   And saying stupid things or doing stupid things.

Zimbardo   Is there some lesson you have learned from your own experience with shyness that you could pass on to others, to your many fans?

Burnett   I tell my three daughters that the important thing is to know that other people have the same problems you have and not to be so selfish as to think the world revolves around what people think you look like, what you're feeling and how you act, or the fact that a boy did not come up and ask you to dance. They're not always evaluating and judging you in critical ways. They're thinking about themselves and you have to come out and reach out to people because when we touch another person we're touching ourselves at the same time—we are helping ourselves. I truly believe we are all one. We really are, and the more you smile and are outgoing to people the more you are going to get that back—you know you reap what you sow. I mean it's a cliché, but it's a cliché because it's so true. Then just to go on and make contact with other people. If you see a kid in school who is a little shy, or isn't getting along too well with some of the other kids and looks a little unhappy, that's when you should reach out. When you do, you are going to open up a little flower there and you'll discover something wonderful.

Zimbardo   Yes, that people are beautiful.

Burnett   Right. And all they need is some TLC—a little tender loving care is the best antidote for shyness.

We turn next to consider the difficulties shy people have in giving or getting their fair share of TLC.

5
friends, lovers, and shy strangers

Which of us has known his brother?
Which of us has looked into his father's heart?
Which of us has not remained forever prison-bent?
Which of us is not forever a stranger and alone?

Look Homeward, Angel

T homas Wolfe's poignant questions have special meaning for all of us, but especially for the chronically shy person. Shyness, as we have seen, is a common experience and one with profound personal consequences.

Many of us have special fears; we're scared of flying or the dark or whatever. However, there are certain things most of us can do to accommodate our phobias. The person afraid of heights can live in a ranch house or a basement. Airplane phobics can take trains, snake phobics can live in cities, and those afraid of the dark can sleep with the lights on. But what about people who are afraid of other people? In successfully avoiding the object of their fear, shy people condemn themselves to become strangers in a strange land. And they suffer for it.

A tale is told of Frederick II, a thirteenth-century ruler of Sicily, who believed that all children were born with already existing knowledge of an ancient language. Without any experience or training, the mature child would begin spontaneously to use this language. To test his belief, the king ordered a group of newborn infants to be raised in silence by foster mothers. They were never allowed to hear human sounds. What did this experiment prove? Did the children speak the king's ancient language when they first talked? The chronicles of history note: "But he labored in vain, because all the children died. For they could not live without the petting and the joyful faces and loving words of their foster mothers."

Ultimately, shy people isolate themselves from the warmth of human contact that is essential to all of us. They often fail to convert acquaintances into friends, and, more often, friends into lovers. Many live by the gold-plated rule, "Give nothing to others as you would have them give nothing to you." No commitment, no sharing, no obligation, no responsibility, no favors to be returned or expected.

But no man or woman can exist happily with the terrible knowledge that they are not needed by some other person. Over a lifetime, the actual pain of feeling inconsequential, irrelevant, and inconspicuous is far greater than the imagined pain of an occasional rejection. So how does the chronically shy person live without the comforts and caring of friends, the loving words of family, and the passionate embrace of a loved one? This crucial problem of interpersonal relationships—the human connection—is what this chapter is all about.

The initial connection

Imagine you are a new inmate in a prisoner-of-war camp. You have a solid escape plan, but you need several others to carry it off. Somehow you will have to find those who can help your escape to freedom. But it's not so easy, because the enemy has informers, paid "snitchers" who look and act pretty much like any other inmate. You must put your trust in someone else or you are doomed to remain imprisoned. If you err in your judgment, your secret plans will be exposed and your life made even more miserable. Do you decide to take the risk, or do you give up your plan and continue to suffer in silence?[1]

This scenario describes the dilemma of all human relationships: does what we expect to get from any encounter offset what it might cost us? Like the prisoner in the example, it is not a simple go/no-go decision, because people are not stamped for ready identification with "You can trust me," "You can sorta trust me," "You can't trust me." So we all make subjective decisions depending on the nature of the immediate situation, our own history of success or failure with encounters like this, and our current state of mind.

When meeting someone new, we all rely heavily on what we see and hear. In making the decision to say, "Hi," "Going my way?" or "Wanna dance?" we take into account the following characteristics: physical attractiveness; body language (an open or closed stance, a relaxed or tense posture or face); communication of warmth and accessibility through a smile or handshake; voice qualities that reveal enthusiasm, boredom, hostility, or confidence; and the obvious reactions of the other person to us.[2]

The setting is also important as an indicator of mutual interests—in books if it's a library, in sports if it's a bowling alley, in socializing if it's a dance. Sometimes settings can be deceiving, or people in them might have hidden agendas. For instance, some people go to a dinner party not for the food or the conversation, but for their own ego trips: "I'm here to show them I'm smart and they're stupid." Others may go to a bar not for the drinks and companionship, but to play their own perverse games: "I'm here to turn guys on and watch them squirm, but don't let them know that, okay?"

These agendas of power, exploitation, and self-interest figure into the risks of opening ourselves to a stranger or acquaintance. In deciding whether or not to connect with another person, we all look at the anticipated social rewards and balance them with the potential costs of being embarrassed, ridiculed, or rejected or found boring, unworthy, or inadequate. We compute the effort required, the time, money cost, distance, and the other opportunities that must be given up once we decide on full-steam-ahead. "Is she going to be worth an hour subway ride home to Brooklyn?" "Will it be worth having to draw him out of his shyness even though he is attractive?" For many people the answer is, "It's not worth the hurt to get some good strokes."

Chronically shy people are overly conscious of this decision-making process, because they are excessively concerned with being acceptable and appropriate. They vividly imagine all the possible horrors of a relationship and become obsessed with the rewards versus the costs of dealing with *anyone,* even in an on-going relationship. They often pay dearly for such an exquisitely tuned consciousness, as is illustrated in the case of this twenty-year-old woman:

> I think that the way I react in my own shyness when getting to know
> someone and liking them a lot is to react almost the opposite in many
> ways. If I *really* like someone, it is hard for me to show it in the way that
> I feel it. In other words, I will put myself on the "buddy" level with the
> person and try to act as casual as possible about my feelings for him or
> her. The shyness comes in the fear of really letting someone know how I
> feel. So I act very casual about the first few encounters and try not to let
> myself get too excited about it. I'm sure that this casualness is just a pro-
> tector for myself, and that the shyness that is behind it is also a basic
> insecurity of letting anyone know the "inside" me.

Shy people often resolve this dilemma of developing new relationships by doing nothing. They choose the security of isolation over the risk of being rejected. But we must all take this risk to establish the important relationships in our lives.

Research shows that strangers, when thrown together in frightening circumstances, as in a hijacked plane or sinking ship, begin to relate to each other almost immediately: "I say old man, I seem to be drowning, can you toss me a life jacket?"

But all too often when people feel anxious, they prefer to be alone. In a study at Yale, students were told they were participating in an experiment on the sensitivity of the mouth and were asked to suck on such harmless things as baby bottles and their own thumbs.[3] The students were being instructed to do something that tapped into their repressed infantile needs of oral gratification and they became visibly anxious. When asked if they preferred to do the experiment alone or with other members of the group, the students invariably chose to isolate themselves.

Most people want to be alone in the face of an anxiety attack because they consider their reactions inappropriate: "Why am I worried about sucking my thumb?" "I'm overreacting, what's wrong with me?" Because shys constantly consider their reactions inappropriate, they almost always choose to be alone rather than risk rejection for their own imagined inadequacy. But in protecting themselves, they lose important feedback from others who might be sharing the very same feelings. This isolation reinforces the person's self-image as shy—"I can't meet any people because I'm shy"— and leads to further isolation.

This protective isolation becomes obvious in a dormitory cafeteria where strangers often end up sitting together. Most shys arrange to eat early or late in the dining period because fewer people will be around at those times. They often will sit at the end of the table instead of the middle so both flanks are not left open, and assault can come from only one side. Some shys erect physical barriers by pushing nearby chairs away or putting books or clothing on them. Others bury themselves in a book or a newspaper. Then there is the "I can't talk with a full mouth" shy reaction. When someone is about to sit in the vicinity and might want to talk, they stuff food down as if they were starving, usually an effective back-off cue to the would-be acquaintance.

Still, many of these shy people long for the small talk, idle chatter, laughter, and friendship that seem to be going on at the other tables. Indeed, quiet anger is a frequent reaction to being left out of the fun, even when the shy person has turned down the invitation to join in. The shy may often become bolder if the other person indicates warmth and a readiness to relate beyond a superficial smile and a shallow greeting. But the other person has to send up obvious smoke signals for the passively shy person to get the message and begin to act on it—cautiously, of course.

Shyness barriers to intimacy

Once we decide to "go" with the initial connection, we are on the road to friendship. But to further develop a relationship with another being, we must open up and reveal something of our private selves. In this process of self-disclosure, we share values, goals, expectations, attitudes, and even some of our personal secrets. There can be no real sense of intimacy without such self-disclosure by each potential friend or lover. However, trust is required before this sharing can take place. And how do you develop trust before you really know anything about the other person?

Psychologist Sidney Jourard, who has written extensively about the self-disclosure process, acknowledges this conflict. "We conceal and camouflage our true being before others," he notes, "to foster a sense of safety, to protect ourselves against unwanted but expected criticism, hurt, or rejection." But without disclosure, others do not know us. Thus, we open ourselves to misunderstandings. "Worse," says Jourard, "when we succeed too well in hiding our being from others, we tend to lose touch with our real selves, and this loss of self contributes to illness in myriad forms."[4]

Both a sense of trust and willingness to disclose require a foundation of safety. This place, the person, the encounter must all assure one that it is safe to venture forth into the open. But safety turns out to be a highly individual matter, as I learned when trying to develop approaches for not-shy people to use in relating to shys. For example, in the cafeteria, a not-shy man would ask for openers, "Do you like the food here?" The shy woman would choke, unable to answer such a "personal" question. Another not-shy might begin with, "Hi, my name is Adam. What's yours?" Ditto on "too personal." No personal topics, no evaluative statements (especially about something the person is doing or wearing *now*), and not too many questions altogether. It can be frustrating to honestly want to get to know a shy person and not know which of these seemingly standard opening moves will be interpreted as a checkmate.

All of us erect invisible boundaries around ourselves to define our personal space. Shy people, however, establish a *series* of buffer zones to keep others from getting too close for comfort. These shyness barriers determine how far the shy person will go in making contact with another person.[5]

A similar set of barriers is erected by people who have phobias of snakes. In one study, a few of the people who answered a newspaper ad for research on snake phobias could go right ahead and pick up a snake.[6] The barrier for them was the label, which made them avoid snakes, but didn't prevent them from picking one up if it was there. Some people with a snake phobia, however, cannot even go into a room where a caged snake is kept. The barrier for others is getting close to a caged snake, or viewing it uncaged held by someone else. Then there is the barrier of touching the snake's skin when it is being held firmly. That achieved, there is the further barrier of holding the snake in one's lap and letting it wiggle around. Even when that much contact is achieved, there is a final barrier to cross: the snake is dropped on the floor and the person is expected to pick it up.

In helping people overcome their snake phobias, researchers recognize that the anxiety associated with the more distant barriers—e.g., walking into a room with a caged snake—must be overcome before the succeeding ones can be breached. Skipping steps or moving the process along too rapidly can backfire and result in a surge of anxiety leading to escape and refusal to try again.

Shy people build similar barriers in their phobia of contact with people. For some, making eye contact with a stranger is a formidable barrier. They feel uncomfortable when the contact is more intense or prolonged than "is called for." (In general, women find eye contact more comfortable, appropriate, and desirable than do men.)[7] For others, the barrier may not be in looking or even in reacting in a structured situation, but in starting action in a new, unfamiliar setting. New situations and unfamiliar people—strangers—make almost everyone feel shy. However, for some people, there is no shyness barrier to cross with strangers, since "they don't really matter"; it is with friends that shyness comes into play.

I was totally unprepared for this reversal of barriers in one of the shyest students I have worked with. Laura was a pretty, twenty-one-year-old senior who could not state her name in class without blushing and twisting in her chair. But after school, Laura worked part time as a nude model. Men would come to her apartment to photograph her in the nude, or pretend there was film in their cameras while watching her assume various provocative positions—for $20 an hour—no touching allowed! She told me how it was possible for her to be nude in front of strangers:

> I am basically modest and shy around men. So I find it slightly weird
> that I'd appear nude for a stranger before I'd appear nude in front of my
> family or in front of friends like in skinny dipping. After I started
> modeling I very quickly began to see the people who came as objects,
> just as they saw me. Then it became very easy. I felt as if I was in a
> power position—it was mostly sad men wanting their kicks. But it
> eventually was so depressing that I stopped.

Another example of this barrier reversal is the prostitute who has a half-dozen clients a night, but reports she is shy when "I'm with someone I like."

It is not simple to chart out the shyness barriers of an individual, because sometimes they are disguised. A single action may look like a free and easy approach, yet be based on hostility or fear. The affectionate pinch, the playful tease, or the backhanded compliment are good examples of this phenomenon.

Researcher and psychotherapist Leonard Horowitz categorizes two classes of behavior that underlie all interpersonal relations: those designed to bring one person *closer* to another—C type actions; and those designed to *distance* one person from another—D type actions. Type C occurs when there is an intention to cooperate, collaborate, be close, agree, share, and, ultimately, love. Type D occurs when there is distance, disagreement, distrust, disapproval, criticism, and hostility.[8]

At times the type D behaviors are barriers others must be willing to overcome before any type C warmth will be shown. At other times, the shy person sends double messages simultaneously: "Go away, I need you." This may be unintentional, as in, "You always hurt the one you love." Or it may be a protective tactic, as in this young man's statement:

I have a strong need for reassurance of affection. I need a great deal of positive feedback to feel secure in a friendship. Occasionally, I deliberately do strange things to reassure myself of my friends' support and my own autonomy. . . .

These "strange things" may not only be a test of friendship, they may be part of an unconscious plan to guarantee failure. Many people have such an intense fear of failure that they avoid situtions that hold the slightest potential for failure, be it academic, social, or sexual. Where the situation cannot readily be sidestepped, a paradoxical effect sometimes occurs in which insufficient effort is expended to pass the test or make the grade. In this way, the failure can be attributed to a lack of effort and not to the really feared source—a lack of ability.

Therapist Richard Beery describes patients whose coping style for their fear of failure is to make it happen—to fail.[9] "They create the situation they most fear, because in creating it they have an illusion they are controlling it, and not the other way around," he reports. People ostensibly concerned with relating better to others socially and/or sexually keep setting things up in such ways that failure occurs again and again—but it is a failure that is under their own unconscious control. It is not their personal inadequacy that is at fault, but rather something about the time, the place, the other people, the system, the anything-but-me. Ordinary looking males who pursue only stunningly attractive women set the stage for failure. And so do women who marry men with full knowledge of their addiction to gambling, alcohol, or drugs.

Fear of failure sometimes gets mixed up with a fear of success, where success means a change of status, a new operating style, giving up comfortable old ways for the unknown challenges of the new. I have known couples that have unexpectedly broken up just when the relationship seemed to be most intimate and close. In several instances, without apparent justification, the man suddenly became cool and distant, to the puzzlement of the woman. And soon the relationship broke down all together, because, "She was just too demanding." Intimacy panicked him.

People often send out mixed messages unaware of the contradictions between what they are consciously doing and unconsciously feeling. In certain structured settings, these double signals become intensified and are further complicated by those that others are transmitting. Nowhere is this more apparent than at a high-school dance.

Want to dance?

Emerson reminds us that "society is a masked ball, where everyone hides his real character and reveals it in hiding." Another way I have tried to

learn how shyness affects the social lives of people is to recreate terrifying situations that shy people often face. One of these is "the dance." The high-school hop is a setting many of us are familiar with—more from memories of our plans for a little body contact than of "scoring" or being carried off in a white Thunderbird by the person of our dreams. (Fortunately, there *is* life after high school, as we learn from author Ralph Keyes—even beautiful Ali McGraw was an adolescent wall flower who never had a date during high school.[10] But that's little consolation for all those who were too shy to ask her to dance.)

To learn more about the dynamics of shyness in this kind of social setting, I arranged a high-school dance—complete with disco music, cokes, and dim lights—for the students in my shyness seminar. The girls, who wore dresses instead of their usual jeans, immediately seated themselves on the "girls' side" of the dance floor. The boys, in sports jackets and ties (also unusual dress for them) quickly huddled together in the male zone.

For ten minutes the music played on, but no one broke ranks. Then, one clump of boys started a caterpillar move around the edge of the dance floor toward the female territory, as the girls eyed them warily.

"Jeff, you go first."

"Don't push, man, I'll go when I'm ready."

"Hey, Mike, Carolyn is giving you the eye."

"You're full of it, if you want her she's yours for the asking. Anyway she's too tall for me."

"C'mon Judy, why don't you ask the foreign student to dance, he looks so out of it."

"Get off my back, will you, Cecilia? This is not a charity dance."

Finally, big Jeff asks Coleen if she would like to dance, and the ice is broken. The music is lively and they dance well together. Just as the caterpillar formation begins to dissolve as other boys decide to make the big move, the music changes to slow soul. The dancing stops, cokes are guzzled, nervous laughter. Too slow, too soon. With fast music you don't have to talk much—you can concentrate on the dance moves, or do your separate thing together, or talk about the music. But slow means close, and close means you'd better start talking pretty soon or else your bodies are going to make their own nonverbal communication. To ask someone to dance to a slow tune is seen by all as an intimate invitation to be close. Fast-music dancers might just like to dance fast—it doesn't matter who they dance with. But slow is something else.

Mike makes his move and asks our very shy, very cute Judy if she would like to dance with him.

"How come everybody is picking on me?" she blurts out, partly in response to Cecilia's former teasing. But the damage is done. Confused and hurt, Mike steps back and thrusts his hands in his pockets. Still, he decides to try someone else rather than return to the pack empty-handed.

"Well, what about you, wanna dance?" he says with defiant nervousness to the girl at the end of the row.

"You're talking to me?"

"Yeah, do you want to dance or not?"

"Well, no, thanks . . . maybe later." How could she agree to be an obvious second choice, or respond otherwise to such a belligerent invitation? Mike is shot down, lost in action. But not being too shy, he tries a new approach with a new partner and it clicks.

The music gets louder and faster and eventually the dance floor is nearly full, except for the two girls who stuck themselves in the back row of seats. To get to them requires more dogged effort and personal commitment on the male's part than to casually pick up one of the front-row girls. They turn out to be among our shyest students and illustrate nicely the power of a self-fulfilling prophecy: "I might as well sit in the back because nobody will want to dance with me anyway." Sure enough, no one asks—because they are planted in the boxed-in section, where they will never blossom.

Everyone knew the dance was a class exercise, but that didn't lessen the tension, because it still made a difference if you were the first girl to be asked to dance by the most desirable boy, or the rear guard forced to accept the leftovers. And the basic issues for the boys remain: "Suppose she rejects me?" "Maybe she won't like the way I dance or make small talk, or maybe I'll sweat too much."

By reading some meaning into every action and gesture, the participants in these formalized rituals are bound into a no-win situation. It is safest, they reason, to follow the rules of etiquette, to imitate others. Doing so gets them paired up, but that's about all. They quickly become characters acting out stereotyped roles. It is only when a person acts independent of what the situation usually calls for that others believe they are glimpsing the "real" individual, and that it is something special about *them* that is encouraging this delightfully deviant behavior. A good example of this is when the man continues to take a few more dance steps and holds the woman close—after the music stops.

When I asked a male assistant to continue dancing after the music ended, his partners invariably rated him as more attractive, considerate, and someone they'd like to know better than when the same young man politely ended the dance as soon as the music stopped. It is safest to do what others do, to conform to the rules, if you want to hide. If you want to be a special person for someone else, then you can't be just another of the obedient sheep.

I offer the following advice to my shy students who really want to meet a particular person at a dance, but are anxious about being turned down. Casually ask, "Do you *feel* like dancing?"

If "No," then quickly counter with, "Me neither, isn't it funny how you come to a dance and after you're there you don't feel like dancing. Sometimes the music's not right, sometimes you worry that someone you want to dance with might not want to dance with you. That's especially a problem for a shy person like me."

"*You're* shy?"

"Sure I am. Do you consider yourself shy?"

Then go into your shyness long suit, and tell your dreammate everything he/she ever wanted to know about shyness but was too shy to ask.

A research program started in Oregon has been designed to assess the reasons why some men and women have dating inhibitions.[11] When men who had fewer than three dates in the last six months and women who had fewer than six dates in the last six months were compared to heavier daters, several interesting findings emerged. For the inhibited males, their negative self-evaluations were more prominent than their lack of social skills. The women, on the other hand, were characterized by problems with social skills rather than overly negative self-images.

Members of the research team prepared a dating manual for the men in the study, based on information provided by their female peers about how to handle dating situations. The manual proved effective in increasing the percentage of dating among the inhibited men, and suggested tactics from it appear in Part II of this book.

But what about the women? With changing sex roles brought on by the women's movement, more and more women are deciding to take the initiative. For many it's less painful than waiting for that magic moment when confidence and skill do merge into that mighty force which carries the male into the giddy excesses of openly asking for the time, a drink, a dance, or a date.

But sometimes these bold beckonings become burnt offerings, as this young woman recounts:

I saw a man dancing at a dance and got very excited watching him. I thought, hmmm, I'd like to dance with this person. But, as soon as I thought that, I was filled with intense fear. It took me all evening to get up the courage to ask him to dance with me and by the time I did, I sort of *hated* him for getting me aroused and was *angry* at myself for being unable to approach him.

So, a few months later, after seeing him again, I walked up to him and said, "I have to tell you something." He said, "What's that?" I said, "You're a beautiful man. I find you very attractive." He said, "Oh, God," and rolled his eyes in embarrassment and mumbled, "Well, that's not important." He also said he felt like falling through a hole in the floor if there had been one. I found out later that he was not very confident about how he looked.

In the meantime, because I was initially shy and he is chronically shy, and I didn't feel like looking longingly at him to give him the *idea* I wanted to know him and instead chose the *direct* method, things got pretty messed up and now I feel we will never interact as just humans.

It's really painful. It was the first time in my life I was not the passive recipient of approaches by men, and it's turned out to be harder than I thought. It must be hell to be a male adolescent, I've decided. In my shyness, I have given up on ever getting to know that person.

What went wrong here? What could Mary have done to make the connection work?

It is only in recent years that women are no longer willing to sit and wait and hope they will be chosen by men to whom they are attracted. They have begun to take direct action and to choose for themselves. But an old Dutch proverb reminds us: "He [or she] who chooses has trouble." Trouble because in the act of making a public choice, we stand out from the anonymous crowd and become responsible for the consequences of our decision.[12] However, it is only through our choices that we define ourselves and come to exert a measure of control over our destinies.

Many women, such as Mary, have grown up with a traditional indoctrination into the passive feminine role. Shyness only intensifies that fundamental passivity. Similarly, men have had their heads programmed by macho sex-role stereotypes. So right off, when Mary asks John to dance, there is a violation of expectancies all around. Even if she had done so with effortless style and grace, John might have balked at the invitation. His man-thing might be a hang-up that requires him to be in the driver's seat on all sexual adventures. But that is *his* problem of control, one which may be alleviated with more positive experiences, further changes in sexual norms, and perhaps even a little therapeutic counseling.[13] Mary never bothered to take his perspective and the context into consideration when deciding on her approach shot. She was too wrapped up in her own fantasies and anxieties.

Furthermore, Mary's approach was anything but graceful; she swooped down on her unsuspecting prey and, in the worst sexist fashion, essentially declared: "Hey, baby I like your body. Want to get it on?" She comes on too strong, too suddenly, without establishing any personal basis for the relationship—other than John's good looks. But it probably didn't seem like too much or too fast from her point of view, brooding as she had been for months over her inability to act more spontaneously and casually when she first saw him dancing. And to make it a total disaster, John turns out to be a shy young man who can't handle personal compliments.

We are also made aware from this example of the mixed emotions involved in what on the surface seems like a simple invitation to dance among shy people already at the dance. Fear, lust, hate, anger, and embarrassment are all excruciatingly blended in a volatile mixture that denies free and easy access to desirable others. There is too much worry about the possible negative consequences of the action to allow it to be casual, too much egocentric concern for it to be an enjoyably shared encounter.[14]

Mary could be more successful in the future by practicing the social skills involved in taking the initiative. She needs to think out and work through her values about being an assertive woman, about how *she* would like to be approached in a nonthreatening way—before going to the dance. Once there, she could be more spontaneous in acting on her feelings. In selecting an appropriate context to deliver her compliment, she might sit next to John during a music break and say, "Excuse me for being forward, I couldn't help but admire the way you danced. Where did you learn to dance like that?" The compliment is clear, but said in such a way that even if he is embarrassed by it, John has an opportunity to reply to the final question. The conversation can then be moved to the fun of dancing, the pleasure of listening to good music, the relaxation it offers after a hard week of work. "What kind of work do you do?" and so on. With this foundation in place, it is more natural for John to take the next step when the music starts again and ask Mary to dance. If he doesn't, then Mary might say, "I enjoy talking to you, would you like to continue while we dance or would you rather sit this one out?" Mary is giving him a choice of reasonable alternatives: he can sit and talk with her, or dance and talk with her. If he rejects both (unlikely), she tells him again how much she appreciates watching a good dancer and moves on to reexamine the available options for a more responsive, less uptight male who would welcome the advances of a liberated woman.

Sex and the shy person

Sex may make the world go round, but the trip usually makes the shy person nauseous. Virtually all of the things that bring on an everyday anxiety attack fuse to ignite a shyness time bomb when sex is concerned. Sexual encounters are the most ambiguous situations imaginable. There are no explicit guidelines for behavior; both partners are nude, exposed, stripped of their outer layers of protection; many don't know the skills required or haven't had much of a chance to practice them; and, besides that, most people have gathered unrealistic ideas about sex from Hollywood romance movies, pornography, soap operas, *Playboy,* or *Playgirl.* Traditional values have made enemies, or at best strangers, of the two sexes, in hopes of keeping young lust uncoupled until marriage. No wonder then that 60 percent of the shy people we surveyed said they are anxious with a person of the opposite sex!

Performance anxiety plagues every stage of the sexual encounter. For the woman, the questions often are: "Will I be able to please him?" "Will he find me attractive?" For the man, the performance is more out in the open: "Will I get an erection, maintain it, and have a climax?" "Will my penis be big enough and will I satisfy her?" No matter how many times these questions have been answered affirmatively, new anxieties well up before each intimate encounter.

The sex act is typically portrayed as a two-step process: the invitation to "go all the way," and, if accepted, then "doing it"—an erroneous and naive simplification. Before step one, numerous barriers must be overcome. There are as many discrete decision points in the romantic scenario leading up to the big moment as there are in a game of chess. Each step along the way is fraught with anxiety and possible rejection. How close to sit, when and how to kiss, when to move your hand from its comfortable place to a more exciting, taboo area. How to move from here to there, down or up, under or in, not too fast, not too hard, but "just right." But what's "just right?" And while the person is thinking and acting and planning and plotting, is he or she also accurately detecting the signals being sent back? When is "playing hard to get" just a teasing come-on and when is it a polite turndown?

Most of us feel shy in some sexual situations, like the one this woman describes:

> I feel my shyness most intensely when making love for the first time with someone. That first time exposing your most intimate self—naked with all the imperfections showing—somehow you fool yourself into thinking he won't notice you, and go on.

As in other matters, too often a "little" learning about sex may be a dangerous thing, especially for the shy person. A fifty-year-old woman recounts:

> I was always uncomfortable with boys and this was complicated by the fact that my physical development and maturity began early—at age ten— and by the fact that sex and things sexual were never mentioned in my presence. Therefore, this was naturally an area of great mystery, concern, and misconception on my part. My real knowledge of things sexual began during my freshman year of college. Aside from learning some French and some Spanish, my greatest learning experience took place during our long "bull sessions" in the dorm. But the newly acquired

knowledge, instead of making me feel freer, further inhibited me and filled me with fears of pregnancy and incompetence.

Shy people have more than their fair share of trouble when interpersonal relations mean sexual intimacy. The following case study sadly illustrates one side of the problem shys have with sex:

> I am twenty-six years old, white, male, from a middle-class background. My shyness can be demonstrated by the fact that I am still a virgin. This is both my darkest secret and the greatest example of self-failure. My family was like a TV family. Sex wasn't described as being bad, it was ignored. I never saw my mother naked and never saw or heard my parents having intercourse. I was always very embarrassed at having an erection and I never masturbated until I was nineteen. Until then, I had only two orgasms (involuntarily in the shower) when I was awake. I enjoyed the feeling but felt it was wrong to masturbate. By the time I knew better, I was so far behind in sexual experience that I was too afraid to ask girls out for dates because I wouldn't know what to do.

Sexual encounters pose a most serious threat for the shy person—for all the same reasons shy people generally feel uncomfortable in novel social situations, where they can be evaluated and are vulnerable to violations of their personal space. On an anonymous sex survey answered by 260 students in my psychology course, shyness was found to have a major impact on sexual behavior.

While only slightly fewer shys have dated and gone steady than their not-shy classmates, the gulf between the groups widens as the sexual relationship becomes more intimate and intense. Comparing the 100 currently shy people with their 160 not-shy peers on their reported carnal knowledge, a consistent pattern of differences can be seen:

	Not shys	Shys
I have petted	87%	73%
I have masturbated	81%	66%
I have practiced oral sex	60%	39%
I have had intercourse	62%	37%

These statistics generally hold equally for shy men and shy women, with some interesting exceptions. Three-quarters of the shy women report being virgins, while only 38 percent of the not-shy women are. For shy males, 59 percent say they are virgins, as compared to 38 percent of the not-shy males. It appears further from the women's results that about a third fewer of those who are shy have had oral sex and, more surprisingly, have ever masturbated. Some shy people report not being able to look in the mirror or even look at or explore their own nude bodies—it is possible for them to feel shy even when they are alone!

Shy and not-shy men don't differ in these ways. But shy men who have participated in various sexual activities report more negative experiences than not-shy men with going steady, masturbation, intercourse, and oral sex. Similarly, shy women get less enjoyment from their experiences with dating, masturbation, and intercourse. More than a quarter of the shy women who have had intercourse recall unpleasant associations with that intimate experience. Although this is a limited sample, it does clearly show that shy men and women have fewer sexual experiences and enjoy them less.

Simple, fast, and in the dark

To the extent that lovers are especially shy about matters sexual, we might predict that their lovemaking will be simple, silent, fast, and in the dark. Adventurous exploration and discussion of preferences are often too anxiety arousing, even when shy people are married. This lack of open communication about sex allows for misinformation and misdirection of both means and ends. For example, the silent quest for the "cosmic mutual orgasm" may lead many perfectly well-functioning couples to feel dissatisfied with their sexual life—unaware that the simultaneous climax is difficult to achieve due to physiological differences between men and women. It's common enough in love stories and those satisfied letters to the editors of sex magazines, but not under ordinary sheets.

Unrealistic expectations unchecked by open talk between husband and wife can lead to a loss of joy in sex, as described by Dr. Lucille Forer:

> Many men have told me they never feel comfortable unless their wives reach orgasm each time they engage in intercourse. Such a high level of self-expectation is almost certainly doomed to failure, because physical love constantly changes and is different according to time, place, and circumstances. Furthermore, the man's *self*-evaluation in terms of sexual performance victimizes his wife as well as himself. He is relating to his role rather than to her as a person.[15]

The general preoccupation with self that is characteristic of the shy intrudes itself into the sex act. For men, the concentration on getting an erection puts anxious thought where erotic emotion should be. For women, the pressure to satisfy and act satisfied destroys spontaneous enjoyment. When our sexual identity is measured by a series of successful physical acts and not by a more all-encompassing set of feelings and reactions, we are inviting failure.

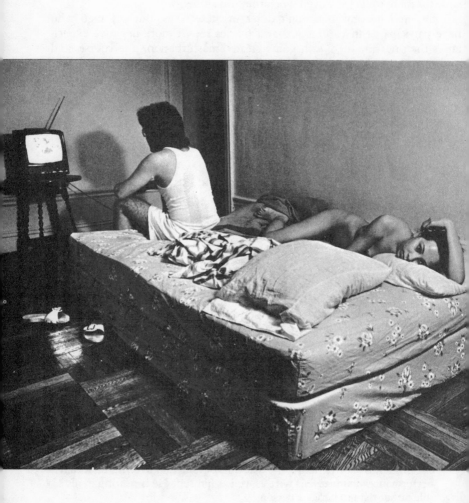

Psychiatrists George and Joseph Solomon warn clinicians to be on the alert for shyness as a cause in cases of sexual inhibition and inadequacy. They offer, as an instance of how shyness may be related to sexual problems, the case of Marsha:

> Marsha, a twenty-nine-year-old unmarried woman, was the epitome of shyness and self-effacement. She was passive, never asserted herself, and frequently put herself in the position of being victimized by aggressive males. She was always afraid to speak and had been a stutterer as a child. She had a terrible fear of emitting bad odors, bathed twice daily, and used "feminine" deodorants and perfumes extensively. In her sexual experiences she had been anxious, embarrassed, frigid, and afraid of passing flatus.
>
> In some individuals like Marsha sexuality equals dirtiness and is not something to be done openly, especially with someone valued and adored. Some persons, in fact, find sexual pleasure only with degraded "dirty" partners. A bathroom quality to sexuality promotes shyness and makes for recoil from intimacy.[16]

Shyness can, on occasion, also result in promiscuity. It may be more difficult to say "no" and "have to hassle the whole scene" than to go along with the boy's advances. Or, it may happen as an active solicitation of popularity, as a physical means of achieving an illusion of psychological security. If everyone wants you, they must find you attractive and desirable . . . right?

Dr. Peter Wish, Executive Director of the New England Institute for Human Sexuality, offered this balanced perspective on the relationship between shyness and sex problems in a recent telephone interview:

> I would say that sometimes shyness is related to sex problems. It would have to do with the amount of interpersonal anxiety the individual experiences, and whether he/she experiences it as a cause or as a result of the sex problems. Many people with sex problems tend to avoid other people because they are unsure of themselves or embarrassed.
>
> Men, especially those who have problems with impotence or premature ejaculation, tend to withdraw into themselves and this lowers their feelings of self-worth. However, withdrawal and what you might call shyness can result after sex problems begin, and it develops into a self-perpetuating problem.

For many shy people, feelings of sexual inadequacy are too embarrassing to even discuss with a therapist, let alone with a mate. One course of action then is to simply downplay or denigrate the importance of sex: "Let's just keep it in its proper place, OK?" Another is to make a reluctant commitment to bachelorhood or spinsterhood, and thereby avoid the unpleasantness altogether. But they obviously lose a lot in the process.

The ideal that we hold out for the shy person is not just *having* sex, or *making* it, or *getting* some, but embracing sexual experience as the vital human experience it is. The great humanist Rollo May affirms what each of us intuitively knows:

> Every person, experiencing as he does his own solitariness and aloneness, longs for union with another. He yearns to participate in a relationship greater than himself. Normally, he strives to overcome his aloneness through some form of love.

But not passive love that waits around for the right time, place, and person to coalesce. Rather, it is the *daimonic love*.

> In its right proportion, the daimonic is the urge to reach out toward others, to increase life by way of sex, to create, to civilize; it is the joy and rapture, or the simple security of knowing that we matter, that we can affect others, can form them, can exert power which is demonstrably significant. It is a way of making certain that we are valued.[15]

The teacher I would choose to guide us away from our shy self-absorption to immersion in the sensuality of living with and through others is Zorba the Greek. Author Nikos Kazantzakis gives us in Zorba, a model of the life force in action.[18] For him, it is "a sin against nature" not to make love whenever you can, not to enjoy the beauty of each season, not to immerse yourself in the community of one's fellows. In the act of teaching his shy young boss, Michael, to dance, Zorba shows him (and us) how in reaching out to another person we come to appreciate emotions too long suppressed within. However, even so prodigious a lover of life as Zorba would have his hands full were he to be faced with the set of problems we turn to in the next chapter.

6
from sad to bad
to slightly mad

S o far we have looked at the ways that shyness affects all of us. We know about the prisons that we construct for ourselves and how they can keep us from leading a fulfilling, satisfying life. But before we can arrive at the promised solution land in Part II, we need to take one more fork in the road: the shyness-as-real-trouble path. It will lead us through places that are often sad, sometimes bad, and occasionally even mad.

In this chapter, we examine the devastating personal and social problems that are both the cause and the result of shyness: impersonal sex, alcoholism, and violent behavior. We also take a look at our possible future as a submissive society—one filled with shy people willing to give up their freedom for security—and what that can mean in our own lives. But first, let's turn to an important personal problem encountered in Chapter 5: As a shy person, how do you satisfy your sexual needs? As our version of the popular song goes, you can't always get what you want, but for a little money, you can always get what you need.

Sex for sale

The main motive for "nonattachment" is a desire to escape from the pain of living, and above all from love, which, sexual or nonsexual, is hard work.

George Orwell, "Reflections on Gandhi,"
Shooting an Elephant

"I never knew making love to a woman could be so beautiful," he said, when he was dressed and ready to leave.

"I think you are cured, and I'm glad. However, I was the aggressor today, but from now on it is up to you. Don't be afraid of women, just try to find the type you like, and act like a man, not like a baby."

Xaviera Hollander, *The Happy Hooker*

It is only through the intimacy of sex that we escape our narcissistic isolation to touch what is essential in another human being. But that same intimacy lays open our own vulnerability; it exposes our secret plans, reveals our private hiding places, and discloses those insecurities that playing "grownup" usually hides from the world. For many shy people, the risk of intimacy is too high an emotional price to pay for a sexual relationship with a friend or with a mate. However, many of these people are willing to pay cash to get what they need.

An analysis by Harold Nawy of erotica consumers in San Francisco suggests interesting similarities between the male purchaser of erotic sights and the chronically shy.[1] Most of the men in the study attend pornographic movies alone; the majority rarely or never saw their parents nude; many didn't have intercourse until after their twenty-first birthday. Over 40 percent were not presently satisfied with their sexual partners; their wives, if they had them, did not know of the afternoon adventures at the movies. More than half spent over $100 on erotica in the past year; three-fourths reported purchasing erotic materials from adult bookstores.

When he puts his raincoat on, Mr. Pornographic Moviegoer is in Nawy's words, "a model of American achievement—the backbone of the nation." Typically, he is white, middle-aged, middle-class, married, neatly dressed, college-educated, and has a white-collar job. Maybe he is also unloved, unloving, and unwilling to take the risk of a truly close relationship. At any rate, over 80 percent of Nawy's sample felt that erotic materials provide an outlet for bottled-up emotions. Another obvious outlet, at least for men, is prostitution.

Miss Kitty, the madam of a local San Francisco brothel recently closed by the vice squad, told me about customers who pay $60 an hour for one of her girls and then are too shy to climb the stairs. "They talk about their marriage and career troubles for much, sometimes all, of our expensive hour," she said. "Sometimes they have to be reminded about what they've purchased."

To gather more information on this connection between shyness and impersonal sex, twenty prostitutes were interviewed during their off-business hours by former prostitutes at the Delancy Street Foundation in San Francisco. About one-half of the interviews were conducted with streetwalkers, the others were with prostitutes who worked hotels, on referral only, or in houses of prostitution. On a good night, each one reported servicing about six men on the average. At the less industrious end were several who had only two customers, while a rate buster at the upper end had sex with twenty different men in one night.

When asked what percentage of their customers they thought were shy, these women estimated about 60 percent. Several prostitutes said that virtually all of their customers were shy, while only two felt that fewer than half were. Unfortunately, we couldn't validate this diagnosis by asking the men if they considered themselves shy, so we will have to be circumspect in our conclusions.

Still, the prostitutes' answers to our questions can help us better understand the shy man's approach to sex.

Q *How do you know when one of these guys is shy?*

A • They usually watch you for a while. That's usually my cue. I don't like to, but I will approach them.

• His approach. They drive around the block four or five times.

• They're reserved. They don't act real steady.

• They're reluctant about taking their clothes off. They want to talk about everything but sex.

• Shy doesn't mean quiet—it means they get awkward and don't know how to handle the whole idea of sex.

• They look lost and lonely.

• They need encouragement and help.

Q *Do shy clients treat you any differently than not-shy clients?*

A • Yes, they're clumsier.

• It's like I'm the leader and they follow me. If they ask for anything they talk in a circle until I suggest it.

• They're not aggressive in any way, you gotta pretty much pull teeth.

• They are more polite. There is a big difference.

• They're gentler at first but get kookier after a while.

• When they're shy and you can make them feel at ease, it is very profitable.

Q *What about the sexual performance of shy men have you noticed?*

A • They're worried about doing it. They're usually very nervous.

• They worry more about getting caught.

• I'd say they take less time to climax, 'cause they're so paranoid.

• It's difficult to keep them hard because they are so concerned about themselves.

Q *Why does a shy man pay to get a prostitute?*

A • They're too shy to tell their wives or girlfriends what they would really like.

- Prostitution is a way of satisfying his sexuality. I found there is a lot of perversion in shy men. They don't feel they can tell their wives these preferences.

- They need someone to show them what to do.

- They might not have a girlfriend, or don't know how to go about getting one.

From this study, we get a sharp picture of the shy man who pays for his sex. He is reluctant to initiate action; he is awkward around sex. He's passive, submissive, worried about being able to perform, and unable to express his sexual feelings and desires. So he buys what he needs. He's not expected to form a relationship, so he doesn't have to risk involvement or commitment. For many men, a prostitute is far less intimidating than a girlfriend or a wife. These women relax him by giving him a few drinks. Most take the lead in directing the sexual activity; they guide and instruct the man in what to do and they make him feel comfortable and competent in whatever he does. They also establish an open sexual contract early on so that the man can stop worrying about what he can and cannot do and what he can ask for without being labeled "pervert."

But what about the prostitutes themselves? Nine said they are definitely not shy, while six do label themselves as shy persons and five describe themselves as situationally shy. When they have a role to play—prostitute—they don't seem to be shy:

- Yes, in some ways I'm kind of inhibited. When I'm making money, though, I don't seem to be too shy.

- Basically, yes. But now that I have to take care of other shy people, it's not a problem any more.

- I'm shy in some situations, but certainly not about sex.

For some, though, shyness intrudes itself into their work: "Yeah, I'm shy to an extent. The only way I can get in bed with a guy is if I'm loaded or drunk."

Preserving shyness in alcohol

There are nine million alcoholics in the United States. About one in five of us lives with a person who drinks too much, and has done so for a decade or more. We often blame our age of anxiety for the high rate

of alcoholism. But in all recorded times people from diverse cultures have attempted to transform the experience within and the reality without by mood-altering, pleasure-giving, intoxicating beverages. But now, proportionally more people are drinking, many are starting earlier, and the social and economic consequences of this personal quest to control the stresses of life are more widespread.

A 1971 task force report to Congress makes it clear that there is certainly not a single, simple cause at work. Rather, alcoholism is best thought of as a response to a combination of physiological and social factors in the individual and his or her environment. "It cannot be said how often excessive drinking is the cause, and how often the effect," the research investigators state, but "it is dramatically evident that alcohol-related problems go hand in hand with other forms of unhappiness." [2]

Alcohol can release the emotional inhibitions that we all feel, as author-journalist Jimmy Breslin points out:

> You've got to understand the drink. In a world where there is a law against people ever showing emotions, or ever releasing themselves from the greyness of their days, a drink is not a social tool. It is a thing you need in order to live. [3]

Some experts believe that the shy person's need to overcome feelings of inadequacy, to be accepted, and to become part of the social group can be directly related to drinking and often to alcoholism. Dr. David Helms of the Washingtonian Center, Boston, comments:

> It is a safe generalization that many people start to drink because of feelings of social inadequacy. However, they don't usually describe their feelings as shyness. They use much more dramatic terms: they are frightened or scared of people. They say they are afraid of letting themselves go. They are afraid they will be rejected if they do. And so they start to drink to loosen themselves up.

Fred Waterhouse, a former alcoholic and now director of the Massachusetts Association of Halfway Houses, offered this personal description of the shyness-alcohol link:

> My problem with drinking was the result of a need to feel mature and equal to my co-workers. With a drink in my hand, I believed I was a more interesting person, a more scintillating conversationalist. Of course, actually alcohol only magnified those feelings of inadequacy, but the alcoholic who is shy has a desperate need to fit in, to belong, in his social

group. I have seen remarkable changes in the personalities of rehabilitated
alcoholics. Even people who had problems with shyness originally were
able to find ways to overcome them after giving up alcohol. Shyness,
or feeling inadequate, is not a trait that you have to live with—you can
change without using a crutch like alcohol.

Another alcoholic put it this way:

Everyone I met in Alcoholics Anonymous was pathologically shy. When
I think of why, I am struck by the reasons for my own alcoholism being
that drinking "turns off" the ever present monitor. Overdrinking turns
it too far off into social irresponsibility, but I suspect that alcoholics do
drink to begin with because they are so shy.

Shy teenagers often start to drink to conform to the social pressures
of their peers. They desire to be accepted as part of the group by not
being different in any way. "I wanted to be lost in the mainstream of
life," confided an older shy woman who had been an alcoholic for years.
"I didn't want to stand out, to be noticed, to be individuated, to be
counted," she said.

But when the alcoholics begin to drink excessively, they suddenly
lose their former social group. So they have to find new places and people
to drink with to validate their own sense of tenuous human worth. It is
never easy for an adult to make new friends; for the shy alcoholic, it
becomes impossible without a few good belts of booze. The fear that
originally helped motivate the need to drink finally becomes a reality as
the drunk is cast out of society for being different, inadequate, and inferior.

Perhaps the most eloquent explanation of the dynamics of the shy
alcoholic syndrome comes from one of my own relatives who only recently recognized she was an alcoholic and began efforts not to be:

It is precisely our concern to love and be loved, to accept and be accepted,
that drives us to that addiction to begin with. We are the terrified. We
are the people who expect every day in various ways for the sky to fall,
and we do not expect that it will fall upon us particularly, but that it will
fall upon those for whom we are responsible. . . . From the man who has
been sober for nine years to the woman who stopped drinking last week,
we will each admit that we like ourselves better and the people we know
find us more charming, loveable, sexy, whatever the criterion of acceptance is, when we have had a drink than they do when we are sober.
The problem is that one drink is too many and one thousand drinks are
not enough. What then is it that alcohol does for us that no amount of
good will can do? Fundamentally it makes us less conscious of the prison

of self, less fearful to venture beyond its peripheries. For us those boundaries that divide the self from the other never go away. The sober alcoholic is the man in the iron mask. What he seeks in alcohol is liberation from himself; what he wants is for the eternal censor to go to sleep for a few hours. And what makes the temptation to drink so strong is that he *knows* that it works to do just that.

From our general survey on shyness it is apparent that shy people with a serious personal problem, such as alcoholism, feel reluctant to ask others for help. To do so requires at least minimal social skills, a realistic self-appraisal, an act of assertion, and the admission of being deviant or helpless in some way. Each of these are typical problems of the chronically shy which will probably prevent them from using available resources. The success of Alcoholics Anonymous and other group-treatment programs may in part be due to the lessened fear of negative evaluation of people who have also been there (unlike those clean, proper, white-coated doctors and nurses). In addition, these treatment groups often become the sought-after source of social contact and approval originally missing in the lives of shy alcoholics. The first step toward rehabilitation is to stop denying that you're an alcoholic; the next step is to turn toward another person for help.

The relationships outlined here suggest that many people drown their shyness in alcohol, but these conclusions must be supported by more rigorous data than case studies and professional opinions. It is hoped that some will be forthcoming; if the relationship exists, then treatment programs must begin to incorporate ways of helping shy alcoholics overcome their shyness if they are to conquer their addiction.

The violent volcano of shyness

In general, shy people are not likely to display their frustrations in overt anger or to act on their hostile feelings. But smoldering embers can flare up if fueled, and bottled anger can pop if shaken enough. Rape, for instance, is an aggressive sexual assault which violates a woman's intimacy but not the man's.[4] The anonymity of the rapist and the impersonal nature of the violent sexual act provides a "safe" sexual outlet for disturbed men who must conquer when they cannot care.

Studies of adult rapists reveal a lack of personal experience with females in adolescence and a non–sexually-oriented home environment. Many rapists report that they never saw their parents nude, that sex was never the topic of conversations, and that they were usually severely punished for looking at erotic materials. Rapists have great difficulty talking about sex and report less enjoyment in sexual relations than do males of the same age and background who are not rapists.

The mentality of the rapist shares much in common with that of the extremely shy male who fears all women and the intimacy and closeness of human sexuality.[5] The rapist substitutes a brute beast for the tender human he cannot be with women. Like the vandal who destroys objects that cannot be appreciated or shared, the rapist destroys the integrity of women and the beauty of love. Indeed, the primitive fear of this sexual assault sometimes acts to render many women shy of *all* men whose power might overwhelm sense and sensibility in the act of sex.

Obviously, not all shy men are rapists, but shy people do have trouble dealing with their strong emotional feelings. People in our shyness clinic repeatedly deny strong feelings of hostility, although they clearly surface repeatedly. They talk about being trapped by boring, aggressive people; they feel they are often made to comply with the wishes of the dominating members of a group; they feel "put upon" by obviously inferior authorities. Who wouldn't feel angry in their shoes?

For some of these people, a cool, formal detached manner of "aloof shyness" is a veneer that protects them from the demands of others. "People expect things from you when you are informal, things you might not be willing or want to give when they want it," said a privately shy, icily cool law student attending our clinic.

If shy people can avoid or escape from a threatening social encounter, they will. But where the confrontation is direct and escape routes cut off, the shy person is in trouble. Unable to negotiate a dispute or pose a plan for conciliation, the shy person is powerless to arbitrate and effect a peaceful, mutually satisfactory settlement. More often than not, the decision is to yield, to give in, to get up, to get out, to do what is expected —albeit reluctantly. For some shy people, this cycle occurs again and again. Resentment builds and builds, but is held in check, along with all the other strong emotions the shy person might feel. And then one day . . .

The therapist of a convicted murderer described just such a scenario leading to a sudden murder. The situation involves a romantic triangle made up of chronically shy Mr. X, the murderer; Ms. Y, the woman he lived with; and his girlfriend. The girlfriend characterized Mr. X this way:

> . . . he speaks of his very great bashfulness (which he states is synonymous with insecurity) as a small child when he wet his pants in school rather than ask the teacher permission to go to the bathroom. . . . He feels

sufficiently worthless that the validity of experiencing and owning his own feelings is not real to him. To this day, he is unaware that he was in love with another woman for some time before he killed Y. . . .

The therapist goes on to describe the critical incidents leading to the brutal murder of Ms. Y:

Y was aware and felt threatened by the fact that he was seeing, and was interested in, another woman. As this situation reached a point too threatening for her, she twice left and then returned to him, finally requesting that they "go steady," get to know one another better, and that he cease seeing the other woman. He wished to continue seeing both, but after wavering for several weeks, acceded to her request and told the other woman twice, in Y's presence, that he would see her no longer, but would give his relationship with Y "everything he had." Y had made no secret of having been grievously hurt in a previous relationship, and he apparently felt responsible not to hurt her again. That same night he choked her to death, in his sleep.

Obviously the factor of feeling for another person's feelings played some factor in Y's death. However a less "shy" person would have said "I'm sorry that this may hurt you, Y, but I want to continue seeing you both, and shall do so."

The convicted murderer now faces a long prison sentence with plenty of time to wonder how it all could have ended differently. If only he could have said what he felt rather than acting on the impulse to destroy the person he could not bring himself to reason with.

The case of a sudden murder is not an isolated incident, but seems to recur often:[6]

- In California, Edmund Kemper III, an unusually tall fifteen-year-old regarded by his classmates as a well-mannered but shy lone wolf, shot his grandmother to death with two bullets to the head "just to see how it would feel." When his grandfather returned from the store, Kemper murdered him in similar fashion.

- In Phoenix, an eleven-year-old boy, described as being very polite and soft-spoken, stabbed his brother thirty-four times.

- An eighteen-year-old boy who assaulted and strangled a seven-year-old girl in a New York church was described as an unemotional young man who planned to be a minister.

- Five days after his graduation, a twenty-two-year-old boy ("gentle, easygoing, good-natured") killed three unarmed victims during a bank robbery.

Not far from where I teach, a young man named Frederick Newhall Woods grew up on a sprawling 150-acre estate. His parents are described by a family friend as being "two of the most courtly people I've ever known, almost to the point of humility. They just didn't live a public life at all, and the kid withdrew even further." Schoolmates say of Fred that "he's quiet," "very cautious," "shy," and "withdrawn." A neighbor told the reporter, "He was never with anyone." Frederick Woods has been indicted along with two others for the bizarre kidnapping of twenty-six Chowchilla, California schoolchildren and their bus driver, who were buried in an underground chamber and were rescued several days later.

The sudden murderer is terrifying to us all because of his lack of predictability and the brutal fury of his attack when it does come. We tend to think of violent people as being impulsive, having poor control over their emotions, and of always being in one kind of trouble or another. Such a person makes sense to us even though we are horrified by his violent act. However, imagine yourself walking into a bar and sitting down on a vacant stool and having someone come over to you and say, "That's *my* seat." Before you can move or say, "Sorry, I didn't know," he starts pummelling you in the face. How do we understand that human transaction? In fact, a similar episode occurred in a downtown San Francisco bar, the only difference being that the "offending" person was stabbed to death.

This incident is instructive because it underscores the apparently motiveless violence that seems to be surfacing in our society. On virtually any city police-department blotter there are a surprising number of such crimes either without motives or trivial motives, such as, "He took the parking space I was waiting for."

Typically the sudden murderer, the mass murderer, is a young man who has been unobtrusive, quiet, and an obedient good citizen before lashing out in the frenzy of violence. It is not a lack of impulse control he suffers from, but rather excessive control. By being extremely overcontrolled in the expression of all strong feelings, including anger, the person has no outlets available. It is all bottled up inside—love, hate, fear, sorrow, and justifiable anger. Without letting others know what he feels, the overcontrolled person has no way of changing bad situations, of having an impact on other people. He is trapped by their demands, ridiculed by their slights, demeaned by their indifference to his needs and rights. This anger smolders until one day it is released in uncontrollable rage, maybe over a very minor irritation or the mildest of frustrations.

I am reminded of a middle-aged Puerto Rican man who was on the hospital ward I was put into after an automobile accident. His poor command of English made it difficult for him to tell the staff where he hurt, what he wanted, or to answer their questions. He just lay there moaning as quietly as possible. I awoke one night startled by the sound of nurses screaming and glass cracking against the tile floor and walls. Mr. Sanchez had blown. He'd had it up to here. When the nurse came around at 3:00 A.M. to wake him to take his temperature, that did it.

He stood astride the bed, defiantly hurling the tray full of rectal thermometers and medicine bottles all over the ward, while shouting: "No more up the ass. No more up the ass." I do not know whether or not he was kept on the psycho ward after being sent there for observation, but I do know that Mr. Sanchez was talking for me and other patients too weak and submissive to strike out against our dehumanizing treatment.

Researcher Ed Megargee asked a group of convicted murderers about their history of handling aggression and also gave them a series of personality tests to see if there were any differences among them.[7] He found they were either undercontrolled or overcontrolled in expression of aggressive feelings as compared to a normal population. The impulsive types had a long history of getting into fights and being charged with assault and battery. On the other hand, for the overinhibited murderers, their crimes were the first times they had made their private feelings public. Despite provocation in their past lives, they rarely or never were able to even verbally express hostile feelings.

This study also discovered that, unlike the murders by the more impulsive types, those by the overcontrolled men were all out of proportion to the immediate situation. We found the extremely shy to be more overcontrolled than the not shy on a personality test (M.M.P.I.). Mel Lee, of our research team, has just discovered that first-time murderers are more likely to be shy than are offenders with a record of repeated assaults. Among a prison sample of 20 of each type, 70% of these murderers reported being shy, while only one-third of the frequently aggressive offenders were shy.

The pathological effects that shyness assumes in women are less obvious than in men. The society does not sanction nor provide outlets for impersonal sex; the neighborhood bars don't welcome women customers. Their isolated existence in the home, removed from the daily responsibilities of the business world, renders the shy woman's inability to function less noticeable than her male counterpart's.

The shy woman can write her diary as a mad, lonely, frustrated housewife without it ever being read by anyone. She may be an alcoholic long before anyone recognizes it, if she can manage to get the kids off to school and dinner on the table.

But the pathology is there even if it isn't lit up in neon lights. The loneliness and isolation of the shy woman are most likely to be expressed in a psychological depression that leads to pill popping, alcoholic excess, institutionalization in a mental hospital, and helplessness that often ends in attempted suicide. (More women than men attempt suicide, but men are better at it—they use more lethal weapons.)

Men who cannot manage or cope in the society and break down one way or another are often cared for by nurturing wives. When wives can't hack it, they are abandoned. It has recently been reported that husbands are far more likely to abandon alcoholic wives than are wives to abandon their alcoholic husbands.

So the shy woman without the outlets available to shy men, and with an even greater degree of solitary confinement, may go more quietly mad, batter her helpless children, seek social stimulation vicariously through her favorite talk and quiz shows, or experience intimacy and sexual fulfillment only in the unreal world of her fantasies.

The extremely shy person in the process of becoming anonymous gives up his or her individuality and becomes just an object on the social scene. To lose oneself in the crowd is one defense against being identifiable in a threatening environment, just like schoolchildren trying to make themselves disappear when the teacher asks a question they can't answer.[8] However, once shy people become objects, then it may be that the only way they can get anyone to take them seriously is through acts of violence and destruction. "If you won't let me play with you, I'll kick down your sand castle and then you will have to recognize my existence and my power."

When driven to the wall by dehumanizing forces, the chronically shy person has two options: to become indistinguishable from the wall, or to assert the strength of his or her individuality and destroy the wall. The many social, psychological, and economic conditions that make all of us lose our sense of personal worth secretly make each of us into a potential assassin.

The point to be made here is that we must encourage our children to express their feelings—positive and negative ones—*when* they are being experienced. They must not just be allowed to do so, they must be supported in these efforts to communicate strongly held emotions, even if these emotions are at first unsettling to others. Without this communication, change is not possible and the shy person is trapped in an intolerable situation. The consequence is sometimes violent rage turned on others, maybe innocent victims of the shy person's own victimization. The mother who batters and abuses her child may very well prove to be a lonely, shy individual without friends and without socially acceptable outlets for her aggression. And then the baby won't stop crying or wets his diapers too often—and the lid is flipped.

However, we must also recognize that the sudden act of violence is the exception. What then of the overcontrolled shy person who never turns his or her aggression outward? There is only one other direction for it to go. When aggression is turned inward, feelings of worthlessness, inadequacy, self-contempt and depression follow. In turn, this sense of despair and powerlessness sets the stage for the final annihilation of self—suicide.

Shyness, submission, and social control

If we could interview people who interacted with one of the sudden murderers on the day before he or she lost all control, what do you expect they might have told us? I believe we would hear how good they were, what a pleasure it was to have them in class, around the house, or on the job. As a group, they would receive top marks for "good citizenship," for "discipline," for "following orders." These shy young people probably never made a fuss or a mess. They weren't boisterous in class and would not get labeled as being one of those hyperkinetic kinds. They knew their place and kept it. They did what was expected of them, conforming to all the rules and regulations.

It is on such a foundation of submissiveness that oppressive forms of social and political control must rest. To a large extent, agents of socialization (such as parents, teachers, and relatives) are unwitting accomplices in preparing the next generation to submit to the existing power structure of the present one. They serve as double agents, talking about "freedom" and "growth" but actually promoting fears of "too much freedom," "being too far out," "not taking chances," and the dangers of "acting up."

Thousands of shy people I have surveyed say that authorities by virtue of their roles in society or their expertise make them feel shy. This finding, interpreted a bit differently, indicates that they have learned to *fear* authority. Not respect and admire, but fear. Shy people do not challenge an authority figure whom they fear. They certainly do not do so openly and publicly. They are like the shy young Carol Burnett who tells us: "I was very quiet in school and I was a good student—I did what the teacher said—I respected the authority." Instead, their silent opposition to injustice, if they perceive it, is manipulated into becoming the nonvocal support of the "silent majority."

From being shy children who were seen but not heard, they have become shy adults, neither seen nor heard as ever making trouble for the powers that be. Most parents are not upset at having a shy child; I think they prefer it to an outspoken, independent child. It is only when he or she is "too shy" that they become concerned. And so the Good Citizenship Award goes to Mr. Shy Guy. This pattern of training a large segment of society to accept the domination of others is exemplified in class and caste practices in many countries.

According to Erich Fromm's brilliant thesis, *Escape from Freedom* totalitarian governments like Hitler's flourish when people are induced to trade freedom for security.[9] When freedom is made into something to be feared, then it seems like a good bargain to get some nice security by giving it up to a leader. A dictator's power is measured by the number of people who escape from freedom for this illusion of security. Shyness abhors freedom with its lack of structure, its individual responsibility, and its many demands to act and initiate, not just react and wait. The shy person is better at playing follow-the-leader than at playing being the leader, or the opposition.

All systems of oppressive social control gain their power by first alienating the people from the natural power of the community of equal citizens. The followers learn to distrust one another and pledge loyalty to ideologies rather than human beings. This isolate-and-conquer tactic was used to full advantage on American POW's in North Korean prisons by the Chinese Communists attempting to brainwash them.[10] Even in the mock prison we created at Stanford, rebellion by the prisoners was met with a strategy of destroying prisoner solidarity by giving some of them special privileges while denying basic rights to others. Privileged classes support whatever system grants those privileges.

Another way that social and political institutions become dominant is by promoting a self-survival, "me first" mentality. By forcing us to be absorbed in our own problems of making it through the day, the social order leaves us with no energy to care for our brothers. It is only by taking responsibility for the well-being and happiness of another person that ours is made more secure.

Through the shyness clinic, it has become clearer to me that shy men and women have abdicated responsibility for taking the risk of freedom, for keeping the life force flowing. Caught up in the web of ego-centric preoccupations, they stop tuning in to what other people are saying and feeling. They rarely notice the tears or hurts of others because their own psychological survival is an all-consuming obsession. When a person is willing to hide behind the security blanket of passive anonymity, not only is freedom sacrificed, but the passion for life as well. Under such circumstances, blind obedience to authority is easier to obtain and fanatical mass movements find ready and faithful followers.

All of us *want* to live a more fulfilling, rich life. But to accomplish this, we must be willing to risk freedom, to break out of our own prisons, to gamble on a new friendship, to take the chance on a love affair. It's not always easy. But there are ways that each of us can build our own self-confidence; there are definite social skills that we can learn; there are specific things that we can do to help the shy people in our lives. That's what Part II is all about.

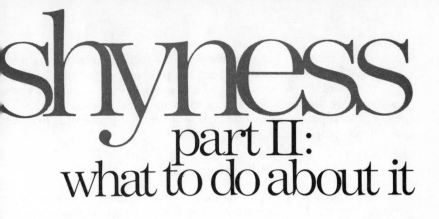

shyness

part II:
what to do about it

A fter spending the past five years conducting research on shyness and teaching seminars about the psychology of shyness, I began to look for ways to overcome shyness. It was not enough just to map out what shyness is, it was time to change what shyness was doing to people. I was spurred on by hundreds of letters and phone calls from desperately shy people seeking help.

Changing your life

I started a shyness clinic at Stanford to try out different approaches to treating shyness. I knew from our research that shyness was a complex problem that would demand a variety of techniques to overcome it. The tactics, strategies, and exercises that have proved most effective in helping our shy clients are presented in this part of the book.

However, the advice and exercises that follow can only be of value if you have made the decision to change your life. If you are tired of being shy, no longer want to survive on a diet of social leftovers, or feel unhappy seeing people you care about too shy to enjoy the opportunities life is offering, the time has come to change all that. Four basic kinds of change are called for. Changes in:

- the way you think about yourself and about shyness
- the way you behave
- relevant aspects of the way other people think and act
- certain social values that promote shyness.

No small order, but, like the building of the great pyramids of Egypt it can be achieved by moving one block at a time. There is no swift and easy magic cure, no certain social success with one application of Doctor Zimbardo's sweet-smelling snake oil. There is, however, one very potent ingredient that you already possess, but probably do not use as often or as effectively as you could or should—*the power of your own mind.*

In order to effect change in oneself or in others, you must first believe that change is possible. Then, you must really want to change away from one kind of behavior pattern toward a more desirable one. Finally, you must be willing to commit time and energy, and to risk some short-term failures, in practicing change tactics that can lead to long-term success.

The myth of unchangeability

The first barrier to conquer is the myth of the unchangeability of personality. Cornelius Bakker, a psychiatrist who believes this myth must be destroyed, reminds us that: "The prevailing idea concerning the nature of man which has dominated Western Civilization since its inception includes the hypothesis that man has an essence, a soul, a personality or a character which stands behind his actions and motivates them."[1]

Psychiatry, religion, and other social institutions promote belief systems that lead us to think of ourselves as possessing such an essence, which, by definition, is static and unchangeable. This inner force allegedly is responsible for what we are and what we do. Such a view makes all change superficial and temporary. Psychiatric patients who improve are described as taking a "flight into health." When these patients are no longer disturbed by the mental problem that brought them to treatment in the first place, they are not "cured," rather their "disease state is in remission" (lurking behind a mask of sanity, perhaps?).

A substantial body of evidence exists (including much of my own research) to support the opposite conclusion, namely, that human personality and behavior are quite changeable when the situation changes. Human nature is remarkably pliable, readily adapting itself to the challenges of whatever environment it finds itself in. Adaptability to environmental change is, in fact, the key to survival; humans and animals that fail to do so soon become extinct. Thus, to change behavior, we must look to factors in the current situation that maintain the undesirable behavior, as well as focus on alterations in the situation that will call forth and support desirable behaviors.

Because many of us have bought this myth of the unchangeable essence, "the real me," we approach therapeutic change with cynical pessimism: "Maybe it works for them, but it can't change me." Or, over time, we find something positive even in our misery and our handicaps. Those "secondary gains" of misfortune often have immediate benefits we are unwilling to give up for the cure. For example, one of my students with an awful stutter unconsciously used his handicap to test the genuineness of his friendships. If people liked him despite the painful experience he put them through, they were "true" friends. In addition, he had a built-in excuse for striking out on dates, one he was not eager to give up even though he wanted to get rid of his stutter. For some of the shy people I've worked with, their desire to no longer be shy is tempered by the knowledge that they will have to take more risks in initiating action. Also, shyness may be a convenient umbrella preventing exposure to even worse feelings—being unwanted, unloved, uninteresting, unintelligent, or an un-person.

Taking the plunge

You can change dramatically if you believe you can and if you're willing to sacrifice some of the ill-gotten gains of shyness. Remember, only a minority of those people who are presently shy have always been so. There are many more people—40 percent from our survey—who have successfully conquered their shyness. Shyness, even of the severest variety, has been and can be changed. But it takes work—hard work.

Many forces of inertia keep us where we are, prevent us from moving on to actualize our potential. Winning over such formidable opposition demands a real commitment on your part. Going through a ten-minute daily exercise in the privacy of your own home won't do it. If you no longer want to be a shy person, you must decide what kind of a person you do want to be, and then invest a great deal of time and energy in realizing your goal. Many of the activities in this book will assist you in doing just that. They are designed to help you:

- understand yourself better
- understand your shyness better
- build self-esteem
- develop specific and successful social skills
- help others who are shy
- learn ways to alter our shyness-generating society.

Read each exercise through once to see what is being asked of you and to determine if you need some special materials or a particular setting. Some simple exercises can be done here and now, others require more time or involve other people. In some exercises, you will be asked to perform one task before reading the rest of the exercise.

Not all of the advice, counsel, recommendations, or exercises that follow in the next six chapters will be appropriate or relevant for your needs. Take what fits; share with others what might better suit them. It is easy to dismiss some or all of these exercises as simple-minded or beneath you, or to passively read them without actively doing them. But, of course; it is also easier to remain shy than to change, and to make these merely exercises in futility rather than an integral part of your personal plan for change.

My interest is only in helping shy people remove barriers to their greater freedom, to their fuller participation in life, and to their personal sense of worth and mastery. These are not gifts that anyone can give you. They must be sought, worked for, and, when gained, held on to. It is entirely up to you, but I hope you will choose to give it your best try.

7
understanding
yourself

A|fter so many years of living with ourselves, it would appear that we ought to know ourselves pretty well. Surprisingly, few of us do. We don't take the time to really get to know what we are like. We often fail to systematically analyze our values, our likes and dislikes, the basis for our beliefs, or the life styles we are living. We just plod on doing today more or less what we did yesterday, and expect to be doing the same tomorrow and hereafter.

What image do you project? Is that image under your control—that is, do others perceive you the way you want them to? Do you tend to feel responsible for the failures of your life? And when something good happens to you, is it more a matter of fate, luck, or your own efforts? Is there anything you would be willing to sacrifice your life for? These are but some of the questions you should start to ask yourself as we begin the process of self-discovery.

The exercises in this chapter will give you a chance to look squarely at your life. They are designed to get you to monitor your thoughts and feelings more closely and accurately. You will be asked to remember your childhood and the influence that parents and others have had on you. You will decide what is important in your life and what isn't. You will discover the messages and commandments you live by. And you will be given ways to determine where you've been, where you are now, and where you're headed.

The purpose of all these exercises is self-awareness, the first step to positive change.[1] We have stated repeatedly that at the core of shyness is an excessive preoccupation with the self, an overconcern with being negatively evaluated. Most of the exercises here will initially *increase* your self-awareness, perhaps making you even more self-conscious, more sensitized to your shyness. It is like learning to drive a car, to water ski, or to play a musical instrument. At first, you are excruciatingly aware of your incompetence, your lack of coordination, your inability to make your body do what your brain tells it to do—"now parallel park," "now get on top of the water," "now play music." You are all thumbs, just dead weight, tone deaf. You are aware of how serious you are, of all your mistakes, or of the discrepancy between what you see and hear yourself doing and the ideal performance in your mind's eye. With practice, separate, jerky actions are integrated into smooth, effortless patterns.

So, too, it will be with your concentrated effort to overcome shyness. You must be patient and expect some setbacks, some failures, some anxiety, and a lot more of *you* to be in the spotlight. But we can learn much from our failures if we are prepared to accept them as an inevitable—but temporary—consequence of trying something new.

These self-awareness exercises are challenging, but they can be fun as well. The objective is simply to get in touch with your inner self and, at the same time, become more aware of the public self you project. Ultimately our goal is to have you more accepting of your inner image while making others more accepting of your public image.

Drawing yourself

This activity will help you discover how you perceive yourself. Take a large piece of paper and an assortment of colored pencils and draw a picture of yourself in any way you want. It might be symbolic or literal, clothed or nude, a portrait or a full figure. Give your drawing a name. *(Complete this before going on.)*

- Do you fill in all or part of your space?
- Is your outline sharp, fuzzy, disconnected?
- Are parts of your body missing? What ones? Out of proportion? Hidden?
- Clothed or nude? Designed to be seen? Touched?
- What colors predominate?
- Are you showing any emotion? Which one(s)?
- Are you feeling anything you are not revealing?
- Are you active or passive?
- Are you an isolated figure or do you exist in some context?

Looking in the mirror

Here is another good self-perception exercise. Look at yourself in the mirror. Spend ten minutes doing so. Look at each part of your body carefully. Study it. What do you see?

- What is your best feature? How would you describe yourself to a stranger who is going to meet you at an airport or train depot?
- Imagine meeting yourself for the first time.
- What would be your first impression?
- How could you make a more positive impression?
- What is your worst physical attribute?
- Imagine that it is as bad, as ugly as it could possibly be.

- Now laugh at that image as you do when seeing your body deformed in a curved mirror at a carnival.
- If you are willing, look at yourself without clothes. First examine yourself in the mirror and then look at your body directly.
- What parts of your body are you satisfied with?
- What parts could use some improvement?
- What features would you like to trade in? For what in return?

The movie of your life

This activity will give you some insights into your life so far. Lie comfortably and close your eyes. Imagine that you are watching an hour-long movie of your life.

- Where does the movie take place?
- What's the plot outline?
- Who are the major characters?
- Who are the minor characters?
- Who is directing the movie?
- What is the audience doing as it watches the movie?
- What is/are the turning point(s) of the story?
- How does it end?
- Are there any morals to be derived?
- What does the audience do when the movie is over?

Labelling yourself

Make a list of ten words, phrases, and traits that describe you best.

Rank

I am _____ _____

I am _____ _____

I am _____ _____

I am _____ _____

I am _____ _____

I am _____ _____

I am _____ _____

I am _____ _____

I am _____ _____

I am _____ _____

Rank each of these from your most important characteristic, 1, down to the least important, 10.

How many of these items are positive values, negative values, or neutral descriptions? Add up the ranks of the items in these three categories.

_____ positive (e.g., happy, intelligent, successful)

_____ negative (e.g., depressed, fat, impotent)

_____ neutral (e.g., student, man, forty-four years old)

Which items would your best friend think were the two most and the two least characteristic of you? Are they the same as your selections? Perhaps ask him or her to rank all ten.

Protecting your secret self

Find out your unique qualities by trying this activity: You discover a sinister plot by a mad scientist to create a carbon-copy duplicate of you in robot form. In every detail, your twin is so identical to you it's uncanny. Since your twin is evil, you do not want other people to mistake it for you.

- What about you is so unique it could not be duplicated?
- How might people who know you best tell you apart?
- Is there anyone who shares a secret with you who would know you by that disclosure?

• Once you reveal anything, the robot twin learns and mimics it perfectly. What personal secret would you save for the final revelation to prove to yourself that you are the real you and not the imitation?

———◆•◆———

The best and the worst of it

All of our lives are influenced by events and people. Here's an activity to help you detect these influences on your life.

List the five best things that have happened in your life.

1. _____

2. _____

3. _____

4. _____

5. _____

Next to each item, list who or what was responsible.

List the five worst things that have happened in your life.

1. _____

2. _____

3. _____

4. _____

5. _____

Next to each item, list who or what was responsible.

How many of each were *you* responsible for?

———◆•◆———

Your metaphor of time

Each of us thinks of time in somewhat different images. The hour glass is one metaphor for time: the sand running through is the present, that yet to pass is the future, and the past is at the bottom where the sand has already fallen. Draw your personal metaphor or time perspective below, labelling past, present and future.

Signify the relative importance of each of the following by the way you divide the time line below: (a) thoughts of the past, how things used to be, your origins, childhood, earlier times; (b) living in the present, experiencing the here and now, getting involved in process and action; and (c) the future, thoughts about goals, dreams, products, what will be.

_____

Put an arrow where you are now. How much of your life have you spent already? How much lies before you?

Which of the following drawings best represent your life time cycle? Why?

Allocating time

How do you spend your time? First, consider the time you spend in each of the following categories:

Work activities that you do because you have to, but don't like to

(such as:_____)

Work activities that you do because you want to (such

as:_____)

Rituals (such as:_____)

Intimate encounters (such as:_____)

Unpleasant games (such as:_____)

Satisfying activities (such as:_____)

Planning ahead (such as:_____)

Idle, down time (such as:_____)

Other, namely_____

Then partition each circle below into segments to reflect these time allocations.

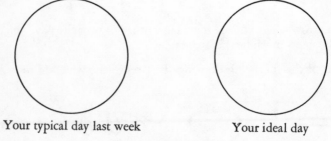

Your typical day last week   Your ideal day

The house you lived in

Draw a detailed floor plan of a house or apartment you lived in before you were ten. As you enter each room, imagine the furniture, pictures, smells, and events you associate with the room.

- What was your favorite room?
- Where were your secret places?
- Are there any rooms that you can't enter? Why?

Plans

You have been put in charge of a five-year master plan to change your life. The public wants to know your three major goals for the next year.

1. _____

2. _____

3. _____

What are you currently doing, or intending to do to achieve each one?

1. _____

2. _____

3. _____

Five years from now, what five goals have you set for yourself, that is, what would you like your life to be at that time?

1. _____

2. _____

3. _____

4. _____

5. _____

Think about how you will get from where you are to where you plan to be. How specific/vague are those means to these ends? What can you do to make them more substantial?

Emotional tuning

When you think about the pain you have suffered, your disappointments, grief, and worst times, do you feel sad or angry? If sad, do you feel like crying? Can you cry now?

If angry, do you feel like screaming? Can you scream now?

When you think about the pleasures you've experienced, the joys, successes, and good times, do you feel euphoric? If so, how do you show it? Or, if you feel unworthy of it, how do you tell it?

Family values

What ten commandments would best summarize the rules, ideals, and taboos your family advocated? List them:

1. _____
2. _____
3. _____
4. _____
5. _____
6. _____
7. _____
8. _____
9. _____
10. _____

What jokes/stories were told over and over again?

Some of the tension/ambiguity we all experience may be a result of contradictory messages we received as children. Can you identify some of the mixed messages your father sent out to you? Can you recall those your mother transmitted?

In many families, there are guards and prisoners, sometimes also a warden. In your family, who played these roles? If you have a family of your own now, are you the guard or the prisoner, or do you alternate roles?

Your fantasy life

If you could be reincarnated as an animal, what animal would you be? Why that particular one?

If you could trade places with another person for a week, who would that be? Why?

If the good fairy granted you three wishes, what would they be?

1. _____

2. _____

3. _____

If you could be invisible for a day, how would you use that power?

If you had the extrasensory ability to perceive one person's thoughts and deepest secrets, who would you choose to tune in on?

If you could take a magic-carpet ride to one place anywhere in the world or outer space, or in any time dimension, where would you go?

If you could make love to anyone in the world for one night, who would that person be?

One month to live

Suppose you have a fatal disease and only one month to live. You have unlimited money and your health is still all right.

• How will you spend your last month?
• Where will you go?
• What will you do?
• Who will be with you?
• How will you spend your last day?
• How will you die?
• Who will be at your deathbed?
• What will be your last words? Your epitaph?
• Who will deliver your eulogy? What will that person say?

Good news! You've been granted a reprieve! You have ten, twenty, sixty years to live. Now how will you spend them?

Imaginary will

Make an imaginary will in which you bequeath your personal/financial possessions. Note which things you value most.

What personal qualities would you like to assign to family and friends? Which do you want to bury with you?

What personal qualities were gifts from people in your life? Who are you living up to?

────── ◆ ──────

Write yourself a letter

A technique that a shy youngster has used effectively involved sitting down and writing herself a letter. She says:

> As for expressing myself, I feel I've taken a really big step. A lot of times I just like to write a letter to myself. It would contain my feelings and it might sound like a dream letter or a hate letter. Since they are letters to myself, I don't censor my feelings. I guess to some people it might sound crazy, but as long as it can help me with my problem, I really don't care what people think. Sometimes I think I've taken a few steps too many or something because I've really changed—a lot. I'm now proud and very thankful.

Write yourself a letter now and get into the habit of doing so whenever you feel the need to express some strong sentiments or to clarify some ambiguous reactions.

You might also want to tape record a state-of-yourself message from time to time and listen to it for content as well as for style of delivery. What messages of hope, anxiety, successes, failures, etc. are you hearing? Are you sending yourself mixed messages?

────── ◆ ──────

8
understanding your shyness

B y now you ought to know quite a bit about shyness from Part of this book. But how much do you know about your own personal brand of shyness? Or, how well are you tuned in to the shyness of those you live with and work with? What turns on those feelings of shyness? How often do they occur? How strong are they? What are you feeling and thinking when shyness comes your way? Which behaviors are telltale outward signs of what you are experiencing inside? What have you done to handle such reactions in the past?

The previous chapter asked you to direct your attention to the kind of person you are in general, to your roots, your current life situation, and where you're headed. Here we want to focus in on just one aspect of your makeup—your shyness. The chapters that follow offer strategies and tactics to help you overcome, cope with, and prevent shyness. You will be able to do so more effectively by first diagnosing what shyness actually means to you. By reflecting on the causes, correlates, and consequences of your shyness, you gain two important benefits. First, you are laying the groundwork for a rational plan of intervention, treatment, or change. In addition, by explicitly analyzing the nature and dimensions of personal shyness, you begin to turn it out, to distance yourself from it by objectifying it. This allows you to get a better perspective on that inner distress you want to avoid or run away from. In a sense, I'd like you to put your shyness on a psychological operating table and approach it with the cool, detached concern of a surgeon carefully inspecting a patient before deciding where and how to proceed with the operation.

This initial assessment of shyness also provides a baseline against which to evaluate later changes in shyness that result from practicing the exercises. It is imperative that you be actively involved in these exercises, complete the shyness survey, and write out your replies to each of the other exercises. You will want to look back on these answers a month from now, six months from now, and next year to see if your views of yourself and of shyness have undergone any change.

If you will take the time to conscientiously chronicle the shyness you suffer, you will be in a more formidable position to profit from the knowledge of what is and was. Therein lies the basis for your new vision of what can and shall be.

Stanford Shyness Survey

This is a version of the survey that we gave to over 5,000 people around the world. Fill it out quickly, then go back over it more carefully to see how exactly shyness affects your life.

_____ 1. Do you consider yourself to be a shy person?   1 = yes 2 = no

_____ 2. If yes, have you always been shy (were shy previously and still are)?   1 = yes 2 = no

_____ 3. If no to question 1, was there *ever* a prior time in your life when you were shy?   1 = yes 2 = no

If no, then you are finished with this survey. Thanks.
If yes to any of the above, please continue.

_____ 4. *How shy* are you when you feel shy?
    1 = extremely shy   4 = moderately shy
    2 = very shy   5 = somewhat shy
    3 = quite shy   6 = only slightly shy

_____ 5. How *often* do you experience (have you experienced) these feelings of shyness?
    1 = every day   4 = one or two times a week
    2 = almost every day   5 = occasionally, less than once
    3 = often, nearly every other   a week
        day   6 = rarely, once a month or less

_____ 6. Compared to your *peers* (of similar age, sex, and background), how shy are you?
    1 = much more shy   3 = about as shy
    2 = more shy   4 = less shy
                               5 = much less shy

_____ 7. How *desirable* is it for you to be shy?
    1 = very undesirable   3 = neither
    2 = undesirable   4 = desirable
                               5 = very desirable

_____ 8. Is (or was) your shyness ever a personal *problem* for you?
    1 = yes, often   3 = yes, occasionally
    2 = yes, sometimes   4 = rarely
                               5 = never

_____ 9. When you are feeling shy can you *conceal* it and have others believe you are not feeling shy?
    1 = yes, always
    2 = sometimes I can, sometimes not
    3 = no, I usually can't hide it

_____ 10. Do you consider yourself more of an *introvert* or an *extrovert?*

1 = strongly introverted   4 = neither
2 = moderately introverted   5 = slightly extroverted
3 = slightly introverted   6 = moderately extroverted
    7 = strongly extroverted

(11–19) Which of the following do you believe may be among the *causes* of your shyness? Check all that are applicable to you.

_____ 11. Concern for negative evaluation

_____ 12. Fear of being rejected

_____ 13. Lack of self-confidence

_____ 14. Lack of specific social skills (specify) : _____

_____

_____

_____

_____ 15. Fear of being intimate with others

_____ 16. Preference for being alone

_____ 17. Value placed on nonsocial interests, hobbies, etc.

_____ 18. Personal inadequacy, handicap (specify) : _____

_____

_____ 19. Others: (specify) : _____

_____

_____

(20–27) Perceptions of your shyness

Do the following people consider *you* to be shy? How shy do you think they judge you to be? Answer using this scale.

1 = extremely shy   6 = only slightly shy
2 = very shy   7 = not shy
3 = quite shy   8 = don't know
4 = moderately shy   9 = not applicable
5 = somewhat shy

_____ 20. your mother

_____ 21. your father

_____ 22. your siblings (brothers and/or sisters)

_____ 23. close friends

_____ 24. your steady boy/girl friend/spouse

_____ 25. your high-school classmates

_____ 26. your current roommate

_____ 27. Teachers or employers, fellow workers who know you well

_____ 28. In deciding whether or not to call yourself a "shy person," was your decision based on the fact that:

　　1 = you are (were) shy all of the time in all situations

　　2 = you are (were) shy at least 50 percent of the time, in more situations than not

　　3 = you are (were) shy only occasionally, but those occasions are (were) of enough importance to justify calling yourself a shy person

_____ 29. Have people ever misinterpreted your shyness as a different trait, e.g., "indifference," "aloofness," "poise"?

　　1 = yes

　　　Specify: _____

　　　_____

　　　_____

　　2 = no

_____ 30. Do you ever feel shy when you are *alone*?   1 = yes 2 = no

_____ 31. Do you ever feel *embarrassed* when you are alone?

　　1 = yes 2 = no

_____ 32. If yes, please describe when, how, or why:_____

　　　_____

　　　_____

(33–36)　What makes you shy?

　　33. If you now experience, or have ever experienced feelings of shyness, please indicate which of the following situations, activities, and types of people make you feel shy. (Place a check mark next to *all* of the appropriate choices.)

Situations and activities that make me feel shy:

_____ social situations in general

_____ large groups

_____ small, task-oriented groups (e.g., seminars at school, work groups on the job)

_____ small, social groups (e.g., at parties, dances)

_____ one-to-one interactions with a person of the same sex

_____ one-to-one interactions with a person of the opposite sex

_____ situations where I am vulnerable (e.g., when asking for help)

_____ situations where I am of lower status than others (e.g., when speaking to superiors, authorities)

_____ situations requiring assertiveness (e.g., when complaining about faulty service in a restaurant or the poor quality of a product)

_____ situations where I am the focus of attention, before a large group (e.g., when giving a speech)

_____ situations where I am the focus of attention, before a small group (e.g., when being introduced, when being asked directly for my opinion)

_____ situations where I am being evaluated or compared with others (e.g., when being interviewed, when being criticized)

_____ new interpersonal situations in general

_____ where sexual intimacy is possible

34. Now, please go back and indicate next to each item you checked whether your shyness has been elicited in the *past month* by this situation or activity:

   0 = not in the past month, but prior   3 = moderately so
   1 = yes, very strongly   4 = only mildly
   2 = yes, strongly so   5 = not at all

35. Types of people who make me feel shy:

   _____ my parents

   _____ my siblings (brothers and/or sisters)

   _____ other relatives

   _____ friends

   _____ strangers

   _____ foreigners

_____ authorities (by virtue of their role—police, teacher, superior at work)

_____ authorities (by virtue of their knowledge—intellectual superiors, experts)

_____ elderly people (much older than you)

_____ children (much younger than you)

_____ persons of the opposite sex, in a group

_____ persons of the same sex, in a group

_____ a person of the opposite sex, one-to-one

_____ a person of the same sex, one-to-one

36. Now, please go back and indicate next to each one you checked whether your shyness has been elicited in the past month by this person (or type of person):

0 = not in the past month but prior
1 = yes, very strongly
2 = yes, strongly so
3 = moderately so
4 = only mildly

(37–40) **Shyness reactions**

_____ 37. How do you know you are shy, i.e., what *cues* do you use?

1 = my internal feelings, thoughts, symptoms only (private)
2 = my overt behavior in a given situation only (public)
3 = I use a mix of internal responses and overt behavior

Physical reactions

38. If you do experience, or have ever experienced feelings of shyness, which of the following *physical reactions* are associated with such feelings? Put 0 next to those that are not relevant, then order the rest from 1 (most typical, usual, severe) to 2 (next most), and so on.

_____ blushing	_____ dry mouth
_____ increased pulse	_____ tremors
_____ butterflies in stomach	_____ perspiration
_____ tingling sensations	_____ fatigue
_____ heart pounding	_____ others (specify below)

_____

_____

_____

Thoughts, feelings

39. What are the specific *thoughts and sensations* associated with your shyness? Put 0 next to those that are not relevant, then order the rest from 1 (most typical. usual, severe) to 2 (next most), and so on. (More than one item can be given the same rank.)

_____ positive thoughts (e.g., feeling content with myself)

_____ no specific thoughts (e.g., daydreaming, thinking about nothing in particular)

_____ self-consciousness (e.g., an extreme awareness of myself, of my every action)

_____ thoughts that focus on the unpleasantness of the situation (e.g., thinking that the situation is terrible, thinking that I'd like to be out of the situation)

_____ thoughts that provide distractions (e.g., thinking of other things I could be doing, thinking that the experience will be over in a short while)

_____ negative thoughts about myself (e.g., feeling inadequate, insecure, inferior, stupid)

_____ thoughts about the evaluations of me that others are making (e.g., wondering what the people around me are thinking of me)

_____ thoughts about the way in which I am handling myself (e.g., wondering what kind of impression I am creating and how I might control it)

_____ thoughts about shyness in general (e.g., thinking about the extent of my shyness and its consequences, wishing that I weren't shy)

_____ others (specify) : _____

_____

Actions

40. If you do experience, or have ever experienced feelings of shyness, what are the *obvious behaviors* which might indicate to others that you are feeling shy? Put 0 next to those that are not relevant, then rank order the rest from 1 (most typical, usual, severe) to 2 (next most), and so on. (More than one item can be given the same rank.)

_____ low speaking voice   _____ inability to make eye contact

_____ avoidance of other people

_____ silence (a reluctance to talk)

_____ stuttering

_____ rambling, incoherent talk

_____ posture

_____ avoidance of taking action

_____ escape from the situation

_____ others (specify):

_____

_____

(41–42) Shyness consequences

41. What are the *negative* consequences of being shy? (Check all those that apply to you.)

_____ none, no negative consequences

_____ creates social problems; makes it difficult to meet new people, make new friends, enjoy potentially good experiences

_____ has negative emotional consequences; creates feelings of loneliness, isolation, depression

_____ prevents positive evaluations by others (e.g., my personal assets never become apparent because of my shyness)

_____ makes it difficult to be appropriately assertive, to express opinions, to take advantage of opportunities

_____ allows incorrect negative evaluations by others (e.g., I may unjustly be seen as unfriendly or snobbish or weak)

_____ creates cognitive and expressive difficulties; inhibits the capacity to think clearly while with others and to communicate effectively with them

_____ encourages excessive self-consciousness, preoccupation with myself

42. What are the *positive* consequences of being shy? (Check all those that apply to you.)

_____ none, no positive consequences

_____ creates a modest, appealing impression; makes one appear discreet, introspective

_____ helps avoid interpersonal conflicts

_____ provides a convenient form of anonymity and protection

_____ provides an opportunity to stand back, observe others, act carefully and intelligently

_____ avoids negative evaluations by others (e.g., a shy person is not considered obnoxious, overaggressive, or pretentious)

_____ provides a way to be selective about the people with whom one interacts

_____ enhances personal privacy and the pleasure that solitude offers

_____ creates positive interpersonal consequences by not putting others off, intimidating them, or hurting them

_____ 43. Do you think your shyness can be overcome?

1 = yes
2 = no
3 = uncertain

_____ 44. Are you willing to seriously work at overcoming it?

1 = yes, definitely
2 = yes, perhaps
3 = not sure yet
4 = no

How did your shyness develop?

Write a letter to me talking about how your shyness developed. In your letter, cover the following points:

- What is the *first* time that you remember feeling shy? Describe the situation, people involved, and your feelings.

  a) What decisions about yourself did you make based on this experience?

  b) Did others say anything to you that made you think that you were shy? What exactly did they say? What decisions did you make at that time about yourself based on what they said?

  c) Can you now see that there was a misinterpretation involved (of motives, responsibility, or missed signals)? Describe what really took place and how it was distorted.

  d) Did anyone do anything to make you feel better (less shy), or worse? Who? What did they do?

  e) Have those decisions you've made about yourself changed over the years or have they remained about the same?

- What is the *next* time that you remember feeling shy?

- Think about another time during your childhood, then during your teen years, and then this last year when you've felt most shy. Do the same things still make you feel shy?

- Do people say things to you now that lead you to think of yourself as shy? What?

- Do you let other people know that you are a shy person? How do you signal this, and how soon after meeting someone do you communicate this message?

- Do you ever do or say things that make other people in your life feel shy?

Costs and benefits

What has being shy cost you? What opportunities have you passed up and experiences forfeited because you are or were shy? Make an itemized cost accounting of each thing you have lost, given up, or settled for less of. Do so on a sheet with the following headings.

Shyness Liabilities

Time in your life	Valued event, action, opportunity, person that was lost, delayed, diminished, etc.	Personal consequence to you
1.		
2.		
.		
.		
.		

Now think very hard about the subtle things you have gained from pasting that shyness label on yourself. Most of us learn how to derive something positive even from adversity. What do you get out of your shyness? Since we don't usually acknowledge these "secondary gains" of our primary disabilities, some examples may be in order: excuses, playing it safe and not taking unnecessary risks, avoiding criticism, keeping aggressive people away, not becoming emotional or too involved in other people's lives, etc. Make an itemized accounting of these gains.

Shyness Benefits

Situation	Action taken, or refused	Benefit realized	Any long-term liability?
1.			
2.			
.			
.			
.			

Rejection

Write down some past rejections that hurt you a great deal. Then, write down the areas in which you are most sensitive to rejection. What is the worst thing that can happen in each of these areas (how could the rejection have been even worse)? In what areas can you tolerate rejection, shrug off put-downs? Is there any basic difference between these two general areas of vulnerability and invulnerability?

Try to imagine scenarios in which some of these unpleasant rejections turned out to be not so bad after all—that is, the rejection was not intended as such, was misperceived by you, was funny, or taught you a valuable lesson. Write brief scripts to accompany these scenarios for several rejection episodes.

When you're anxious . . .

When you're anxious, what do you *do?*

_____ pace the floor

_____ smoke a cigarette

_____ wring your hands

_____ call a friend

_____ do some distracting activity, like _____

_____ jog, ride a bike, mow the lawn, clean the house, or engage in some other physical activity

_____ take a drink

_____ pop a tranquilizer

_____ smoke a joint

_____ go to the movies

_____ play music

_____ spread the misery, complain to others

_____ overeat

_____ get a headache

_____ go shopping

_____ turn it into anger at myself

_____ turn it out as hostility toward others

_____ become dependent and passive

_____ imagine how Woody Allen would handle it, if Woody would

_____ write a letter or diary entry

_____ other actions taken: _____

_____

Which of these actually work and which are useless rituals? Which help to contain the anxiety, but don't help you with the underlying problem that aroused the anxiety in the first place? Which of these make matters worse for you in the long run?

What could you do that has positive, lasting consequences?

Test anxiety

Imagine that without warning one of the following events takes place in your life: (a) a surprise quiz is announced in your favorite, major subject, but you didn't do all the homework; (b) a telephone call informs you that you have been chosen to answer the $100,000 question on a TV quiz show.

What emotional reactions are you experiencing at that moment? What negative thoughts and sensations are you having?

This response might be called "test anxiety" aroused by being publicly tested when you feel less than competent to perform up to your expectations and ideals.

Now, scrutinize these feelings and decide in what ways they are similar to or different from your feelings of being socially anxious.

Taking risks

You can try for the $100,000 prize—winner takes all, loser gets nothing —or you can pass it up and be certain of winning $5,000. Do you take the risk or settle for the sure thing?

You can go on a date with a so-so person who you know will definitely accept, or you can let your ideal person know you are ready and willing, although you have no idea what his/her response will be. Do you stand pat with your two pairs or gamble on a full house?

List all the important chances, risks, and gambles that you have taken in your life. Next to each, note whether it proved wise or foolish. (*Complete this before going on.*)

Now go out and take a risk. Do something "scary" that you would like to, ought to, but have been avoiding. Do one scary thing every day this week, first writing down what you intend to do and why it is scary for you. Then record whether or not you did it, and what happened when you did. Of course, I mean socially scary, not scary like robbing a bank or jumping from the Golden Gate Bridge.

Loneliness

- Do you often feel lonely?
- When do you feel most lonely?
- Who or what is (was) responsible for your loneliness?
- Do you ever enjoy the solitude of being alone?
- What can you do about your loneliness that you have not already done?

Imagine being snowed in your home for a weekend with no way out, no communication possible with anyone else, and no help to come until Monday. You are alone and have no obligations, that is, no "homework" to occupy your time. Plan how you will turn this emergency into a joyful, self-indulgent weekend. You do have stores of good food, wine, music, books, cards, games, hot water, pen and paper, but no TV or radio.

Rough out a plan for your solitary survival, stressing sensual, sophisticated, or sloppy strategies sure to sweeten such solitude. (*Complete this before going on.*)

So why wait for the snow job? Go have yourself a good time. Who deserves it more than you?

Memorize and assimilate into your own thinking the profound meaning of the following view of aloneness (by the Greek philosopher Epictetus):

> When you have shut your doors and darkened your room,
> remember, never to say that you are alone; for you are
> not alone, but God is within and your genius is within.
> *Discourses,* 2nd century

Shyness barriers

Between you and some of your goals are shyness barriers that inhibit or make difficult getting to those goals. Select one highly desired goal that gets blocked by the shyness barriers you erect. In the diagram below, note what that goal is, and then indicate along the path to it each of the barriers that in turn interfere with attaining that goal.

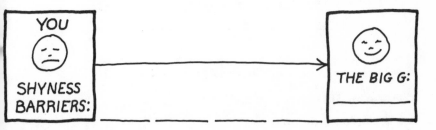

Like a commander in battle, formulate a plan to eliminate and overcome each of these barriers to the freer movement of your troops. Can you detour around some, redefine others, suffer some temporary losses, bluff through others, bite the bullet on some, use a better mine detector in other places, or reappraise your strengths while concealing the weaknesses in your forces? Develop a battle plan for each of your shyness barriers.

Sample Shyness Journal

Time	Situation and setting	Symptoms
Time of day	Where am I? What am I doing? (Or what do I want or need to do?) With whom?	How am I experiencing shyness?
Examples noon	Dorm lunch. Stranger sits next to me, introduces self, starts asking questions, etc.	Heart pounding, nervous, uncertain, don't know what to say. Start to look him in the eye.
3 P.M.	At the library, have first class assignment. Went on library tour but can't remember what to do. Have to ask the tour lady for help.	Hands sweaty, shaky. Blushing, tight stomach Wish I could leave.

Shyness journal

Keep a journal of the times you feel shy.

> Write down the time
> what happened (situation and setting)
> your reaction
> the consequences to you

Carry a small pad around in your pocket or purse so you can jot down the basic information as soon as possible after a shyness episode. Do this for a week, then transfer your observations into more formal journal entries in notebook pages arranged as in the sample above.

Name _____Sample_____ *Date* _____

Reactions	Consequences
What are my thoughts and feelings? (What's causing these feelings? What are others thinking, etc.?)	What do I do or not do as a result? Do I gain or lose something or someone? What should I have done or wish I had thought?
Why did he pick me? What does he want from me? I think he's too aggressive. He probably thinks I'm boring. I hope he doesn't tell everyone.	Don't finish lunch. Leave wishing I'd been more interesting. He might have been nice to know. Feel kind of lonely.
She'll recognize me and feel annoyed that I didn't listen. Why do I get so nervous that I can't remember? Worried I can't remember this time either. Maybe I should have taken another course. The course is dumb, the assignment is ridiculous— and I am too.	Decide to get a coke. Decide to try to watch a guy from the dorm who has experience. (It doesn't help.) Try to buy a book at the bookstore instead. Just can't ask the librarian. Worry about my inability to do this. Worry assignment will be late. I've lost time. Lost self-respect, feel angry. Ask for help, she doesn't remember me, tells me what I need. Not too bad after all.

Look for recurring patterns and themes that characterize your shyness episodes. Make new observations in your note pad every other week for a month of entries.

Now examine how often you experience shyness. Can you detect any changes in shyness frequency, intensity, type of reaction, and action decisions? Have you logged situations you've avoided altogether?

————◆•◆————

It is surprising to discover that Johnny Carson, TV's premier talk-show host of the *Tonight Show,* considers himself to be shy. Instead of trying to overcome it or hide it, Carson has learned the secret of making it work for him instead of against him. "I don't fight it, I use it," he said in a recent interview.[1] "I get a lot of my energy on the show from compensating for my shyness." Judging from the amount of energy Johnny Carson puts out nightly on his show, he ought to share his energy conversion secret with the rest of us.

9
building
your self-esteem

The way we think about ourselves has profound effects on all aspects of our lives. People with a sense of positive self worth typically display poise and radiate confidence as outward signs of inner satisfaction. Such people are not dependent on the praise and social reinforcement of others, because they have learned how to be their own best friends and biggest boosters. They are the participators, the initiators, the facilitators who make the social machinery move, and they get the lion's share of whatever goodies are being passed out in society.

The people I know who enjoy this high-self-esteem niche in life do not crumble under criticism or feel devastated by rejection. They thank you for the "constructive advice." When confronted with a "no," it is never construed as a rejection of *them*. Instead, several alternatives are considered: their act needs more work, the approach was too fast, too gross, too subtle, too complicated; the situation and timing were not right; the no-sayer has a problem that needs counsel or sympathy. In any event, the cause of the "no" lies not within them but without; it can be analyzed and plans made to regroup forces and return again with a more polished act. It's easy then for them to be optimists; they get what they want more often than not.

Being your own worst enemy

In contrast, the person with low self-esteem seems star struck. He or she is likely to be more passive, persuasible, and less popular. These people are overly sensitive to negative criticism, thinking it confirms their inadequacy. They have difficulty accepting compliments ("You can't mean me, aw no, it was nothing, no big deal, you're just saying that to make me feel good"). With all that grief going for them, it is not surprising that researchers have found people with low self-esteem to be more neurotic than those with high self-esteem.[1]

A graduate student of mine hysterically informed me ten minutes before his Ph.D. oral examination that he couldn't go on, he wasn't prepared, he would make a fool of himself. Since it had taken my blood to arrange for five professors to be free at the same time for the next two hours, and since I knew that Gabe was talented, I gently pressured him onward. He performed admirably and passed with flying colors. When I conveyed the examiner's praise for his excellent presentation, he said of this distinguished panel of professors: "I'll have to reevaluate what *I* think of *them* if they thought that terrible performance was any good."

Gabe's case illustrates an important point: objectively positive feedback may not have much impact on beefing up a depressed sense of esteem;

"I don't suppose it's much compared with other inferiority complexes."

© 1976 *Punch* (Rothco Cartoons, Inc.)

people can still maintain a self-image that departs sharply from reality. Even very intelligent and talented individuals can be their own worst enemies once they let their self-esteem guard down.

If you don't think much of yourself, why should I, since you obviously know yourself better than anyone else? And if I persist in my delusion that you are a worthwhile and interesting person to know, will you behave so that I will see the error of my ways and agree that you are worthless? I've seen this happen many times with the extremely shy students in my shyness seminar and patients in the shyness clinic. Sharon, a pathologically shy young woman who hid her attractive face behind a mass of uncombed hair, resented being told to brush her hair back. It was only after ten sessions, while zooming in on her face with the close-up lens on the TV camera, that I happened to notice she was attractive. She had kept it a secret even in the closeness of a therapeutic relationship. But she balked at the suggestion to change her hairstyle so people could see her face better. "Damn it, that's the way my hair *is,* I've always worn it this way."

Shyness and low self-esteem go together. The research by Paul Pilkonis and other investigators in our shyness program has uncovered a significant correlation between the two; when shyness is high, self-esteem is low and when esteem is high, shyness moves out of the picture.[2]

A word of caution

Self-esteem is an evaluation of your own worth based on your perception of how you compare to others. But in making these comparisons, you need to be aware of several potential problems.

First, be careful of whom you choose as models for comparison. It is well to acknowledge certain others as "ideals," but not as the sole reference point for knowing when you have made it. Some people are inappropriate comparison targets because they are uniquely gifted with looks or with brains, or with a desirable physique or other inherited qualities. I'd like to look like Robert Redford, think like Einstein, talk like Richard Burton, and write as prolifically and as well as Isaac Asimov. Ideals can be emulated, but should not be the established measures of success, status, or accomplishment.

Second, by focusing on inappropriate models for comparison, you may not only be letting yourself in for frustration, you may also be encouraging envy, status seeking for its own sake, and a loss of enjoyment in the *process* of becoming, since it is only the *product* you're after.

I recently became aware of my own drift away from the process and joy of living because I had gradually accepted the values of a highly competitive, goal-oriented environment. I picked up a hitchhiker on the ride from my home in San Francisco to Stanford University, some thirty miles away in Palo Alto. He was a handsome, robust young man entering his twenties. We talked about college, about good campgrounds, and about vacations—he was obviously on one. When I asked where he was going, he answered, "South." "Los Angeles?" I inquired. "No." "Mexico, that far?" "No sir, just south."

I now became aware of a slow anger rising in my voice. Here we are having a good conversation and this ungrateful hippie is uptight about telling me where he's headed. As I pulled off the highway at the Palo Alto exit, I asked one more time, my curiosity and sense of injustice aroused, "Say, what city are you headed for?" His answer was a sweet remembrance of times past, when life was not so timebound for me.

"I'm not going anywhere in particular. I have two weeks off and I'm just heading south. I'll go as far as my money and rides take me and then come back. You see that way I don't have to worry about not getting there. In a way, I'm already there."

He couldn't be frustrated at not having achieved his goal. He could enjoy himself now since his satisfaction was not tied to future-oriented goals. He was the model of a person for whom the process was the product.

Third, you may be unaware of the hidden costs of success. The quota-busting salesman in your department may be forever relinquishing his chance for intimate contact with his children because he can't be with them at home and nailing down those extra orders on the road at the same time. Or your ideal "hostess with the mostess" may never have time to read a good book or enjoy nature or the less fashionable things in life. Many times if you *were* aware of these costs, you probably wouldn't be willing to pay them.

Fourth, success, achievement, brain power, beauty, and most other much-sought-after goals are relative to the standards of a given time, setting, and society. We tend, however, to think of them in more absolute terms as possessions we do or don't have. This kind of thinking may get you in trouble when the standards change. You've moved on to a new level of comparison, but, as you perceive it, the change is in you. This is the phenomenon of the big fish in the little pond moving to the major leagues.

The dramatic star of summer stock in Podonk can't hack it on Broadway. The high-school football center is not a candidate for the college team, because at only 200 pounds he's not hefty enough. Think about the bevy of Miss America beauty finalists who win none of the awards. All of their lives, from the nursery on up, they have been the most beautiful girls on the scene. Suddenly they're not even one of the top ten.

Every year as a college teacher I witness the toll taken by this dangerous obstacle to self-confidence. Students have to be outstanding in order to be accepted at Stanford University. But, within a few months of arriving there, half of the freshman class find themselves functioning below average on academic tests. They have not become dumb, but are victims of statistical averages and grading practices in which half of the class is above the median performance level, and, by definition, half *must* fall below. They are now forced to swim against a sea of virtually all "once outstanding" ambitious competitors.

Fifth, you must come to recognize the extent to which you are living out other people's scripts. You cannot have a well developed sense of self if you are acting out programs written by or for others. After your recognition of their existence must come attempts to cope directly with those alien scripts. You must find the courage to confront them, so that you can reject them if they diminish you or modify them to suit your own needs and values.

Often, we are not even aware of how the script got deposited into our head in the first place. Sometimes pervasive cultural values ghostwrite them—for example, men can't cry, women can't express anger, boys must be tough and virile, girls must be tender and nurturant. Parents, teachers, and other well-meaning agents of social control obviously write all or most of our scripts when we are young. Many of those scripts are quite good, so that we are willing to accept them as our own after reaching the age of reason. The danger lurks in the scripts passed on to us that contain the unfinished, unresolved business of our parents. The frustration of an unloved wife becomes the basis for a "men don't appreciate women" script for her daughter. And there are the fathers who want their boys to be everything they wanted to be—but couldn't be, for one reason or another. One such father threatened to get me fired from my former job at New York University because his son, Mark David, accepted my advice to go into the Peace Corps as a teacher in Nigeria. "He should be a doctor, a dentist at the very least," foamed the furious father. "He was supposed to be. I named him Mark David so that he would have M.D. before *and* after his name." It didn't matter to dear old dad that his son was happy as a teacher in Africa, that for the first time in his life he had a sense of purpose, and that he hated medicine. To some extent, Mark's low grades may have been his rebellion against having to play out the Mark David, M.D. scenario. But rebellion scripts are still built on someone else's story line.

To be an autonomous person with a sense of integrity, you will have to become aware of your script, then write, rewrite, or actively participate in sharing the writing of the scripts that govern your life. These scripts can be new and exciting ones or, like the "new" TV season, just a rehashing of the same old programming. It all depends on how much or, for shy people, how little you want out of your time on stage before the final curtain.

You gotta accentuate the positive

If you have but one life to live, live it with high self-esteem! It is your choice, a decision not made in the heavens but in your head. It is *your* General Accounting System that posts the report that your self-esteem is high or low. If you are shy, you probably have tagged the low self-esteem label on yourself. But, unless you have carved it in granite, we are going to begin to change that label. Low has got to go! Think positively of yourself, set meaningful goals that require some measure of ambition, industry, and perseverance to attain. Then, learn to evaluate your accomplishments in an honest and realistic fashion.

Dorothy Holob is a dynamic woman who teaches workshops in California to help students and business people build up their sagging self-confidence. Her boundless energy and infectious enthusiasm cast a glow about her. You feel good simply being in her presence. What is unusual about that reaction is that Dorothy has a speech impediment and her face is distorted—features that usually make us feel distressed. Suppose you had to trade places with Dorothy Holob. Would you give up, faced

© United Features Syndicate, Inc.

with the stark reality she had to come to grips with, or would you emerge from tragedy a new and better person? She tells us what it was like to one day become disfigured, and how she overcame her self-loathing and depression.

In 1963, I returned from a major operation for a serious brain tumor. I was handicapped cosmetically, my face was changed, and the voice I heard when I talked was not familiar. I walked with a stagger. I just knew I would never be accepted by society like this, and I kept thinking, "Why did this have to happen to me?"

Did I receive sympathy from my family? No. Instead they initiated me into a program of reverse psychology. They insisted that I practice talking plainly—as a matter of fact, they told me that if I wanted to remain a member of the family, I had better speak up or ship out. I cried a lot, and then I finally decided that I would show them that I certainly was not going to ship out.

For recreation, my family persuaded me to accompany them to shopping centers, out to lunch, or to concerts. They were gentle and considerate and guided me over curbstones, up and down escalators, across streets, and through crowds of people who eyed me curiously. They urged me to stand on my own two feet and face the world alone. I tried walking around my block, but I simply could not stand the mocking laughter of children nor the giggles of some neighbors. When I walked to the shops alone, clerks gave me disdainful glances and occasionally would toss my purchases at me. Once in a while some crank would telephone me and taunt me. How did I react to the jeers and sarcastic remarks? Usually, I came home and cried, and sometimes even enjoyed my suffering. For months, I became a recluse.

One day this thought occurred to me, "Why are you wasting your energy in feeling sorry for yourself—you don't have time for that. You cannot help the way that people perceive you to be—an ugly derelict." So I forgave myself for looking like I did, I began to feel sorry for everyone who could not empathize with another's problem. I watched for quiet, sad-looking people on the street, in the stores, on the bus. I spoke to them, we shared a lovely day, a bird's song, a rain shower—whatever. Suddenly, each day was brighter, I was smiling again—just like the doctor said I would be able to do—I found another way to smile. I practice putting enthusiasm into my voice. I even developed a pretty good sense of humor.

We can all learn valuable lessons from Ms. Holob's story. She not only overcame a physical disfigurement, but also a more serious psychological one—the self-hatred that drives us to cease hoping, to vegetate into nonbeing.

The activities in this chapter can help you overcome feelings of low self-esteem and develop a stronger, more confident self. Try to do every activity. Each one will help you build toward a more positive self-image. You might find the following fifteen steps useful in providing a structure for your efforts.

Fifteen steps to a more confident you

1. Recognize your strengths and weaknesses and set your goals accordingly.

2. Decide what you value, what you believe in, what you realistically would like your life to be like. Take inventory of your library of stored scripts and bring them up to date, in line with the psychological space you are in now, so they will serve you where you are headed.

3. Determine what your roots are. By examining your past, seek out the lines of continuity and the decisions that have brought you to your present place. Try to understand and forgive those who have hurt you and not helped when they could have. Forgive yourself for mistakes, sins, failures, and past embarrassments. Permanently bury all negative self remembrances after you have sifted out any constructive value they may provide. The bad past lives on in your memory only as long as you let it be a tenant. Prepare an eviction notice immediately. Give the room to memories of your past successes, however minor.

4. Guilt and shame have limited personal value in shaping your behavior toward positive goals. Don't allow yourself to indulge in them.

5. Look for the causes of your behavior in physical, social, economic, and political aspects of your current situation and not in personality *defects* in you.

6. Remind yourself that there are alternative views to every event. "Reality" is never more than shared agreements among people to call it the same way rather than as each one separately sees it. This enbles you to be more tolerant in your interpretation of others' intentions and more generous in dismissing what might appear to be rejections or put-downs of you.

7. Never say bad things about yourself; especially, never attribute to yourself irreversible negative traits, like "stupid," "ugly," "uncreative," "a failure," "incorrigible."

8. Don't allow others to criticize *you* as a person; it is your *specific actions* that are open for evaluation and available for improvement—accept such constructive feedback graciously if it will help you.

9. Remember that sometimes failure and disappointment are blessings in disguise, telling you the goals were not right for you, the effort was not worth it, and a bigger letdown later on may be avoided.

10. Do not tolerate people, jobs, and situations that make you feel inadequate. If you can't change them or yourself enough to make you feel more worthwhile, walk on out, or pass them by. Life is too short to waste time on downers.

11. Give yourself the time to relax, to meditate, to listen to yourself, to enjoy hobbies and activities you can do alone. In this way, you can get in touch with yourself.

12. Practice being a social animal. Enjoy feeling the energy that other people transmit, the unique qualities and range of variability of our brothers and sisters. Imagine what their fears and insecurities might be and how you could help them. Decide what you need from them and what you have to give. Then, let them know that you are ready and open to sharing.

13. Stop being so overprotective about your ego; it is tougher and more resilient than you imagine. It bruises but never breaks. Better it should get hurt occasionally from an emotional commitment that didn't work out as planned, than get numbed from the emotional insulation of playing it too cool.

14. Develop long-range goals in life, with highly specific short-range subgoals. Develop realistic means to achieve these subgoals. Evaluate your progress regularly and be the first to pat yourself on the back or whisper a word of praise in your ear. You don't have to worry about being unduly modest if no one else hears you boasting.

15. You are not an object to which bad things just happen, a passive nonentity hoping, like a garden slug, to avoid being stepped on. You are the culmination of millions of years of evolution of our species, of your parents' dreams, of God's image. You are a unique individual who, as an active actor in life's drama, can make things happen. You can change the direction of your entire life any time you choose to do so. With confidence in yourself, obstacles turn into challenges and challenges into accomplishments. Shyness then recedes, because, instead of always preparing for and worrying about how you will live your life, you forget yourself as you become absorbed in the living of it.

Building self-confidence

By successfully accomplishing difficult tasks, you can begin to build your self-confidence. Start with small tasks and then work up to more major goals.

The first thing to figure out is what you want to accomplish. List three goals that you would like to accomplish within a month. Make them as specific and as practical as possible.

Becoming the premiere hostess of Boston is not a realistic goal. Going to a party and talking to two people is. Choose one of your goals and break it down into smaller parts. What would you have to do first? What second? And so forth. Make a chart so that you can check off each part as you accomplish it. Formulate a plan for reaching the first part of your goal. If you want to talk out in class, for instance, decide exactly what you'll say. Write it down and practice it.

Right after you reach the first part of your goal, reward yourself with a compliment, a bath, a movie, a cup of coffee, reading a novel or magazine, or some other pleasurable activity you have earned.

Then, go on to the next part of the goal. And so on until you accomplish your entire goal.

Savor your feelings of accomplishment. Tell yourself out loud what a good job you did.

Then, turn to your next goal, break it down into small parts, and start working on it. Anything that you want to do in your life can be broken into smaller parts and accomplished bit by bit.

You may want to use some of the exercises in Chapter 10, "Developing Social Skills," to help you reach your goal.

Undoing downers

Keep track of what triggers negative self statements in you for two weeks (chart them). What seems to happen over and over that causes you to put yourself down?

Become actively conscious of your negative self talk. Every time you start to put yourself down, say, "Stop." Practice this until you stop putting yourself down all the time.

Keep a chart of how many times a day you can keep yourself from thinking these negative thoughts. Reward yourself for suppressing them.

Opposing forces

Make a list of your weaknesses. Put them on the left side of the page. Then, put the opposite positive statements on the right side. For example:

Weakness	*Opposition*
No one who knows me likes me.	Everyone who really knows me likes me.
There are few things about me that are attractive.	I have a lot of attractive features.

Expand on your statements in the "Opposition" column. Give examples. Begin to think of yourself in terms of the right-hand column instead of the left-hand one.

Shyness by any other name

Many times we are shy in only one or two situations, yet we think and speak of ourselves as *shy people.*

Instead of thinking and saying, "I am a shy person," start thinking and talking about yourself in more specific terms; describe specific situations and specific reactions. Say, "I get nervous when I have to talk to groups," or, "Parties make me feel out of place and cause me to feel weak inside," or, "I feel anxious around the president of our company," or, even more specifically, "My heart starts to pound and I get butter-flies in my stomach when I know a girl is checking me out."

Make as complete a list as you can of these situation-specific reactions. Then, plan what you have to do to control and change that reaction. For example: *If* hands shake when talking to a girl, *then* clasp hands, rest them on leg, put them in pockets.

Sit them on the hot seat

Make a list of all the people who make you feel shy, or who reject you. Then, take two chairs and arrange them facing each other. Sit in one chair and imagine that the first person from your list is in the other chair.

Talk to that person, yell at them, blame them for all of your shyness problems. Then switch seats and answer as if you were that other person. Go back to that first chair and explain why you feel shy around the other person. Then switch chairs again and respond the way you think that person would respond.

If only I weren't shy . . .

Make yourself comfortable and close your eyes. Think about a person or a situation that has repeatedly made you feel shy. Go over it in detail—every word, every action.

Now, imagine what you would do in this situation if you weren't shy. What would you have done? Said? What would have happened?

Think about this positive image every day for a week.

The next time you start to feel shy in this situation, think about your positive image. Try acting that way.

You know what I like about you?

Choose a friend that you trust and do this activity together. Each of you should list things about the other person that you really like. (Try to make a list of ten items.) Take turns telling each other why you listed an item. Start out with, "What I really like about you is _____."

How do you feel when your friend compliments you? Learn to accept these compliments (say "thanks," if nothing else), and immerse yourself in the positive feelings compliments generate.

Learn to pay your friend straightforward compliments. Apply this to your everyday life by adding to the people you compliment even for small, ordinary things.

Strength collage

Each of us can do at least one thing better than anyone else. It might be cooking a ham and cheese omelet or writing with flair, telling a joke, being a listener, or giving the best shoe shine. What is your best thing? Are there other good things that you can do?

Gather a bunch of magazines and newspapers. Cut out headlines, pictures, cartoons, etc. which illustrate all your strengths, and make a collage of them.

Put the collage someplace where you and others will see it.

Self-esteem—a role model

Think about someone that you admire a lot. It could be a friend or a relative or a movie star or a hero or heroine in a book. Imagine some situation in which that person is shy. What are they doing? Saying? How could you help them? What are the strengths of that person?

List them here:

_____

_____

_____

If you had all of those strengths, what would you be like? How would having those strengths affect your shyness? Close your eyes and imagine yourself in several situations in which you weren't shy. What does it feel like?

Feel good chart

Keep a note pad with you and jot down every positive experience you have for two weeks. Do this on the in-between weeks when you are not charting your shyness experiences.

Make a day-by-day chart showing these good-feeling times. Examine the chart and determine the following:

- How many of these events were initiated by others?
- How many were initiated by you?
- How many were good times alone?
- How can you fill up your chart with more good feelings?

From now on, when you have a positive experience, recognize it as such and immerse yourself in it. *Really* enjoy it.

Be a maven

Develop a skill or become an authority on something that you could share with others in a social setting. Have at least one attribute that others can enjoy, profit from, be entertained by, or be wiser for. Learning to play the guitar, harmonica, piano, or some such social musical instrument is often welcome at social gatherings. You might learn to tell jokes well or perform magic tricks. Dancing is easy to learn and will score a lot of points, especially for men who are always in short supply when the music starts. Take the time to be up on current events or some particular world issue of importance (overpopulation, the ecologists versus the developers, the decline of heroes both in our culture and internationally, etc.) Read and be able to discuss some good books—from both the fiction and the general best-seller lists.

Relax yourself

It is difficult to concentrate on these new positive self-messages when you're distracted by tension, fatigue, and irrepressible anxiety-provoking thoughts.

Total relaxation is the key to opening your mind to its own potentialities and ridding it of unwanted distractions.

- Set aside fifteen to twenty minutes for this exercise.
- Find a quiet place where you will not be disturbed.
- Sit in a comfortable chair, or lie on a couch, the bed, or the floor. Support your neck with a pillow.
- Loosen or remove tight clothing and jewelry. Remove contact lenses.
- You will first exaggerate your muscle tension before relaxing it. First, do the following steps one at a time.

  a) Make a clenched fist ... tighter ... tighter ... release.
  b) Suck in your stomach, try to make it touch your back. Hold it. Release.
  c) Clench your teeth, lock your jaws ... firmer ... firmer' ... release.
  d) Close your eyelids tightly. Press them down more and more. Release.
  e) Push your head and neck into your shoulders. Further down. Release.
  f) Inhale. Hold it as long as you can. Release.
  g) Stretch out your arms and legs ... stiffer ... stiffer ... release.

  Now try all seven steps at the same time.

- Release and let a warm, soft wave flow over your body, relaxing each part in turn as it slowly moves from your head down around, over, and into every muscle. Especially let it loosen the tension around your eyes, forehead, mouth, neck, and back. Tension out, relaxation in. Let the wave of gentle relaxation dissolve all muscle tension.
- Open your eyes. Hold your thumbnail a few inches from your eyes and focus all attention on it. Your hand will move down slowly. As it does, allow your eyelids to get heavy, your breathing to become fuller, and your whole body to enter a deep state of relaxation. Eyes closed. Hands down at your side or on your lap.
- Breathe in and out deeply, with each breath counting to yourself: 1 ... deeper, 2 ... deeper, 3 ... deeper, up to 10 (very deeply relaxed).
- Now imagine yourself in the most relaxing situation possible. See it, feel it, hear it, smell it, touch it. Float on a raft on a warm summer day, or in a hot bath. Go for a walk in a forest after a refreshing morning rain. Whatever your relaxation image, go to it.
- Now your body and mind are prepared for the Message of the Day. You should plan for important coming events by imagining the setting and seeing yourself as an effective, competent actor in it. You

will not be anxious, you will not be tense. You will not be shy. You will enjoy it. You will master it. These are the messages you communicate to yourself. You will find over time that you can be even more specific in what you tell yourself and how you prepare for events that used to arouse anxiety in you.

- Enjoy the good mental state and the relaxed physical state.
- Before counting yourself out of the relaxation state (saying 10, 9, 8 ... 1), be aware of how good it now feels to be *you* and how you are gaining control of your thoughts, feelings, and actions. Tell yourself this awareness and the positive feelings will persist. You might want to throw in a suggestion that you will sleep deeply and fully that night or that you will be alert, refreshed, and ready to put your social-skills exercises into practice.

You are on your way to greater self-efficacy[3] and personal contentment. The more you practice, the more completely and easily you gain control over the relaxation response.[4]

10
developing your social skills

We have seen throughout our explorations into the world of the shy that shy people avoid responsibility both for starting social encounters and for lubricating the machinery of interpersonal contact. Many of us, for whatever reasons, never learned the basic ingredients of social life. We don't know how to meet people; we can't talk up in a group; we get nervous about parties.

If you have a problem with social skills, you can be helped readily by simple and direct applications of the principles of behavior modification. In this chapter, the emphasis will be on what you can do to change your behavior patterns in order to get more of the social rewards that you want. You'll need to learn, practice, and be rewarded for effectively dealing with others. And you must be taught techniques that make you more physically and socially attractive to those you want to impress and be closer to.

Much of the advice to be given comes under the heading of "assertion training." Some of it is old hat, part of the common folklore of "how to win friends and influence people." But other wisdom is derived from scientific research on principles of behavior change and theories about the transactional process that takes place whenever two people come into the same life space.

Whenever I talk about the assertion techniques that we use to help shy people become more effective, invariably I hear the complaint that there are already too many aggressive bodies throwing their weight around. But, to be an assertive person is not to be a selfish, pushy bully, nor an insensitive clod who insists on getting his or her way. Assertive people get a fair share of what life has to offer by communicating their needs, relating to the needs of others, and having the courage to choose a life style that is in harmony with their values and the ecology of their life space. You could say they succeed by polishing the too-often tarnished Golden Rule and living the democratic ideal. Nothing new in that. But we have been led to believe that in a world of hard knocks, you'd better become an aggressive dictator unless you're willing to accept the role of passive slave. Those models are all too available for inspection . . . we looked at them earlier in their guise as guard and prisoner. In my opinion, the appropriate model for the shy individual is that exemplified by the appropriately assertive person.

Actors must act

The basic principle behind any program to make you more effectively assertive is *action*. We have seen over and over again that inaction is the most characteristic feature of shyness. "To act or not to act" is the question to be resolved for the shy person. Shakespeare's Hamlet dallied around for the entire play before he stopped talking to himself about whether or not he

ought to do what he wanted to do. By the time he finally did what he should have done five acts earlier, the play was over for him.

The energy to act isn't always there, however, because anxiety, boredom, and passivity generate more fatigue then does the heaviest of labors. But you need to get *moving.* You will discover untapped sources of energy when you are doing what you want to do and reaping rewards for your actions.

"Hello," "Hi there," "How is it going?" "Good to see you around," "Where have you been?" "I liked what you said," "Have a good weekend." A nod of recognition, a smile, a wave of the hand, a look in the eye. That little action starts you on your new career as an actor. To go further, you will have to put some energy behind it and some skill into it.

Start with small goals that you feel could be achieved if only you could do some simple things. Begin by working on situations and people where your shyness barriers are the smallest and least threatening.

At first you will probably find it useful to base your act on scripts you prepare in advance (see pg. 185). Later on, when stage fright is no longer an issue, you can try more spontaneous, improvised performances. Rehearsing your act before doing it helps to make it have the impact you'd like it to. Visualize the specific assertive actions you will engage in, running them through your imagination. Rehearse specific lines, gestures, and movements. Practice in front of a mirror what you will say and do.

Can anyone hear you? Talk up! Develop a voice style and manner that are appropriate for the scene—forceful, interested, concerned, upset, angry, or tender. An illustration of how crucial voice and manner can be occurred in our shyness clinic recently. Most of the clients had real problems talking in a small group and wanted to have practice in doing so. After a long while, an interesting topic, ESP, came up, and for the first time most members of the group began to talk to each other and not to the therapist. "What?" said Bob softly. On went the discussion without stopping for Bob. "Wha?" Bob murmured still more demurely. In a few minutes he moved his chair back from the table, sighed, expressed boredom, and opened a newspaper. He perceived that he had been ignored or rejected, so he wanted none of their stupid conversation.

When we discussed what had happened, a very different interpretation emerged. Some of the others hadn't even heard Bob ask a question. Those who had weren't sure what his "what?" was referring to, and they were too involved in their first enjoyable conversation to stop the show to find out. For Bob's part, his low energy "what?" expressed his anxiety that he didn't know much about the topic of the discussion, since parapsychology wasn't his field and he didn't talk about things he didn't already know a lot about. Bob was not one to make a fool of himself. Thus, his initial genuine curiosity to find out what someone meant when he said, "ESP has been proved by scientific tests," ended with a "So what? Who cares anyway?" Finally this defensive maneuver became an offensive one, in which Bob made it condescendingly clear that that conversation was beneath him. It takes practice and scripting to learn how to interrupt without disrupting, and how to ask questions that get answered.

The real you and the role you

Shy people are often too concerned with whether or not their actions reflect their *real* selves. Like a method actor, you must learn to dissolve the boundary between the so-called real you and the role you play. Let your actions speak for themselves and eventually they will be speaking for you.

I have found that one way to get shy people to initiate actions they would never attempt on their own is by having them role play. Given a part to play—as an "interviewer" for a shyness survey, for example—even extremely shy people are able to give convincing portrayals. They can step out of their timid, bashful, sensitive self and play at being someone else.

In this way, *they* are not vulnerable, for the *real them* is not being evaluated. When, in addition, the role is sanctioned by the setting or by authority and the script is provided, their egos are completely off the hook. "What the hell, anything goes, what do I have to lose. Why not?"

"Hello, I'm conducting an interview for the Standford Shyness project. I'd like to make an appointment to talk to you about your reactions to the Shyness Survey you completed. When would it be convenient for us to get together for about fifteen minutes or so? Fine. Thank you. Then I'll be seeing you Wednesday, 7:00 P.M. at your address. By the way, my name is Robert Roleplayer and I do appreciate your cooperation."

Starting out with a scenario like this, shy students in my seminar arranged for nearly a hundred interviews. Acting as interviewer, they not only were able to make these usually feared telephone contacts, but they enjoyed the interview immensely. Many of the interviews went for an hour or two, and ended with an unplanned social event like a walk or coffee. For some, even good friendships developed out of this role-induced initial contact. They had transcended the limits of the role and allowed it to merge with their other roles (which, taken collectively, constitute the "real self" according to some sociologists).

Another special feature of becoming involved in a particular role is "forgetting yourself" in the process. Bandleader Lawrence Welk tells this story about the development of his shyness and how being cast in the role of a performer made a big difference in his life.

A childhood illness and a serious operation forced me to miss an entire year of school. When I returned the following semester, I found myself a head taller than my classmates and became convinced I was truly the "dummer-esel" which my father sometimes called me. The experience seemed to aggravate what I assume was an inborn inferiority complex. Shortly thereafter, I became a "fourth-grade dropout."

Having been raised in a German-speaking household, I became acutely aware of my heavy accent very quickly after leaving my farm home at the age of twenty-one. I was terrified at the prospect of speaking in public. I loved to play my accordion and entertain, and secretly hoped to be asked to play whenever a few people were assembled. Yet, I was basically afraid of people and usually felt like crawling into a hole rather than face an audience.

A man named George T. Kelly helped me tremendously in overcoming my shyness and building my self-confidence. George had a small vaudeville troupe called the "Peerless Entertainers," and he offered me a job. He billed me as the "World's Greatest Accordionist" (obviously, a masterpiece of overstatement) and taught me everything he knew about show business.

When I first became a leader of my own band, I had learned a few things about pleasing an audience, but I still dreaded the thought of having to talk to them. It took me something like twenty years as a bandleader before I uttered my first words from the stage. Those words were, "a-one and a-two."

On radio (and later on television), I found myself fighting the multiple handicaps of a strong accent, a limited education, and that abiding fear of speaking in public. When we first signed a contract for a weekly TV show, our producers almost scared me back to the farm when they told me I was expected to do the "M.C." chores. My reaction was something like, "You gotta be kidding" (or a heavily accented slang equivalent of that period).

With the passing of time, twenty-six years on TV, countless talks for the American Cancer Society, plus many appearances on behalf of my book publishers, I believe I have lost much of my early timidity and, I hope, acquired at least a respectable amount of poise. Also, I am completely at ease when fronting my band or when in the company of close friends. You might say that learning my business has played a very important part in overcoming my shyness. . . .

If, over the past fifty years I have managed to lose some of my shyness, I believe that it can be attributed largely to the fact that I try to avoid embarrassing situations and make sure I know what I'm saying. Of course, if things get desperate, I can always let my Musical Family do the talking for me with their superb singing and playing. When the old bugaboo, "Shyness," crops up, I can always count on these wonderful people to bail me out.[1]

Role playing is a vital ingredient in the development of social skills. It involves taking action and experiencing how it feels to take those actions. By suspending the "self" for the "role," you are granted permission to engage in behaviors that are normally off-limits. Your overbearing, all-monitoring consciousness is not allowed into the show. And so you can show off what you could do if you weren't *you*. But once having played the role, it is a part of you. You cannot deny the knowledge that you can do and can feel what you have done and felt while role playing. Research has demonstrated that enacting a role different from that which is usual for the person results in corresponding private changes in attitudes and values.[2]

A fifty-year-old shy woman describes the effect of dramatic role playing in these terms:

I found that my shyness and embarrassment vanished when I assumed a role in a play. I have real dramatic flair and ability—after all, it was not me on the stage, it was a role, a character, someone else—again a chance to shed the uncomfortable me, to "lose myself." My passionate nature had many outlets which saved the shy me from serious emotional trouble, and provided me with personal reward and feelings of some significance and achievement.

It is not uncommon for performers to have entered their profession, in part, to cope directly with their shyness. Richard Hatch, taking Michael Douglas's place on the TV serial *Streets of San Francisco,* said in an interview: "I used to be shy. I went into this business to try to get rid of my self-consciousness and to conquer my inhibitions. Really, the money means nothing to me."[3]

Changing behaviors

Psychologists are becoming increasingly aware of the lack of social skills in the behavior of many clients and psychiatric patients. Previously, psychologists thought that problems could be traced to deep-seated pathological emotional-motivational states. But a newer approach focuses less on unobservable inner mechanisms and more on specific behaviors and their consequences. Behaviors are the target of change, not *people.* This analysis omits mention of inferiority complexes, underdeveloped egos, and the like. Rather, it identifies actions that do and don't have desired consequences. Then the behavioral approach sets out to change those behaviors, so there will be more positive and fewer negative consequences. Instead of analyzing the oedipal complex of someone who is afraid to go on a job interview, psychologists now concentrate on giving that person the specific skills to have a successful interview.

The two primary reasons for failing to behave appropriately in a given situation are: not having mastered the necessary social skills involved, and the disruptive impact of high levels of anxiety. Anxiety-reducing techniques such as relaxation and meditation are used to bring the anxiety under the individual's control. However, a successful social-skill program (of the kind to be outlined in this chapter) has been shown to lead also to anxiety reduction, as self-confidence improves and assertiveness increases.[4]

Make a contract with yourself

No labor leader negotiating for improved working conditions would be satisfied with only a vague, general plan for change. An explicit contract which lays out the objectives and enumerates specific measures to achieve those goals is requisite. Only in this way can progress be charted and reneging be exposed.

To begin improving your life style, you must impose similar demands on yourself. The time has come to write out a detailed, explicit self-contract. Your contract should specify the following.

- **The changes you want to make**

  Decide on realistic changes. Talking to a group of 400 is not a realistic goal for someone who is afraid to meet one other person. Many times you might want to divide your goal into smaller, more manageable parts. For instance, if you'd like to make more friends, perhaps the first step would be to say hello to four new people this week.

- **How you will monitor your progress**

  You can use a chart or a journal to note your progress. Or, you can ask friends to monitor you.

- **How you will reward yourself as you fulfill each part of the contract**

  "Every time I say hello to someone new, I will feel good inside and reward myself with a bath or a long walk or a movie." Be ready, willing, and able to reinforce any and all behavior that meets (or exceeds) your desired standards of performance. It is especially crucial not to be stingy when it comes to dispensing rewards to yourself. Be generous with immediate verbal approval. Say to yourself: "That was a good thing I did," "I'm pleased by the way I went about that," "I really like that about me."

- **How you will know when you've completed the contract**

  "At the end of next week, I will have said hello to four people and be ready to move on to the next step in making friends."

- **What you will do if you fail to meet the contract**

  Choose a punishment and make it stick. Cleaning out the basement, raking the leaves, straightening out the silverware drawer all qualify.

Often it's a good idea to write down your contract. That makes it more official and increases the chances that you'll honor it.

You can form a contract around any or all of the activities in this chapter. They are designed to increase your stock of social skills so that you can relate more effectively to the people in your life. Select the ones that are most important to you and design a program to accomplish each one. With concentration and practice, these skills will soon become second nature to you.

First time talking

If you find that you have a hard time talking to *anyone,* you might try some of these things:

- Call the information operator and ask for the telephone numbers of people you want to call. Besides getting practice, you'll know you have the correct number. Also, thank the operator and note his/her reaction.

- Call a local department store and check on the price of something advertised.

- Call a radio talk show to say you like the programming and then ask a question.

- Call a local movie theatre and ask for show times.

- Call the sports desk at the local newspaper and ask for the scores of the last hometown basketball, baseball, or football game.

- Call the library and ask the reference librarian what the population of the United States is, or for some other information you'd like to have.

You can use the phone to get yourself talking to someone while still remaining anonymous. Gradually, you can transfer this experience to calling particular people you want to contact and to greeting people on the street, as in the exercise, "Saying 'Hello.' "

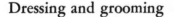

Dressing and grooming

Very few of us look like Lauren Hutton or Paul Newman. But each of us can look as good as possible, and probably better than we usually do.

Get a haircut that is good for *you*—not just the latest style. Keep it clean. Use make-up (but not too much) if you want to emphasize the good points of your face.

Figure-out what clothes look the best on you; if you don't know, ask your friends. What are your best colors? Use them. Make sure your clothes are clean and pressed. When you dress assertively (and comfortably), you will naturally start feeling more assertive. At the very least, you should minimize or eliminate this source of apprehension.

Saying "hello"

For the next week, greet every person that you pass on the street, in your office, or at school. Smile and say, "Hello, nice day," or, "Have you ever seen so much snow?" or some other short greeting. Since most of us aren't used to being greeted on the street, you may find that many people are surprised when you talk to them. Some may not respond, but in most cases you'll get an equally pleasant response.

Anonymous conversations

A good way to practice your conversational skills is to strike up a *safe* conversation with strangers in public places, like:

Grocery-store lines
Theatre lines
A political rally
The doctor's waiting room
A sports event
The bank
The PTA
Church
The library

You can start the conversation with the *common experience* you are sharing at the time. For example:

• "This line is so long, it *must* be a good movie."
• "I had a horrible time parking around here, do you know a good place?"
• "Is that a good book (good buy, etc.)? I've never read it (tried it)."
• "That's a nice sweater (briefcase, etc.). Where did you get it?"

Giving and accepting compliments

An easy way to start conversations and to help others (as well as yourself) feel good is to give compliments. You can comment on:

• What someone is wearing: "I like your suit."
• A person's grooming: "Your hair looks great."

- A skill: "You are an excellent gardener." (Or, "You have quite a green thumb.")
- An aspect of personality: "I love your laugh, it's infectious."
- Possessions: "What a terrific car."

To get into a conversation, simply add a question:

- "What a terrific car. How long have you had it?"
- "You're an excellent gardener. What do you do about bugs?" (Or, "How do you find the time to grow such lovely cockle shells?")

Learn to enjoy the compliments you receive. Never discount a compliment made to you, as for example: "I like your suit."—"Oh, this old thing. I should throw it away." Doing so makes the other person look foolish and feel worse. At the very least, say "Thank you" to every compliment. The best reply would be to add some of your own positive feelings to the compliment: "I like your suit."—"Thanks. I like it too, it's really comfortable," or "It's nice of you to say so."

For the next two weeks try to give at least three compliments a day—keep track of the compliments made to you. Concentrate on accepting them graciously. Allow yourself to feel good about them, and show the person who compliments you that you really appreciate it.

You might also try giving a compliment to people whom you admire, but who probably don't get many direct compliments because of their positions of authority or power—like a teacher after a good lecture, your parents after a good deed, your boss about some action taken or change in company policy. A complimentary note is easy to send and wonderful to receive. Try sending some to deserving people.

——◆•◆——

Meeting people

Try to meet a lot of people. At first, it's the quantity that's important, not the quality. It is practice in general social mixing that you need.

You can go to places where you feel comfortable: The supermarket, a book store, the library, a museum. Strike up at least one conversation wherever you go.

You can go to places that interest you, but that aren't as "safe" as your comfortable spots: a coffee house, a writers' workshop, a hiking group, a women's study group, a "Save the Whales" group. At first, if you feel uneasy, take a friend. But gradually go alone. Again, start at least one conversation based on your mutual interests, "What kind of coffee are you drinking? Mine's French roast and it's great." A note of caution: Dating bars are usually the worst places to meet people. There is obvious tension in the air and the chances of rejection in an explicitly singles pick-up place are too great.

You can go to places with friends: accompany them to courses or sports events or parties, and get them to introduce you to *their* friends. Be alert for others who are on the fringe of the event. They are likely to welcome your approach.

Now, make up a calendar of planned outings. Go someplace at least three times a week for the next month. Plan week-by-week where you will go and whom you will go with. If you plan to ask friends along, get them to agree in advance. Start out with your comfortable places, then move on to those that are less familiar. If you need to, make a contract (page 173) with yourself for each week.

After each experience, write down where you went, what happened, and how you felt. Figure out what made your experience positive or negative and work to improve future outings.

—◆—

Have something to show-and-tell

To get into good conversations, you need to have something to say. The easiest way to do that is to keep yourself informed.

- Read the newspapers and/or newsmagazines.
- Know what the political situation is in your city, state, or nationally.
- Read movie and book reviews—then, go to some movies and read some books.
- Delve into a couple of political, cultural, or whatever topics, and become knowledgeable about them. Jot down notes if you want to.
- Come up with four or five interesting or exciting things that have happened to you recently. Turn them into brief interesting stories by practicing in front of a mirror or with a tape recorder.
- Write down two or three interesting stories that other people have told you. Jot down jokes if you feel comfortable telling them. If you have trouble remembering the punch lines, jokes aren't your best bet.

When you meet people, be ready with several stories to tell or interesting comments to make. Practice ahead of time with friends or an empty chair or the mirror or a tape recorder.

See how many different stories you can tell other people in the next week. Gradually expand the number of stories in your repertory. Always evaluate the audience for the appropriateness of your material. Your septic-tank back-up story might not be compelling for some listeners.

———————◆●◆———————

Starting a conversation

So there you are in the library or investment course, or at a dinner party or mixer. How do you start a conversation? First of all, choose someone who looks approachable, a person who is smiling at you or sitting alone or wandering around. Don't choose someone who's obviously busy doing something else.

There are a number of ways to start a conversation. Choose the one that is most appropriate to your situation and most comfortable for you.

- *Introduce yourself.* "Hello, my name is _____."
  Best for gatherings where everyone is a stranger. Exchange information on where you live, what you do, your families, etc.
- *Give compliments* (see pg. 176). Then, follow up with a question: "This is a great drink. How do you make a Tequila Sunrise?"
- *Request help.* Make it obvious you need it and think other person can provide it:
  "I can't find this law case. Can you help me?"
  "Can you show me that dance step?"
  "I don't know anything about commodities, can you explain them to me?"
- *Try self-disclosure.* You'll find that when you make an obviously personal statement, it will elicit a positive, sympathetic response. Try:
  "I'm not sure what I'm doing here, I'm really quite shy."
  "I'd love to learn to sail, swim, ski, etc., but don't know if I can make it."
  "I just got a divorce and feel a little shakey."
- *Use the normal social graces:*
  "May I light your cigarette?"
  "Looks like you need a refill, can I get you one? I'm headed that way."
  "Here, let me help you pick up those groceries."
- *If you're at a total loss, fall back on some trite, but very workable openers:*
  "How do you like this weather?"

"Haven't I seen you somewhere before?"
"What's happening?"
"Do you have a match?"

Practice these openers in front of the mirror or with your tape recorder. Test out several openers in the next week. See which ones work out the best and why.

Keeping the conversation flowing

Once you've started a conversation, you can use several techniques to keep it going.

- Ask a question that is either *factual:* "How did the Dodgers do yesterday?" or *personal:* "How do you feel about President Carter's selection of Cyrus Vance?"
- Offer one of your personal stories or opinions (see pg. 178).
- Get the other person talking about himself or herself: "Where did you grow up? Do you like your line of work?"
- Express interest in the other person's expertise: "How does a book get published?" "How do you start a day-care center?"
- Most important, share your reactions to what is taking place at that moment while you are interacting. Relate your thoughts and feelings about what the other person has said or done.

Active listening

Become an *active* listener by paying attention to what people are saying around you. You can pick up a lot of information and clues to personality by listening carefully to conversations or discussion.

- Pay attention to what is being said and give clear indications that you are doing so: verbal cues—"Yes," "uh, huh," "I see," "That's interesting," "Incredible," "Really?"—and also nonverbal cues—lean forward, sit up, stand closer, nod appropriately, etc.
- Do not make assumptions about motives and the person's inner states without checking them out, as in: "It seems to me that you are really

feeling hurt by not being invited to the party. Is that so?" Or, "Are you saying you're upset because I didn't answer your letter?"

- Active listening also involves identifying with the other person's situation, when possible. Or, if not, recasting what you're hearing into a similar experience that you can relate to: "I've never been in the military, but I can relate to having to take petty orders that are meaningless. When I worked as a camp counselor . . ."

- When you're in a conversation, don't hesitate to ask for clarification if you don't understand something: "Is this what you're saying _____ _____?" Or, "I don't understand that, can you explain it?" Don't be afraid to admit that you don't know something. People often enjoy explaining things to others.

------◆◆------

"So long, it's been good to know you"

The rhetoric of leave-taking is a complicated ritual that has considerable significance for interpersonal relations.[5] How you take leave of another person and the manner in which you bring a conversation to an end can either facilitate your next encounter or undo all the effort you've put into trying to make this one work.

When you are finished saying all you have to, or your allotted time is up, you must signify that you are about to take leave. Three messages must get across: you will be leaving soon; you have gotten pleasure (benefitted in some way) from the present talk; and you hope there will be more contact in the future. There are a number of ways that you can do this:

- *reinforcement*—short words of agreement to the last thing the partner said ("sure, O.K., right, etc.")
- *appreciation*—a statement of pleasure derived from the interaction ("I really enjoyed talking to you.")
- *completion sentence*—"That's about the sum of it."

Breaking eye contact, moving legs or feet toward the exit, leaning forward, smiling, nodding, and a handshake are some nonverbal behaviors used to say you are shipping off.

Watch the ways in which your friends, acquaintances and people you interact with end their conversations. Right after you take your leave from various conversations, write down all you recall saying or doing in the last minute(s).

Decide on which leave-taking signals are clearest, feel most comfortable to you, and seem to leave the other person also feeling positive about the conversation. Work them into your personal rhetoric of goodbye.

Becoming a social animal

Here are a number of exercises that will help you get used to socializing. Choose several to accomplish in the next week. If you need to, make a self-contract to do them. Start with the easiest and progress to those that are more difficult for you. Record your reactions to each of these reaching-out exercises, as well as the reactions you've elicited.[6]

- Introduce yourself to a new person in your office building, the grocery store, or in a class.
- Invite someone who is going your way to walk with you.
- Ask to join the next game or bull session you see in progress. If you're in an office, join a coffee-break talk group.
- Conduct a personal opinion survey. Ask ten people their opinions on a current topic. Ask one question about their opinions.
- Ask someone you don't know if you can borrow ten cents for a phone call. Arrange to pay them back!
- Find out the name of someone (opposite sex) in your office or class or social club. Call him or her on the phone and ask about the latest work issue, class assignment, or upcoming event.
- Go to a coffee house. Smile and nod at the first three people who look at you. Strike up a conversation with at least one person of the same sex.
- Stand in a line at a grocery store, bank, or movie. Strike up a conversation about the line with whoever is near you.
- Converse with the gas-station attendant as he is filling the tank with gas and checking the oil.
- Sit down beside a person of the opposite sex who looks interesting (on a bus, in a lounge, at a class or movie). Make some sort of opening commentary.
- Ask three persons for directions. Shift at least one of them into general conversation for a brief minute or two.
- Go to a jogging track, beach, or swimming pool. Converse with two or three strangers you come close to there.

- Notice someone who needs help in your neighborhood or class or office. Offer to help.
- Carry a copy of a controversial book with you for one day. Count how many people you can get to start a conversation over it.
- Organize and throw a small party (say three to five people). Invite at least one person you don't know well.
- The next time you have a problem, find someone in your dorm, office, or neighborhood who is not close to you, and ask his or her advice.
- Invite someone to go eat with you—someone you have not eaten with before.
- Practice your openers and follow-up statements before a mirror and tape record yourself. Listen to yourself, then do it again, trying repeatedly for improvement in the liveliness and enthusiasm in your voice.
- Say "Hi" to five new people today whom you would not usually greet. Try to provoke a smile and return "Hi" from them.

Friends from acquaintances

Friendships are usually based on: being physically close; being involved in mutual activities; similar attitudes, values, background, personality, and interests; and expressing mutual liking.

Of the people you know only casually, which ones would you like to be closer to, to have as friends? Decide on several people that you will make a serious effort to get to know better—in the hope of making new friendships out of casual acquaintances.

Write down everything you think you know about each person, and what you have in common with each.

Prepare for and make a brief initial contact by phone call, or face-to-face. Decide on possible conversation topics and natural openers. Be sure to identify yourself. Announce that you want to chat for only a short time, to get some advice, to check something out, to share something that he/she might be interested in. End with a positive expression of feeling and a supportive goodbye.

Follow up within a few days with an invitation to join you in some casual activity, like a coffee break, a pizza, attending a local event, or going for a walk.

If you feel like it, express warmth toward the person by your attentiveness, support, encouragement, self-disclosure, and by saying so. Expand your circle of friends by using this "getting to know you" approach a number of times.

------•◆•------

Make a date

Dating is a social contact that is often anxiety-provoking for shy people, because of its promise of intimacy and the more than usual emotional intensity it demands. Shy daters feel great vulnerability to imagined threats of rejection. For many, this anxiety outweighs the anticipated rewards and they "just don't date." Perhaps for this reason, more and more dating is becoming a group activity: "A bunch of us are going bowling. Why don't you come along?"

Make your date by telephone. That way you can at least avoid worrying about body language. Plan ahead; have two specific activities in mind.

When you reach the person, clearly identify yourself by name and explain where you met, if necessary: "This is John Simmons. I met you at the Clark's open house last week." Then:

- Be sure you are recognized in turn; if not, establish who you are.
- Pay the person a compliment related to your last meeting, one that indicates your regard for his/her ideas, values, position on an issue, sense of humor—that is, some nonsuperficial attribute.
- Be assertive in coming to the point of requesting a date: "I was wondering if you'd like to come to a movie with me this Friday." Be specific in your request, state the activity in mind and the time it will take place.
- If "yes," decide together on the particular movie and times (have alternatives ready to allow the other person some freedom of choice). End the conversation smoothly, but quickly, and, of course, politely.
- If "no," assess whether the activity or the time are not appropriate, and suggest alternatives for each. Or, suggest a more informal get together if your unexpected request proves too anxiety-provoking for the shy person on the other end of the phone line: "How about getting together then for a cup of coffee (or a drink) after work sometime?" If the answer is still "no go," the interest is not there at this time and you should politely end the conversation.

Refusal to go on a date does not mean *you* are being rejected. Health, work, previous commitments, excessive shyness, etc. can all account for a turndown.

Suppose *you* are asked for a date and are not interested in getting to know the person. Never say "yes" out of sympathy or guilt. Do not hesitate to say, "No, thank you. I appreciate your asking, but I'd rather not." Do so without hurting the requester (he or she may also be shy and have spent hours practicing this exercise). You have the right to say "no" to anyone, to be pleased that you are desirable to someone, without offering an explanation of your refusal.

Handling interpersonal conflict

Sharon and Gordon Bower, in their book *Asserting Yourself,* present a unique technique for handling most interpersonal conflicts—from the car repairman who is "ripping you off" to your husband who criticizes you in front of other people. The technique is called "DESC Scripts." (DESC is an acronym for Describe, Express, Specify, and Consequences).[7]

Describe	Begin your script by describing as specifically and objectively as possible the behavior that is bothersome to you:
	"You said these car repairs would cost $35 and now you're charging me $110."
	"The last three times we have been with other people you have criticized me in front of them."
Express	Say what you feel and think about this behavior:
	"This makes me angry because I feel I'm being ripped off." (to the car repairman)
	"This makes me feel humiliated and hurt." (to the husband)
Specify	Ask for a different, specific behavior:
	"I would like you to readjust my bill back to the original estimate unless you can clearly justify these extra charges."
	"I would like you to quit criticizing me and I will signal you every time that you start to do it."
Consequences	Spell out concretely and simply what your reward will be for changing the behavior. Sometimes you have to specify the negative consequences of not following the changes:
	"If you do this, I will tell all of my friends that I have gotten good service at Bob's repair shop."
	"If you quit criticizing me I'll feel a lot better and bake you your favorite apple pie."

The best way to make these scripts effective is to write them out ahead of time and practice them in front of a mirror. After doing this a few times, you'll be able to make up a script on the spot and deliver it effectively.

Now write a script for a troublesome situation that you would like to resolve and change. Practice it, deliver it, note the results, and work on improving your assertive delivery.

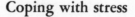

Coping with stress

Following are several techniques to help you cope with stress and/or anxiety. You can use these when you're anxious about going to a party, calling for a date, making a speech, etc.

- Be as prepared as possible. If necessary, practice beforehand.
- If you can, relax or meditate for twenty minutes.
- Lie down and imagine the entire coming scene in your head, detail by detail. Don't stop at any one point, but keep moving through your scene.
- Think of your comfort zone. This is a place where you feel the most comfortable. It might be on a beach or in the bathtub or walking through a field. When you're feeling anxious, think about this experience in detail—the feelings, the smells, etc.
- Say self-coping statements like, "I know I can do this. I'm going to be good at it. I'm going to enjoy it," over and over in your head.

Sometimes one or two of these techniques will work. Sometimes you may need to use all of them.

These skills can help you to become a more effective, assertive social being. They must be practiced, just as any other new set of skills you wish to acquire. Initially, they may seem artificial, too planned, or manipulative. With practice and positive results, however, you will be able to adapt them into a personal style, your own style. They will no longer be externally imposed strategies for self-improvement, but self-initiated plans for enjoying a more satisfying life with other people.

Hopefully, as your self-confidence builds and your social skills develop, you can begin to deflect some of your awareness away from *ego* and toward *others*. There are so many people out there who need *your* help to overcome their shyness and feelings of inadequacy. Won't you try to help them?

11
helping others overcome their shyness

B obby Kennedy was a politician I could respect and openly admire. I admired the forceful intelligence that marked his decisions and the tough stands he took against organized crime and racial discrimination. When I chanced to meet him at a political rally in New York, it came as somewhat of a shock to see my bold hero so timidly shy meeting people at this social gathering. In fact, rarely have I seen anyone who looked more uncomfortable in the midst of well wishers.

Being aware of his shyness has made me appreciate even more the story of how he helped someone else overcome shyness. Roosevelt Grier, the ex-New-York-Giant football star who, as we saw in Chapter 2, was painfully shy, recounts what Bobby Kennedy did to help him conquer this formidable adversary.

> It was Bobby Kennedy who finally got me out of my shyness, not only because of what he stood for, but because he was the first person ever to say, "Go on, Rosey. You can do it. Get up there and say what you feel!"

> It worked. Then and after 1968, because I wanted so desperately to carry on his work for all of us, I not only found that I could speak, could get out of myself, but that people would listen. Big as I am, there was something bigger in that beloved man and his philosophy, and I shall be forever grateful for what he gave to me—and gave to us all.[1]

We all can help others overcome or cope better with their shyness in many ways if we are willing to reach out and make the effort. Sometimes we can help by what we say and do; sometimes it is by the supportive environment we help create; and, more often than we are aware of, we help indirectly by the examples we set.

Not only *can* we help our shy children, mates, friends, and neighbors, we *should feel bound* by the social contract to do so. In helping anyone win the battle against shyness, we help ourselves. If we are shy, involving ourselves in another's problem diminishes our self-absorption. For the not shy, contributing to the defeat of shyness has several advantages. Not only will more socially attractive people be available, but a wealth of human resources will be freed, ready to assume useful roles in all areas of society. And, most importantly, there will be less loneliness and more joy all around.

Much of what you have already learned about the nature of shyness provides the foundation for your new role as shyness change agent. In addition, many of the personal exercises outlined in Part II can be adapted to the particular people you plan to help. In this chapter, we add some other ideas, general principles, and specific exercises designed to assist you in helping your children, your mate, your friends and co-workers, and others in your community. Some of the exercises are designed for individuals, others for small groups. Some can be carried out easily and informally, while others require more planning and formal arrangements. With imagination, ingenuity, and a commitment to help others, you can not only make these ideas work for you, you can expand on them or create better ones of your own design.

Be something to other people that will enable them to be more to themselves.

Parents and teachers

Because of the central role you occupy in the lives of our young people, you can create and intensify shyness in more ways than you can imagine. You and I often do so unintentionally, because of the powerful needs our children and students have for so many of the rewards we can grant. By recognizing each young person's individual integrity, we help them to develop a sense of personal worth. By being understanding of their problems, we ease their difficulties in learning to live in a complex, changing adult world. By supporting their attempts to grow and to extend themselves, we encourage them to be something special while being themselves. Perhaps most of all, they need our unconditional love, given openly and freely, so that they can accept what they are while trying to become something more.

The power coin you hold obviously has two sides: the power to induce shyness by not acting in these ways, and the power to reduce shyness by being the parent or teacher that grants these essential rewards. You must use the coin one way or the other, so plan your investment in advance to ensure that you will use the resources at your disposal to get the best return. Be aware of the power you possess, the needs of others for what you have, and then consciously decide how you will balance that demand with your supply. Don't let it "just happen," because, either way, the responsibility is yours. Choose your investments wisely, so that they will make things happen for the next generation(s) and for you—things that promote life, not diminish it.

Expressing love, empathy, uncertainty, and emotions

It is your task to make your children, your neighbor's children, and your students feel good about themselves. Help them discover everything that is attractive about themselves. Start today to compliment your children and students for all that they do and all that they are that you find attractive. Say, "I think that the way you've done your hair is beautiful," rather than "Your hair looks nice." Or, "I really like your sense of humor (or the way you solve a problem). I find it a very attractive quality."

Encourage others also to be more generous in giving compliments, perhaps by directly suggesting to your spouse or colleagues the appropriateness of certain compliments.[2] But never force them, since false compliments, like starched underwear, always show through.

Teach your children or students how to accept compliments, so that in return they reinforce the giver of the compliments.

Learn to see with your own eyes and hear with your own ears what a child is doing, saying, being. Too often we use filters provided by what others have told us about the child. Someone else's evaluation should be acknowledged as exactly that—a judgment made in a time and place different from now. The reports of the child's "bad" behavior by last year's teacher, a neighbor, or one's spouse typically don't include mention of their own role in eliciting or defining the behavior as bad, or the things in the situation that provoked the child's reaction.

Behavior always occurs in a context; try to understand the context before evaluating, judging, and reacting to the behavior. We look in at a classroom and see little Alfred not paying attention while the teacher is starting her lesson on caring and compassion. What's wrong with the child? Cognitive deficiency? Behavior problem? Attentional impairment? Actually, little Alfred is just weaving revenge fantasies. He is imagining his teacher is dead and he's in charge of the funeral arrangements. "How awful of him!"

Dr. Alice Ginott, a psychotherapist especially sensitive to the ways adults mistreat children, provides the context for Alfred's awful act of revenge:

> [The] teacher said to a group of children: "Take your seats!" Everyone took his seat except Alfred who remained standing. The teacher turned to him and shouted: "Alfred, what are you waiting for? A special invitation? Why must you be the last one! Why does it take you forever to sit down? Are you naturally slow or is someone helping you?" All the children laughed as Alfred sat down.[3]

As we can see, it's not so unreasonable for Alfred to want to punish the teacher. Unfortunately, however, Alfred's justified anger outward is likely to become unjustified guilt, and he will probably wind up feeling badly about himself. The teacher didn't intend to enrage Alfred. She was just doing her job, may have been behind in her schedule, and had to impose rules, and so forth.

In reporting a child's behavior, it is important to include as much of the context as possible. Be sure to indicate any role you might have played in the scenario. Before passing this report on to another person or having it become part of The Permanent Record, add the child's version as well.

You should want to explore areas where your two versions don't mesh. Remember, of course, that simply by virtue of your adult caretaker status your story will carry more weight in courts of appeal. Compensate by listening more carefully to the other side, and by empathizing with the way the world looks through the opposite end of the telescope.

Please pass me an emotion

A good exercise to demonstrate how our biases and memory distort the way we perceive and communicate important events is through a telephone rumor chain. Gather your family together, or break into small groups in the classroom.

Write out a brief story about a newsworthy event. Read it to the first person (out of earshot of the others). That person transmits it to the next, and so on down the line. The last person relates the story to the group as he/she heard it. You then follow by telling it like it was supposed to be.

Examine where and how distortions entered—was it in the words and labels, stereotypes, forgetting, combining things, misplacing emphasis?

Then, pass along a nonverbal communication from person to person. Again the purpose is to demonstrate how easy it is to misperceive what others are feeling and what they are telling us about how they are feeling. Give the first person the following written scenario.

> You have been hit with a lot of bad news in the past few days—sickness in the family, lost your job (or failed an important test), house burned down, broke your arm, and your pet (child, spouse) ran away. You feel hurt, depressed, and dejected. Feel it. Pass the emotion along to the next person without using any words.

Each of the next people in line is to receive the emotion and then send it along the transmission chain until it reaches the last person. That person tells the group what he/she is feeling and makes up a story that would justify that emotion.

Compare both emotions and scenarios, while also discussing the ways in which individual pairs communicated and where distortions crept in. Let pairs that did not communicate accurately try to figure out where the problem was.

Sometimes the problem in a family, school, or work setting is not accuracy of communication, but communication itself, getting things out in the open. You must know what is troubling people before you can begin to make changes. And that means they have to express it. An effective exercise for doing just that is to "let it all hang out, out loud."

Hit 'em again, louder!

Sit with eyes closed. At the signal, "Begin," all start to complain about a common situation (the job, the team, the family vacation plans, etc.). Do so simultaneously and forcefully. As soon as there is a lull in the complaining, signal, "Eyes open." Now repeat it again, looking at each other. Only this time *shout* out the complaints as if all the others are nearly deaf.

Next, see how many similar complaints there are and begin to discuss them. Finally, discuss the special complaints that bother only one or two people.

This exercise lets off steam and turns quietly building anger and resentment into loud and usually funny bickering. It allows people to hear that others are dissatisfied also and then leads naturally to discussion of problem-solving solutions.

Sometimes the issue is not that we can't admit what we feel, but that we feel inhibited from saying anything at all. "Cat got your tongue?" we say to the silent child. But making the reticent child more self-conscious will not break the ice. Suggestions for thawing frozen tongues are contained in these exercises, which vary with the age of the tongues and how frozen they are.

Roar, lion, roar—chug, train, chug

To break the ice with a group of children who seem inhibited and unresponsive, get them to be less self-conscious by roaring like a lion and then chugging like the Little Engine that Could.

- "We are all lions in a big lion family, and we are having a roaring contest to see who is the loudest roarer. When I say, 'Roar, Lion, Roar!' let me hear your loudest Roar."

- "Who can roar louder than that? Okay now, lions, Roar . . . You call that a lion's roar? That's a pussy cat. I mean really roar." Then get them moving in a line around the room, each child with a hand on the shoulder of the child in front. You be the "big engine" at first. Start slowly, moving in a circle, chugging and hooting as you go. When you come back to the starting point, go to the back of the train to become the caboose while the child next in line is the engine. He or she should chug a *little* louder and move a little faster. Continue around the tracks replacing engines until everyone has had a turn and the train is really chugging and moving. End with a derailment, "and all fall down."

Letting another you come through

Excessive self-preoccupation can be set aside by arranging conditions for children to express themselves through another voice, another self. My research and that of my colleagues has shown that masks and costumes liberate behavior that is normally inhibited and restrained. If the setting you help to create is one that encourages joyful, playful exuberance, open expressions of feelings, and tender sentiments, then anonymity will help make it happen. (If, however, hostility or aggressive games are sanctioned, all hell will burst forth instead).

Provide masks, or have the children make them from paper bags or out of papier-mâché. Have available old clothes to use as costumes for dress-up time, especially for dressing like grownups. Have each child assume a new name and go along with that new identity. Face painting is another way to turn a shy child into whatever he or she would like to be. Don't wait for Halloween to provide an excuse for masks (for adults as well as children).

Also have children use puppets to express their feelings. When your puppet is the child and the child's puppet is you, some interesting revelations often come through. Be ready, willing, and able to be a child again. Your children will respect you more for it, not less, as many grownups fear.

Sharing

Encourage the open sharing not only of feelings but of talents and knowledge as well. You don't have to join the Peace Corps and go to foreign lands to share your abilities and specialized knowledge, you can do it here and now, and your children should be encouraged to do so as well. Any child's gifts then become treasures for all to share and rejoice in. Once a child has internalized this attitude about his or her talents, "performing" is no longer shyness-inducing. It becomes an act of sharing, entertaining others, or helping them—and not merely of basking in the spotlight of attention.

Jigsawing knowledge

Create conditions where children learn to use other children as a resource, seeking help from and giving help to each other. The purpose of the exercise is to promote cooperation, sharing, and friendship by creating a democratic community of scholar-experts.[4]

Prepare a set of materials that can be divided into as many equal segments as there are children (in groups from two to six). Each child is to receive one piece of the total, which will then be put together in the manner of a jigsaw puzzle. If there are several such groups, the same material is distributed to each. The material might be information about another society. For example, one child gets a paragraph about geography and climate, another about economy, another learns a paragraph about political conditions, while others in the team may get information about child-rearing practices, sports, or other aspects of the culture. Only by combining all the parts does a whole story of the culture emerge.

Each child masters his/her paragraph and then teaches it to the others. To determine how well the child-teachers taught their child-students the lesson, a diagnostic test is given to each child on all of the material. Children in different groups with the same paragraph to master can compare notes first before communicating and combining information within their own group.

Obviously, any materials can be used that are dividable; history lessons, stories, art projects, or mechanical-electrical devices will do nicely. In addition, toys and games that require two or more players should be available to encourage cooperative play behavior.

Self-reliance

We live and ultimately survive as social animals interdependent on one another. But the strength of the group depends on the self-reliance of each individual. We are too ready to nurture dependence in our children in order to feel needed. But the result is that we turn our children into "yes people" —"Yes Momma, yes Poppa, yes teacher, yes world, yes, I will be what you want." They become quiet, passive, well-mannered children, rewarded by all for being obedient nonentities. Rewarded, but taken for granted, and ultimately ignored. They fade into the woodwork or become part of the standard operating procedure.

- Recognize that passivity is an alien state for children and all living things.
- Do not encourage dependence in your children or students simply because it allows you to better control and manage them. Dependence is like taffy candy, however good it tastes at first, it always ends up stuck to your teeth.
- Teach your children to be responsible for themselves as soon as they can.

- Make a list of all the activities each child is responsible for, and a second list of all the things you now do *for* the child you wish the child could be responsible for. Try shifting items from the "wish" to the "do" list. Discuss these responsibilities with your children. See if there are other items they would like or feel ready for. Negotiate on those where there is disagreement. Responsibilities are not just house chores, like taking out the garbage. They include grooming one's self, caring for one's property and common property, making arrangements for various events, and so on.

- Encourage children to be responsible for others, not just for helping old ladies across streets, but for helping brothers and sisters with homework, you when you are distressed, or classmates who need assistance.

- Allow for mistakes and permit the child sufficient time to become more self-reliant. Shy children fear taking any action because of their anxiety about failing or doing it wrong. Teach children to take calculated risks and to handle failure. The message to get across is that the child's *attempts may fail* to get a desired goal, but *the child is never a failure.* Failure means either the goal was wrong or the means to it were wrong. Or, of course, it could mean that the game was rigged against the child and he or she should take the play elsewhere.

- Prepare children to be comfortable with themselves when they are alone. Solitude can be a positive experience when it is chosen as a means to get in touch with one's self. This means making available private space and personal time for the child. It also means not filling up the child's life with planned group activities. On occasion, it might even mean encouraging the child in a solitary activity, such as a walk down the block, a trip to a museum, the library, a movie, or, for older children, a hike in the woods.

Works and plays well with others

What grade did you get on your report card for "works and plays well with others?" Did you ever think how ridiculous it is to grade one's sociability quotient?

We should be sensitive to how our children relate to their peers. Teachers and parents need to take greater pains to observe the conditions in which the child does and doesn't work and play well with others. (I might not want to play baseball with the other kids if they only want me to be second base.) We need to ask the children themselves. Are they being invited to play? Is the work task at their level? And we need to know from the others why they have not issued an invitation to, or have ignored the advances of, our child.

Sociogram of friendships

Teachers can get a better insight into the social atmosphere of their classes
by means of a sociogram. Have each child check off on a separate list all
the children he/she plays with (P). Then, indicate those who are good
friends (GF), and just friends (F). From these evaluations, you can construct a diagram of the patterns of association within the classroom. From
this pattern, it will be evident who are the "stars" and "loners," whose
friendship choices are not reciprocated, and whose play is not welcome.

With this information you are in a position to institute activities that can
realign some of the allegiances to achieve greater mutuality of interest and
caring. A sociogram of seven children might look like this:

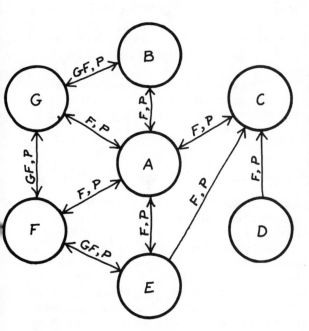

*D is left out, no
one's friend, plays
only with C; A is
everyone's friend,
but no one's good
friend; F and G
have several good
friends; C does not
return the friend-
ship of E and D.*

You can also do this exercise with your own children and those in the
neighborhood.

Popularity takes practice

Children need the opportunity to practice their social skills, to communicate, to express feelings to other children and to you. At as early an age as

possible, encourage social play with other kids and make time to be with your child.

Speech therapist James White maintains that adults with successful careers were talkers as children—it is the verbal child and not the unheard one who makes it in the home, school, and out in the verbal world of careers and professions. "The shy, reticent child usually doesn't get any-where with adults," White believes. "He doesn't give the adult enough to go on. Youngsters who don't talk and respond usually don't read very well and generally don't do well in school. It's up to an interested adult to draw a child out and help him verbalize his thoughts and feelings."[5] Among other recommendations White makes is to get down to the child's level or pick him or her up to yours in order to have better eye contact during your conversation.

Popularity can be taught to shy children who are left out of the social action. They can be coached in ways to communicate, to cooperate, and to be more attractive to other children. Some of the skills in Chapter 10 can be made to work for your shy child or shy pupil. A research team from Ro-chester and Illinois proved that third- and fourth-grade children who were rated low in acceptance by their classmates came to be accepted and chosen as friends after a month of supervised coaching and practice in social skills.[6] You too can achieve similar results if you're willing to be your child's informed coach.

Touch, trust, and tenderness

"Have you hugged your kids today?" Rosita Perez poses this question on her bumper sticker. She hugs hers and thinks we should hug ours because it's good for their well being. Researcher James Prescott goes further in ad-vocating physical contact as a means to reduce violence between people and nations. His research shows that cultures where physical contact is minimal are more aggressive, and people who do not like close physical contact with others are more punitive in their values toward lawbreakers, endorse the death penalty for capital crimes, and are more bigoted and authoritarian.[7]

Cultures vary in their support for, or taboos against, touching and physical expression of love. People from Mediterranean and Latin nations tend to be more openly expressive than those from Nordic and Oriental cultures. In the United States, we follow Anglo-Nordic norms, which pro-hibit tender physical contact among males and place restrictions on other public displays of affection. For many people, the only times they get touched are when a doctor takes their pulse, when they are caught in a crowded subway, or when they score a touchdown on the football field.

Touching connects us in a direct and primitive way with others. It keeps us from drifting away, from getting lost. It gives pleasure and reaffirms the physical reality of our existence. Hugging a baby is a special delight that many parents give up when the child is supposed to start growing up.

Reflect on your answers to each of these touch questions:

- Do you touch, pat, hug, kiss your mate, parents, relatives and close friends? If not, why not?
- Do you do so in front of your children? If not, why not?
- Do you or did you hug, touch, kiss your baby?
- How often?
- How often do you do so now?
- When and why did you stop or do so less ?
- Do you enjoy being touched?
- Do you enjoy touching?
- Do your children enjoy it or not? How do you know?

Unless it makes you nauseous, try a little more touching with your children, especially your shy ones. If it makes you nauseous, take a Dramamine and try again. I recall with great joy memories of Saturday night rubdowns my uncle used to give us after our bath. Try setting up a family massage center where you feel comfortable giving and receiving massages.

Trust is perhaps the most important dimension of human relationships. It washes away fears of rejection, ridicule, and betrayal that haunt the shy person's existence. It paves the way to friendship and intimacy. It is at the core of love for another person and acceptance of one's self.

You can create a climate of trust in your home or classroom by:

- expressing support and unconditional acceptance of the children, even though you disapprove of some of their behaviors (make them aware of this difference);
- making it acceptable to talk openly about themselves;
- reciprocating with your own openness;
- not making promises you do not intend to keep, or cannot deliver;
- being consistent, though not rigid in your standards, values, and behavior;

• and finally, by being available to listen, express warmth, and empathize even, when you don't have an answer, a solution, or spare change.

Several physical exercises can be utilized to help build trust and make children and students more aware of the experience of trusting.

------◆◆------

Jump, baby, jump!

Since the time my daughter Zara was able to stand up unassisted on the changing table, I have played the jump baby, jump game with her. I encourage her to jump off the table into my arms. At first I tilted her off as I signaled, "one, two, three, jump." As she got the idea, I moved my hands back, then my body back, so she would have to jump further. As trust in you grows, you can observe the child's tentative nervous early behavior change to freer, bolder leaps into space—accompanied by squeals of delight. Be sure to have a clear jump signal that indicates you are ready to play the game. You don't want standing up on any table to be the cue to jumping—whether or not you're ready. Children can make this discrimination very early if you are consistent at your end.

------◆◆------

Blind walk

To experience how our overdependence on vision makes us mistrust our less-used senses, arrange for one member of a pair of children to be blindfolded for twenty minutes (or more) and the other to act as guide. Guide the "blind" person around the room, down the hall into an open area outside. Ask him or her what is being sensed. Have the guide try to make the sensory experience a rich one. In a safe place, preferably an open field or large uncluttered room, let the guide leave the blind person for a short time. Invite the blind person to run to the guide's voice, then to explore the guide's head and hands through touch. Reverse the roles and after repeating the exercise have all participants share their feelings about:

• trust in their senses
• trust in their guide
• dependence on vision and the guide, initially
• frustrations and resentments

- being left alone
- being reunited with the guide
- reversing roles

———————◆•◆———————

Tenderness means different things in different relationships; for me, it always means at least the expression of feelings of caring, warmth, and gentle loving. It does not mean treating children, students or friends as if they were fragile, porcelain dolls. Tender is the opposite of tough, but in this context it is also the opposite of cold, indifferent, demanding, and not affectionate. Tenderness is the sunshine of human warmth that enables us all to grow, to flourish and radiate inner confidence. And it is evident in the faces and demeanor of children who have been nourished on a diet of it.

- As the song says, try a little tenderness next time.
- Don't be afraid to say to your children, "I love you"—regardless of how old they are or who is listening. Say it and show it.
- Make it possible for them to express tenderness toward you, as well. If you can't, then face it as a hang-up *you* ought to be dealing with.

Lovers and mates

When you want to help your lover or mate overcome shyness, much of what we have covered thus far will also be of value in that effort. Here we shall add only special concerns for intimacy, freedom, and autonomy.

To be intimate is to be close to another person in body and mind. Shyness often serves as a protective shield insulating shy people from the heat of intimacy. Thus, they are less likely to enter intimate relations and, even when in one, they erect shyness barriers that prevent total intimacy.

- Take time to develop the necessary trust and show that you care for the whole person.
- Offer reassurance and emotional support.
- Provide the recognition and attention that confers a feeling of being special in your eyes—both in public and in private.
- Be willing to take the first step in declaring feelings, initiating action, disclosing, taking the big risk. You may have to do this not only at the beginning of the relationship, but at each point a shyness barrier has to be scaled. Again your sensitivity to timing and tenderness will keep

you from seeming too assertive and pushy—especially if your shy mate is a male who believes men ought to be in the driver's seat.

- Avoid judgmental evaluations; especially avoid making sex a performance open to evaluation. Focus on the natural pleasure of physical closeness, on the joy of sharing that pleasure.

- Express your needs, your uncertainties, and also your confusion about what your partner wants, or is not clearly communicating about your sexual relationship.

- Help create an atmosphere of love in which either of you is able to say "no" to a sexual union on any given night without being pressured into it or feeling guilty for not feeling passionate.

- Share responsibility for making sexual love mutually satisfying—and for the times when it isn't.

Freedom and autonomy

The poet Khalil Gibran expresses beautifully the seeming paradox of lovers being separate though together:

> Sing and dance together and be joyous, but let each one of you be alone,
> Even as the strings of a lute are alone though they quiver with the same music.
> Give your hearts, but not into each other's keeping,
> For only the hand of life can contain your hearts.
> And stand together yet not too near together,
> For the pillars of the temple stand apart,
> And the oak tree and the cypress grow not in each other's shadows.[8]

Shy lovers and mates are not possessions, neither rare jewels to be kept in your safe, nor doormats to be stepped on. They need freedom to continue to grow and to help you grow. They must have an independent identity, so they can continue to be what you loved them for in the first place—and not become just a silent reflected dimension of you.

- Choose friends and situations you both feel comfortable with, or enjoy them separately.

- It should not be so important to your image to have your mate be positively evaluated by others that you straitjacket him or her into being what others want.

- Support activities, hobbies, and friendships that your mate can enjoy independent of you—it will give you new things to share.

- Learn to negotiate differences, to fight openly and fairly and work together at solving problems.
- Your shy mate may have learned habits that close down all channels of communication when anxiety or anger builds up. Learn how to gently reopen the flow of communication, and don't include silence as a weapon in your arsenal.
- Encourage a sense of humor in both of you that laughs at mistakes and human frailty—such as shyness.

Shyness self-help groups

Self-help groups can provide a nonthreatening way for shy people to meet one another. Of the possible forms these groups could assume, the most promising, I believe, would be to organize them around a primary interest that the members already share, such as sports, drama, religion, literature, recreation, and so forth. What would differentiate them from existing clubs and groups is the members' shared knowledge that another common reason for joining was their shyness.

Announcements on the library bulletin board, for example, of the formation of a play-reading group primarily for shy people could bring together those with the same interest and common concern. Other interests and hobbies are equally plausible common denominators: bible reading, bowling, camping, acting, exercise, magic, ESP, miniature soldiers and railroads, guns, and science fiction.

Shyness clinics

There are a handful of treatment centers that provide therapeutic help for those who are shy. Three deserve mention here. The most ambitious is The Friendship Clinic, directed by Dr. Gerald Phillips in University Park, Pennsylvania. The clinic's emphasis is on developing competency in communication skills. Staff members use many elements of a behavior-modification approach to help reticent clients overcome stagefright, speech apprehension, and "whatever it is that plagues people before they have to perform in public."[9]

Another similar program is conducted by staff psychologist Dorothy Smith at the counseling center of The Claremont Colleges (Claremont, California). She found that more people were interested in enrolling in a "shyness workshop" than an "assertion training workshop," because their difficulty was a general one of not relating to others, rather than a specific

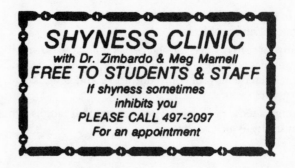

need to be assertive in a more specific area of their lives. Like the Pennsylvania Friendship Clinic, the Claremont Shyness Workshop stresses the importance of learning and practicing conversational skills.[10]

At the Stanford Shyness Clinic, we use specific techniques to help clients deal with the various components of their shyness. To control generalized anxiety and bodily tension, there is training in progressive relaxation. To change negative self-images and build self-esteem, we use techniques to help clients become aware of their own self-statements, recognize inappropriate ones, and learn to stop them and to increase the frequency of positive self-statements and self-images.

Skills building assumes considerable importance in our program to remedy problems in relating to others. Using video-tape feedback, we train clients in listening, self-disclosure, expression of feelings (especially of taboo feelings like anger, rage, and tenderness), ways to build trust and to be more socially attractive. For areas where the person feels inadequate and gets put down by others (or puts himself or herself down), we use assertion training.

Role-playing that realistically simulates situations of high anxiety—for example, a dance, a job interview, calling for a date, making small talk, conducting an interview, or even engaging themselves at a party—is especially valuable in putting all the learned elements into action.

An essential part of our shyness clinic is "real world" homework activities. Clients must contract to keep records and engage in a variety of exercises (like those outlined in Part II of this book) to remain participants. In this way, the reduction in shyness we note within the clinic setting can better generalize to the person's life setting and be of more permanent value.

But beyond specific tactics and therapeutic strategies, we try to communicate to our clients several basic messages that have been regularly reiterated throughout this book.

- You have control over what you feel and do.
- You are responsible for those feelings and actions and for creating the consequences you want.
- You have chosen to be shy and learned how to act like a shy person. You can now choose not to be, if you are willing to unlearn those old habits and substitute ones that work for your best interests.
- You are free to do X, even when others say you cannot; you are free to refuse to do X, even when others say you must.

And, perhaps most important, we acknowledge the need to penetrate the isolation of solitary existence with the touch of humanity that gives it meaning and purpose beyond narcissistic survival. Theologian Martin Buber puts it this way.

> Man wishes to be confirmed in his being by man, and wishes to have a presence in the being of the other—secretly and bashfully he watches for a "Yes" which allows him to be and which can come to him only from one human person to another.

12
preventing shyness in society

T here is a tale my grandfather was fond of telling that sets the theme for our final chapter on ways to overcome shyness:

One day in the waiting room of a small Sicilian village medical clinic, three patients were arguing the merits of their physicians.

"There is none more skilled in surgery than my doctor," proclaimed Mr. Ninni. "He can painlessly remove from my feet the thorns and burrs I happen to step on while herding the sheep."

"That's nothing compared to Doctor Baccigaluppi, who has invented the most outstanding ointment to soothe the rope burns I get on my hands from pulling in the fishing boats."

"Simple cures for simple ills," said the third young man. "Whenever I get obsessed with the worry of how I will feed my poor family, the good Doctor Odrabmiz has taught me to hypnotize myself and take away my cares by imagining that there is pie enough for all in the sky."

Unable to resolve the issue of which of their doctors was preeminent, they turned to the old janitor who had been listening to their debate: "Old man, you have heard their cures, now which of our doctors do you think is the best?"

"They are all great and wonderful specialists to be sure, with much skill and imagination in their treatment. Being but a simple, unschooled man I cannot really help you decide which cure and which great physician is the best. All I can offer is a pair of shoes to you, Mr. Ninni, my gloves to you, rope puller, and for my hungry friend over there, a bowl of pasta today and a job as my assistant for tomorrow."

Moral: Sometimes simple prevention proves wiser than the most wondrously complex cures.

Thus far in Part II, the focus has been on what can be done to make ourselves and others less shy. Many alternatives have been outlined and different proposals suggested that could reduce the undesirable impact of shyness on our lives. However, common to all is the emphasis on *changing people*—the way they think, feel, talk, and act. A second common feature is doing something to modify shyness *after* it occurs.

In this final chapter, I want to consider with you a quite different approach to the problem of shyness: *preventing shyness before it occurs by changing cultural values, social norms, and situational forces.* A tall order to be sure, but one with broader, more lasting effectiveness, if it can be achieved.

Consequences or causes

There are two ways to go about changing an undesirable behavior: change its consequences or change its causes. The first is a basic tenet of behavior modification; the second is the foundation of preventive strategies. The one involves treatments and cures of what ails you; the other involves innoculating you to keep you from ailing. *Individuals* may get cured of diseases by applying the appropriate treatment; *populations* are prevented from getting the disease by appropriately altering *conditions* that generate the sickness. Which approach to utilize is not just a matter of whether you decide to take action before or after shyness occurs. At issue are fundamental differences in the philosophy of helping people in need and the politics of social change.

Given that shyness exists and is an undesirable, unwanted problem for most shy people, there is a need to offer them (and you) immediate help. But at the same time, we can work to prevent others from ever having to face this devastating problem. Both approaches to dealing with shyness can, and should, go hand-in-hand. Of course, translating this ideal into practice is not always easy.

In our analysis of shyness, we have scrutinized the shy *individual,* and made the shy *person* responsible for making the changes needed to overcome shyness. But what about the social and cultural root causes of shyness? How are *they* changed by assertion training, progressive relaxation, and other *self*-help exercises? Of course, they are not, and so the next generation of shy people is currently being prepared to take the place of all those "presently shy" who successfully defect to join the ranks of the "formerly shy." Despite changes in individuals, the system remains. Despite any miracle cures, the epidemic continues.

Sometimes we don't make the necessary changes because of our over-eagerness to change people rather than situations or social values. Other times, we don't see the solution because we are part of the problem, or we don't recognize the problem because we don't see alternatives.

We can shake off these blinders by first briefly examining some instances where situational or social changes have worked better than direct attempts to change the "problem people." Consider the examples offered below.

In a Washington, D.C. facility for delinquent boys, violence was an ongoing problem that the staff dealt with in all the usual ways. They voiced their concerns, rewarded nonviolence, gave counseling and therapy to repeated offenders, and punished the incorrigible troublemakers—all exercises in futility. It was not until they decided to analyze the situations in which aggressive behavior occurred that the violence was controlled. Most of the incidents of aggression took place in the hallways, particularly at corners, where one boy often bumped into another coming around the bend. One bump led to another, push came to shove, and another fight erupted. The simply solution was to break down the wall with its blind turn, widen it, and curve it. No more traffic accidents at the intersection, and the incidents of violence were significantly reduced.[1]

To keep drivers from speeding on residential streets, traffic signs, stiff fines, and media appeals have proven much less effective than just putting speed bumps in the roadway. Once bumped is better than twice warned in preventing future speeding.

A persistent problem that has plagued me in all my years of teaching (and surfaces every so often at our military academies) is cheating by students on examinations. A variety of preventive techniques have been tried, but they are invariably less ingenious than the cheaters are and less persuasive than the reasons that compel cheating. Ultimately, when honor codes don't work, nor close surveillance, then the cheating few are removed from the institution so they won't spoil the other apples. I have come to believe it is the barrel that is contaminated.

While sitting at one after another judicial hearing regarding students accused of repeated cheating in my course, I was struck by the futility of these proceedings in deterring future cheating. On trial were the *whos* of cheating rather than the *whys*. Intense competition for a limited and too valuable commodity—the sacred A—was the primary reason given. Then, there was the anxiety over being evaluated, the uncertainty that what you knew and had studied would even be on the test, the absence of a second chance in case you weren't prepared or blew it, and, finally, the impersonal and hostile testing situation—each individual student pitted against all the others out to prove their superiority.

The preventive strategy I have since adopted is designed to render these reasons for cheating irrelevant; as a consequence, cheating has become irrelevant. Grades reflect each student's mastery of the material to be learned, not superiority over others. Everyone can earn an A if each performs above a specified criterion of test mastery (for example, 80 percent correct). Competition is not with other students, it is against a personal standard. Test anxiety is reduced by having students take the many exams in the course whenever they are prepared to, repeat performances that are below the mastery level several times without penalty, and take the tests in a personalized setting individually administered by a student-proctor. The result has been that the students put in more work than they do in virtually all other courses, enjoy it more, and most get A's. The new social norms adopted have made cheating a meaningless concept in this setting, and have promoted student-proctor friendships as a side effect.

These examples are illustrative of alternatives to traditional treatment approaches. They prevent undesirable behavior patterns by altering aspects of the context in which those behaviors usually occur. It may be that the only way to prevent shyness is to radically change those values in our culture that foster its development.

Cultural programming

In which hand do you hold your fork while eating? In the left when you are cutting your food, and in the right when you eat it? Probably so, *if* you are an American; Europeans always keep a fork in their left hand. Do you bow when meeting a friend on the street? Americans probably don't, but it would be rude for Japanese not to. Would you be more willing to help a foreigner or a compatriot? Depends on the way your cultural background defines ingroup and outgroup. For Greeks, ingroup includes family, friends, and tourists, but not other Greeks who are strangers. This is not so with Parisians or Bostonians, both of whom, as a group, have been shown to be more ready to grant help to compatriots than foreigners.[2]

To an extent we often fail to appreciate, our culture conditions our perception of reality while programming the structure of our thoughts, feelings, and actions. Even so fundamental a reality as pain has been shown to elicit very different reactions depending on one's cultural background. Italians are very sensitive to pain and exaggerate its intensity. Jews also react strongly to pain, but are more concerned than Italian patients about its implications for their future health. Anglo-Saxon Protestants display emotional reactions to pain only in private. In contrast, Irish patients "bite the bullet" and silently endure pain without complaint or showing their suffering, even in private.[3]

How do cultural values and practices program people to be shy? You might frame an answer to this question by designing the shy society you would develop if you were minister of the interior. On your list of ten ways to promote shyness, you'd probably want to mention:

1. Valuing rugged individualism (making it on one's own, going it alone, doing it my way).

2. Promoting a cult of the ego (narcissistic introspection, self-absorption, and self-consciousness).

3. Prizing individual success and making failure a source of personal shame in a highly competitive system.

4. Setting limitless aspirations and ambiguous criteria for success, while not teaching ways of coping with failure.

5. Discouraging expression of emotions and open sharing of feelings and anxieties.

6. Providing little opportunity for intimate relations between the sexes and strict taboos on most forms of sexual expression.

7. Making acceptance and love contingent on fluctuating and critical social standards of performance.

8. Denying the significance of an individual's present experience by making comparisons to the unmatchable glories of past times and the demands of future goals.

9. Fostering social instability through mobility, divorce, economic uncertainty, and any other way possible.

10. Destroying faith in common societal goals and pride in belonging to the group.

Consider whether this prescription of a shyness-generating society has already been filled for you. Don't many of these values exist in your work, school, and everyday life? I believe that in any society where shyness is a prevalent, undesirable problem, we will also find variants of these ten elements. Where shyness is less prevalent, we should expect to discover fewer of these values in operation. If we look at the variations in shyness from culture to culture, we might be able to recommend changes in those values that generate shyness. First, let's look at a culture where a couple of these values are promoted so strongly that they almost guarantee shyness. (A summary table of cultural variations in shyness is given at the end of the "Notes" section, p. 233).

The "inscrutable" Oriental

Our studies show that shyness is more prevalent in Japan and Taiwan than in any other culture we surveyed. Among the Japanese, 57 percent reported being currently shy, as compared to 53 percent of the Taiwanese. For three-fourths of the Japanese, shyness is viewed as a "problem," over 90 percent report having labelled themselves as shy in the past or currently, and, more than any other nationality, the Japanese report feeling shy in virtually all social situations. Shyness is a special problem for males caught between conflicting cultural demands: to be the dominant authority in the household, and to be passively deferential to all other authority. A significantly greater percentage of Japanese (and Taiwanese) men than women report being shy. In every other culture we have surveyed, there is either no difference between the sexes (as in the United States), or women are more shy than men (as in Israel, Mexico, and India).

An interesting contradiction arises between the general devaluing of shyness in these Oriental cultures and the traditional values that make virtues of modesty and reserve. More Japanese subjects than any other group reported they "liked" being shy and extolled its positive consequences. But this 20 percent of the population is, nevertheless, in the minority. Reflecting perhaps the growing rebellion of the younger generation against the formal, stylized structure imposed by traditional Oriental values, the majority of our student respondents do not view shyness as a desirable attribute and do not like being shy.

Japanese society is the model of a shyness-generating society. My own observations underscore the analysis by my Oriental colleagues and other scholars of Japanese culture that the Japanese child is caught in a net of cultural values that make shyness inevitable. Studying how cultural values are transmitted to the child is a difficult and complex undertaking, open to misinterpretation. But a number of different sources have come to similar conclusions about the effect of Japanese cultural values on child-rearing practices, and about how these practices produce a shy person. One of the best investigations of Japanese and American children (and their parents) from the time they were three months old through six years of age concludes:

> Compared to Japanese, Americans are more active, more vocally and
> physically emotional, more independent, and more likely to manipulate
> functionally both their social and physical environments.[4]

Training in emotional control, inhibition of self-expression, and compulsive attention to details, planning, rules, and rituals not only stifles action and spontaneity, it denies legitimate expression of anxieties and justified anger. When the Japanese become mentally ill, they are likely to perceive the major source of their problem as being within themselves and, as a result, they turn against themselves. This inward turning of emotions and hostility is fostered by other cultural values that emphasize a strong sense of duty (*giri*) and obligation to others, deference and politeness to authority, self-effacement, and personal responsibility for failure to live up to the expectations of others.[5]

Basic to the Japanese character development are *"amae"* and *shame*. *Amae* begins as a passive dependence of the child on his or her mother (wanting to cling, be comforted, indulged). But it comes to pervade every level of Japanese social structure and to control social, political, and cultural actions. *Amae* encourages passive dependence and unquestioning loyalty to all those in higher positions, regardless of one's ability and talent. One must patiently wait for the appropriate time to be "recognized" for merit, often by far less worthy superiors. As the president of a large Japanese firm informed me, to choose to stand out, to push one's self forward, or to show impatience at not being recognized sooner are marks of "immaturity." Holding such an assertive person back is seen as a wise decision by the superior. It is a self-fulfilling prophecy which breeds further passivity, dependence, and excessive concern for the favorable evaluation of critical others.

The other basic mechanism of social control in Japan is the use of shame. In fact, much energy is devoted in Japanese society to avoiding shame, because of the devastating consequences. Any action that violates the expectations of others is a potential source of shame for the individual —and for all those others. Japanese life is lived in groups—the family, the neighborhood, the school, the team, the work group. Loyalty to each of these groups is strong, as is one's feeling of obligation to maintain and enhance the group's prestige. Any failure, ridicule, or embarrassment, however small, that one's actions create for the group is a cause for shame. Once experienced, shame can be undone by new acts that compensate for the wrong done to the group—or by removing one's unworthy self from the group, often by the route of suicide. There is no failure, however trivial in the eyes of foreigners, that could not become a reason for suicide. A high-school baseball player took his life for committing an error that lost a game, college professors have done so for being criticized by their students for lack of preparation, and so forth.

"In Japanese," writes Giyoo Hatano, "the word 'shyness' is closely related to the word 'shame.' This is seen in the tendency for Japanese to be shy for fear of being laughed at.'" The group's reliance on social control through fear of shame then encourages shyness as a safe life style. This is equally true in Taiwan as in Japan.

The use of *amae* and shame tactics provides strong psychological group control of antisocial behavior, and helps to account for the low crime rate among Orientals in Asia or in America. While shyness or inscrutability is prized at a social level, its effects on the personal lives of Japanese and Taiwanese are extremely disruptive. The mainland Chinese, on the other hand, have been able to effectively prevent the devastating effects of shyness.

Walling out shyness in China

Like the other Oriental cultures we've discussed, life in mainland China is group centered. But, unlike them, the group is the source of positive self-regard, and the destroyer of self-doubt. Communal life (following the cultural revolution) in China bears more resemblance to that in Israel than it does to other Oriental societies. The philosophy of collectivism means that no single individual will consider his or her own interest above that of the group. As practiced in China (and in Israel), individual potental is not suppressed by group domination, but enhanced by sharing in the

pride and common achievements of the group. Individualism is rejected when it means "selfish or undisciplined action divorced from the group." "Friendship first, competition second" is a motto on classroom walls and in athletic-team locker rooms. Individual success is measured in terms of its value to the group and to the society as a whole. For instance, some children are selected for special education at "Children's palaces," but they then have the responsibility to learn all they can in order to teach it to the other children. Knowledge, talents, and achievements should "serve the people" and never only one's personal needs.

To get survey data on the experience of shyness in mainland China, I sent a Chinese-speaking research assistant, Larry Leo, to Canton. We were not permitted to distribute our questionnaire, however, because an official said that it had been determined by a review committee that the act of filling it out "would force people to be too introspective and focus too much attention on themselves." Here was the cultural principle being put into practice.

Unfortunately, we do not have comparative statistical data to present, but there is every reason to believe from behavioral observations that shyness as we know it is an uncommon reaction in the People's Republic of China. My assistant reported that in village after village, young children would come up to him, start a polite conversation, ask questions, and give responsive answers. Although he was there to investigate them, he quickly became the object of their curiosity. He experienced similar sociability with older children and with families he visited.

Strong support for the "shylessness" of the Chinese child comes from a recent report of another American delegation that studied early childhood development in the People's Republic of China. This group of child psychologists visited a great many schools, hospitals, health clinics, and Chinese homes. From their observations, they conclude that the children are remarkably self-controlled, psychologically secure, independent, and lively.[7]

It seems that shyness is minimized or prevented in this culture by giving everyone a place in the social order and responsibility for achieving group goals, by believing in the perfectability of children and the power of concerned education to transform everyone, and by placing the blame for failure on bad social influences and external conditions, not on defects in the individual.[8] In only a few decades these cultural values have removed the Oriental mask of shyness worn for so many thousands of years.

Chutzpa, pride, and not-shy Jews

Among the students who answered our shyness survey, Jewish-Americans were the least shy. Compared to the more than 40 percent shy figure that appears again and again for thousands of people we've surveyed, only 24 percent of the Jewish-American group reported themselves as presently shy. In addition, they were less introverted, more extroverted, and, when they were shy, they tended to be more situationally shy.

Although the small size of the sample cautions against generalizing the results too far, the very low prevalence of shyness among Jews is a provocative finding. When we compare the kinds of things that elicit shyness in this group and in their non-Jewish peers, several significant differences emerge. Fewer of the Jews are distressed by being the focus of attention in large or small groups, by social situations in general, or by situations where they are being evaluated by others. Strangers and members of the opposite sex do not induce as much shyness for them as for their peers of similar age, education, and social class.

Interviews and personal experience with Jewish students, friends, and relatives suggests one source of this difference may be in the cultivation of Chutzpa among Jews. There is really no direct English translation of the word, perhaps because the concept is alien to the Anglo-Saxon mentality. Chutzpa might be defined as a unique kind of prideful self-confidence that motivates action, regardless of the risk of being discovered unprepared, untalented, or unwise. For Israelis, Chutzpa connotes a sense of daring, a willingness to fight against incredible odds. Many feel that the existence of the state of Israel is itself an act of Chutzpa. The important thing about having Chutzpa is it enables the Chutzpa-bearer to say and do certain things without becoming obsessed over being wrong or inappropriate. The practical consequence is getting more rewards in the long run by acting as if you deserve them—if you can tolerate some short-term setbacks when you do not measure up. With Chutzpa, you ask the best-looking girl to dance, apply for the better position, suggest that your raise could be bigger, your grade could be higher, and your work could be lighter. "What could they do to me but say 'no,' which never killed anyone, or 'yes,' which is all I want?"

But what are the origins of this personal style that is the antithesis of shyness? Some answers are provided in data collected on the nature of shyness in Israel by Dr. Ayala Pines, who surveyed over 900 Israelis between the ages of thirteen and forty years old—schoolchildren, college students, military service personnel, and kibbutz members. The percentage of Israelis who report being shy (35 percent) is the lowest of any of eight countries for which we have survey data. In addition, more of them have *never* been shy, and the vast majority of those that have been experience feelings of shyness only occasionally and primarily in specific situations.

Shyness is seen as less of a "problem" by Israeli Jews than it is by people from any other nationality. Only 46 percent of the sample describe shyness as a problem behavior; this compares with 64 percent for American students, 73 percent for other Americans, 75 percent in samples from Japan and Mexico, 58 percent in Taiwan, and 82 percent in India.

The situation most likely to make an Israeli squirm is one in which he or she feels vulnerable (about equally so in the American groups). But almost every other situation that makes Americans feel shy is much less likely to do so for an Israeli. Similarly, the types of people who have the power to push the shyness button for Americans lose that power in Israel. The Israelis make their American kin look uptight by virtue of their minimal reaction to all authorities or strangers, to being evaluated, to having to be assertive, to being the focus of attention in large or small groups, in new situations, or in social situations in general.

According to Dr. Pines, and others, the antishyness orientation characteristic of Israelis is the inevitable consequence of powerful forces operating throughout the culture. Jews are acutely aware that, for centuries, they have been discriminated against in every nation where they have lived as outsiders. But while people have rejected them, they have been comforted in the belief that God has made them the chosen people. This knowledge has fostered a sense of pride that could not be extinguished by oppression, nor dampened by nonacceptance and apparent failure.

Their fear of persecution also had the effect of forcing Jews to withdraw into their own community life, and made the family the important unit and children the center of existence. Thus, communal life is strong, even when individuals are weak; and children are priceless resources, even though their parents are poor or not accepted by other peoples. Pines says:

> Children are seen as the symbol of life and as the promise of the future for a nation constantly in danger of extinction. Thus Israel can be characterized as a child-centered nation where attitudes toward children are very positive and very permissive. Children are viewed by everybody as a very important national resource—it is thus common for strangers to approach children in the street, talk to them, take care of them, and give the mothers generous advice about how to raise them. In addition to this national symbolism, there is a special personal meaning that an Israeli child has to his or her own parents. Since many of them were immigrants who never had a chance to fulfill their potential, they see their children as the materialization of their dreams. Thus, they are prepared to sacrifice everything and anything for the sake of the child. The result is that most Israeli children grow up feeling that they are the center of the world—which indeed they are! [9]

These positive attitudes toward children are seen functioning in many different ways. Children are usually included in adult conversations, invited to perform their tricks, "chockness," for family and friends, for which they are lavishly praised even when the show is not special or outstanding. They come to expect support and reinforcement from those who love them, and to regard negative reactions as a reflection of the critic's lack of appreciation or personal bias. Everyone who is concerned about children belongs and, although he or she may not be known personally by the child, is treated as a "guest" and not as a "stranger" by the trusting Israeli child.

The institution of the kibbutz, where children are raised communally, reduces and prevents the development of shyness by encouraging self-reliance and leadership. Kibbutz children are not economically dependent on their parents nor limited to them as a source of reinforcement and love. Since parents are not responsible for disciplining their children, their primary functions are to give the children attention, praise, and an unconditional love that breeds security and trust.[10]

Finally, the Israeli commitment to direct action, to confronting people and situations one fears, comes as a reaction to the "phony bourgeois" life style that Israeli emigrants have left behind in the cities they grew up in, and to the passivity of Jews in the holocaust. To be straightforward, open, and unrestrained is consistently reinforced. On the other hand, to be shy is to be weak and ineffectual. "Shyness is associated in the Israeli mentality with weakness, with an inability to answer a challenge, with giving in, with spiritual surrender—like those Jews who did not fight for their lives, but accepted their fate like sheep on the way to the Nazi slaughter," says Dr. Pines.

These threads of the Israeli culture are woven into a tough fabric that protects the Israeli child from the social anxiety and feelings of inadequacy experienced too frequently by children in our culture.

Synanon: a shyness-shunning society

No need to go to an Israeli kibbutz or a Children's Palace in China to discover a world relatively free of the problems of shyness. Right in our own backyard is a community where children know little about the experience of shyness. They are outgoing, friendly, sociable children who express their feelings openly and directly. These are the children of Synanon. Synanon is an alternate-life-style community, begun in 1958 largely as a drug treatment program, but now the permanent home for thousands of adults and children in cities and rural areas of the United States. Many "straight" newcomers join this community not for treatment of "character disorders," but to escape a society with disordered priorities.

On a visit to the Synanon community in Northern California's Marin County, it became evident to me why many people would see the Synanon life style as attractive. There is work enough for everyone, and everyone works to earn the right to the good housing and the nourishing food provided. The tight communal structure and strongly shared values severely limit physical violence, crime, and addictive behaviors. There are no privileged classes in this democratically run society to breed inferiority feelings in the less fortunate. Self-reliance is a prized virtue and much rewarded wherever practiced by children and adults. With limited mobility, stability in social relationships flourishes, so that children develop lasting friendships.

The most unique features of life in this society are its communal living arrangements and the Synanon Game. From early infancy on, children live apart from their parents in specially designed bunkhouses. Organized by age levels, children, like adults, take their meals in communal dining rooms with their peers. There is considerable adult supervision, much attention to the developing needs of the children, and obvious respect, trust, and love shown them. Children are, in effect, born into a large communal family, but one in which there aren't favorites, and where there are enough parents so that no child is ever lost in the shuffle or ignored. It is enjoyable to be around these children, in part because they are active, interesting, emotionally mature young people who show a concern for you—even when you are a stranger. Ongoing psychological studies of the social and thought development of these children reveal that they are advanced in their intellectual attainments and socially competent, adept, and comfortable around other children and adults.[11]

The core activity of Synanon is the Game. All members of the community, from the age of six on, meet regularly for Games that may last anywhere from one to forty-eight hours. There are Games every day, with formally scheduled ones at specified times and informally arranged ones at any time. No physical violence is allowed, regardless of the verbal provocation.

In the Games, members openly express their resentment, frustration, and anger at the behavior of others and publicly share their fears and insecurities. Assuming that people can change undesirable behavior when they learn of its negative effects on others, it becomes the responsibility of members to give others "verbal haircuts" when they need it. It is through criticism, and then group suggestions and support for nonoffensive or nondetrimental alternatives, that behavior changes. The Game provides group solidarity and acts as an effective social control, directing members toward more appropriate behavior.[12]

This strong emphasis on the group allows little room for shyness at Synanon. Children clearly weren't shy in the classroom or in their bunkhouses or around adults. When adults bring their shyness to Synanon, they are told to act as if they were not shy. And when they do in that cultural setting, many lose what shyness they once suffered.

Leveling individuality or celebrating life?

What lessons can we learn from this cross-cultural perspective on shyness? When the prevalence of shyness is high (as in the Oriental cultures we've examined, and to a similar extent in our own culture), we find children are made to feel that their worth and the love they desire from adults is contingent on their performance. They have to prove they are deserving in a world where success is modestly taken for granted and rewards are given sparingly, while failures are magnified in the spotlight of shame. Children of shyness-generating societies are often not encouraged to express their ideas and feelings openly, nor given adequate opportunity to interact with adults or play freely with their peers. They learn to live too much within a private world of their own thoughts, devoid of action.

In contrast, those societies where shyness has not gained a stronghold on the minds of the young appear to be alike in the following ways: In the People's Republic of China, in Israel, and in the Synanon subculture within the United States, the emphasis is on common goals beyond the narrow concerns of the individual ego. Children are made to feel special, the prize of this generation, the promise of the next. Love is given unconditionally by parents and is not confused with training in responsibility and discipline. People learn from mistakes and are not stigmatized by them. There is considerable opportunity to relate to others, to practice both conversational skills and sharing within the communal setting. The orientation toward taking action, when combined with that of not allowing others to become isolated or alienated, is another antidote to the social disease of shyness.

Often when I describe how shyness is being prevented in these cultures at home and abroad, I hear, "I'd rather my child be shy than one of their conforming, docile robots without any personality!" But who's the robot? After all, it is the shy person who conforms to the will of others and submits to tyranny. It is the shy person who turns away from the joys of social community into the isolation of a nonbeing.

I am not suggesting that we trample individuality in seeking a solution to the shyness in our society. But we must recognize that shyness is but a symptom of the existence of cultural values and social practices that impoverish the quality of human life. Those values can be modified without necessarily adopting the political and economic orientations of the shyness-preventing societies we know. In creating social structures where people can live in harmony, we do not need to diminish the spirit of the individual —rather, we can multiply his or her own strength. But it is only by beginning to critically examine our own cultural priorities that we can start the social revolution needed to overcome shyness and prevent its appearance in the next generation of children.

I do not support the mindless anonymity of any group existence that denies the richest expression of the human potential. Rather, it is Zorba's song that I dance to. It is love of life that I celebrate. But I am able to dance and love and be free only because I am a social animal who lives in and with and for a community of people who give meaning to my existence. In overcoming shyness, we celebrate life and discover in ourselves a capacity to love and an energy for living that we dared not recognize before. It is worth any effort to make that discovery in ourselves, our children, our mates, and our friends. The time to begin is *now,* the place to begin is *here,* and the person to head the expedition to overcome shyness is *you.*

notes

Introduction

1. The power of roles, rules, and forces in the situation to overwhelm individual personality and values is demonstrated in a number of social psychological experiments, especially:

P. G. Zimbardo, C. Haney, W. C. Banks, D. Jaffee, "The Mind Is a Formidable Jailer: A Pirandellian Prison," *New York Times Magazine,* 8 April 1973, Section 6, pp. 38–60.

P. G. Zimbardo, "On Transforming Experimental Research into Advocacy for Social Change," in M. Deutsch and H. Hornstein, eds., *Applying Social Psychology: Implications for Research, Practice, and Training* (Hillsdale, N.J.: Lawrence Erlbaum Associates, 1973), pp. 33–66.

S. Milgram, *Obedience to Authority* (New York: Harper & Row, 1974).

N. J. Orlando, "The Mock Ward: A Study in Simulation," in P. G. Zimbardo, and C. Maslach, eds., *Psychology for Our Times,* 2d ed. (Glenview, Ill.: Scott Foresman, 1977), pp. 243–248.

R. Jones, "The Third Wave," *No Substitute for Madness* (San Francisco: Zephyros Press, 1976).

J. Elliott, "The Power and the Pathology of Prejudice," in P. G. Zimbardo, *Psychology and Life,* 9th ed. (Glenview, Ill.: Scott Foresman, 1977), "Research Frontiers Section," pp. 13A–13D.

Chapter 1

1. Malcolm Brenner of the University of Michigan has convincingly demonstrated how this special kind of anxiety operates in his study of "the circle of apprehension." His subjects, all men, were seated around a large table and asked to perform one task: each one in turn had to read aloud one simple word (like "grocery" or "October") from a printed card in front of him. They were told in advance that they would be asked to recall all the words that had been

read aloud. On each round, half of the subjects would read their words while the others listened.

"The *listeners* could remember about an equal number of words that each of the speakers had read aloud," Dr. Brenner reported. "However, we found a curious outcome in the recall patterns of the *speakers*. Of course, they could remember their own words and did pretty well on those most of the others had read with two exceptions—they had a very difficult time remembering the words spoken just before and just after their own turn."

Even when the readers knew exactly what to say (and had a printed card to help them), the anxiety of having to perform in front of an audience was enough to affect their memory. If saying one simple word could cause such anxiety, just think of the consequences when a shy person gets in a situation where he or she doesn't *know* what to say or to do!

2. Robert Young, quoted in *Family Circle,* February 1976. Reprinted by permission.

3. Letter to Ann Landers, *San Francisco Sunday Examiner and Chronicle,* 25 January 1976. Reprinted by permission.

4. Melvin Belli, quoted in article by Charlotte K. Beyers, "Don't Worry If You're Shy," *Parade,* 18 January 1976, p. 12. Reprinted by permission.

5. Many of the sensitive, personal accounts of extreme shyness I've quoted in this book were generated from listeners to a talk-show discussion of shyness I led on Carlo Prescott's program on station KGO, San Francisco.

6. F. A. Hampton, "Shyness," *Journal of Neurology and Psychopathology* (1927–1928):124–131.

7. Isaac Bashevis Singer, quoted in Charlotte K. Beyers, "Don't Worry If You're Shy," *Parade,* 18 January 1976, p. 12. Reprinted by permission.

8. For a fuller analysis of the function of anonymity in liberating behavior from the constraints of convention, see P. G. Zimbardo, "The Human Choice: Individuation, Reason, and Order versus Deindividuation Impulse, and Chaos," in W. J. Arnold and D. Levine, eds., *1969 Nebraska Symposium on Motivation* (Lincoln, Nebraska: University of Nebraska Press, 1970), pp. 237–307.

Chapter 2

1. Shirley Radl offers other personal insights into shyness and its treatment in her article: "Why You Are Shy and How to Cope with It," *Glamour,* June 1976, pp. 64, 84.

2. Phyllis Diller, quoted in *Family Circle,* February 1976, also described her shyness in a personal communication, 26 August 1976. Reprinted by permission.

3. See D. C. Murray, "Talk, Silence, Anxiety," *Psychological Bulletin* 24 (1971): 244–260.

4. G. M. Phillips and N. J. Metzger, "The Reticent Syndrome: Some Theoretical Considerations about Etiology and Treatment," *Speech Monographs* 40 (1973).

5. T. Williams, *Memoirs* (New York: Doubleday, 1976), p. 12.

6. Cornell MacNeil, in *Family Circle,* February 1976. Reprinted by permission.

7. A Modigliani, "Embarrassment, Facework, and Eye Contact: Testing a Theory of Embarrassment," *Journal of Personality and Social Psychology* 17 (1971): 15–24.

8. A. Fenigstein, M. F. Scheier, and A. H. Buss, "Public and Private Self Consciousness: Assessment and Theory," *Journal of Consulting and Clinical Psychology* 4 (1975):522–527. See also C. S. Carver and D. C. Glass, "The Self Consciousness Scale: A Discriminant Validity Study," *Journal of Personality Assessment* 40 (1976):169–172.

9. P. A. Pilkonis, "Shyness: Public Behavior and Private Experience" (Ph.D. dissertation, Stanford University, 1976).

10. Roosevelt Grier, quoted in *Family Circle,* February 1976. Reprinted by permission.

11. See A. Bavelas, A. H. Hastorf, A. E. Gross, and W. R. Kite, "Experiments on the Alteration of Group Structures," *Journal of Experimental Soical Psychology* 1 (1965):55–70. See also R. N. Sorrentino and R. G. Boutillier, "The Effect of Quantity and Quality of Verbal Interaction on Ratings of Leadership Ability," *Journal of Experimental Social Psychology* 11 (1975):403–411.

12. Johnny Mathis, quoted in a newspaper interview, verified in personal communication, 16 August 1976.

13. Nancy Walker, quoted in *Newsweek,* 29 December 1975.

14. Elizabeth Taylor, quoted in *San Francisco Chronicle* newspaper feature by Lester David and Jhan Robbins, "Liz and Dick—Meant for Each Other?" Her shyness was verified in a personal communication from her agent, John Springer, December 3, 1976.

15. Barbara Walters, quoted in newspaper feature, "Tough on the Outside, but Shy on the Inside," *San Francisco Chronicle,* 26 November 1976.

16. Barbara Walters, quoted in newspaper feature, "TV News Queen Barbara Walters Reveals: My Battle with Shyness," by Christina Kirk, *The Star* (Washington, D.C.), 26 October 1976. A fuller portrait of this shy super-celebrity appears in Jean Baer, *How to Be an Assertive (Not Aggressive) Woman* (New York: Rawson, 1977).

17. Joan Sutherland, quoted in Charlotte K. Beyers, "Don't Worry If You're Shy," *Parade,* 18 January 1976. Reprinted by permission.

18. Carol Burnett, quoted in *Family Circle,* February 1976. Reprinted by permission.

Chapter 3

1. H. Campbell, "Morbid Shyness," *British Medical Journal* 2 (1896):805–807.

2. R. Cattell, *Personality and Mood by Questionnaire* (San Francisco: Jossey Bass, 1973). Another psychometrician who has studied shyness as a personality trait is Andrew Comrey. See A. L. Comrey and K. Jamison, "Verification of Six Personality Factors," *Educational and Psychological Measurement* 26 (1966): 945–953.

3. John Watson's classic statement is found in J. B. Watson, "What the Nursery Has to Say about Instincts," in C. Murchison, ed., *Psychologies of 1925* (Worcester, Mass.: Clark University Press, 1926), pp. 1–34.

4. G. V. Solomon and J. C. Solomon, "Shyness and Sex," *Medical Aspects of Human Sexuality* 5 (1971) :15.

5. D. M. Kaplan, "On Shyness," *International Journal of Psychoanalysis* 53 (1972) :439–453.

6. M. Mahler, *On Human Symbiosis and the Vicissitudes of Individuation,* vol. 1 (New York: International Universities Press, 1968).

7. Michael York, quoted in the *San Francisco Chronicle,* 1976.

8. V. Packard, *A Nation of Strangers* (New York: McKay, 1972).

9. R. C. Ziller, *The Social Self* (New York: Pergamon, 1973).

10. See T. Szasz. "The Myth of Mental Illness," in P. G. Zimbardo and C. Maslach, eds., *Psychology for Our Times,* 2d ed. (Glenview, Ill.: Scott Foresman, 1977), pp. 235–242.

11. D. Rosenhan. "On Being Sane in Insane Places," in P. G. Zimbardo and C. Maslach, eds., *Psychology for Our Times,* 2d ed. (Glenview, Ill.: Scott Foresman 1977), pp. 249–261.

12. See the work of A. Farina, C. H. Holland, and K. Ring, "The Role of Stigma and Set in Interpersonal Interaction," *Journal of Abnormal Psychology* 71 (1966) :421–428.

13. Angie Dickinson, quoted in *Family Circle,* February 1976. Reprinted by permission.

14. An adaptation of Nietzsche's view of Greek tragedy. See F. Nietzsche, *The Birth of Tragedy* (New York: Doubleday, 1956).

15. R. D. Laing, *Self and Others* (New York: Pantheon Books, 1969); and *The Politics of Experience* (New York: Pantheon Books, 1967). See also Jean Paul Sartre, *Existentialism and Human Emotions* (New York: Philosophical Library, 1957).

Chapter 4

1. T. Solomon, "The Correlates and Consequences of Shyness in School Children" (Unpublished report, Stanford Shyness Project, 1976).

2. S. L. Hedrick, "A Study of Achievement as Related to Intelligence, Achievement, and Self-Concept," *Dissertation Abstracts International, A. Humanities and Sciences* 33 (September/October 1972) :3–4.

3. S. Schachter, *The Psychology of Affiliation* (Stanford, Ca.: Stanford University Press, 1959). See also N. Miller and P. G. Zimbardo, "Motives for Fear-Induced Affiliation: Emotional Comparison or Interpersonal Similarity," *Journal of Personality* 34 (1966) :481–503.

4. L. Forer, *The Birth Order Factor* (New York: McKay, 1976), p. 128.

5. N. Miller and G. Maruyama, "Ordinal Position and Peer Popularity," *Journal of Personality and Social Psychology* 33 (1976) :123–131.

6. J. W. Macfarlane, L. Allen, and M. P. Honzik, *A Developmental Study of the Behavior Problems of Normal Children between Twenty-One Months and Fourteen Years* (Berkeley, Ca.: University of California Press, 1962). See also J. W. MacFarlane, "Studies in Child Guidance. 1. Methodology of Data Collection and Organization," *Monographs of the Society for Research in Child Development* 3 (1938) : No. 6, entire issue.

7. Norton's problem appeared in a "Dear Abby" column in the *San Francisco Chronicle,* 15 April 1974. Reprinted by permission.

8. The insensitivity of teachers to shyness in their students is reported in studies by Ziller (1973) and Hedrick (1972) cited previously.

9. Marilynne Robinson's analysis of shyness in her second-grade pupils is excerpted from a personal communication, 1 November 1976.

10. Teacher quotes on opening-day stage fright are taken from a featured story by Anita Kay, *San Francisco Chronicle,* 10 September 1976.

11. N. Hatvany, "Shyness, Emotional Arousal, and Information Processing" (M.A. thesis, Stanford University, 1976).

12. A popular account of how some children appear to be invulnerable to early life traumas is Ruthe Stein's article, "Children—Thriving on Calamity?" in the *San Francisco Chronicle,* 29 June 1976. For example, Eleanor Roosevelt's "mother died when she was eight; two years later, her father, a self-destructive alcoholic whom she adored, was also dead. A painfully shy little girl, Eleanor was raised by a stern grandmother in a gloomy house where her friends were never made to feel welcome." (p. 19).

13. H. Renaud and F. Estees, "Life History Interviews with One Hundred Normal American Males: 'Pathogenicity' of Childhood," *American Journal of Orthopsychiatry* 31 (1961):786–802. See also E. L. Cowen, A. Pederson, H. Babigian, L. D. Izzo, and M. A. Trost, "Long-Term Follow-Up of Early Detected Vulnerable Children," *Journal of Consulting and Clinical Psychology* 41 (1973): 438–446.

14. Quotes from Carol Burnett taken from typescript of an extended telephone interview, 13 January 1977. Used with Ms. Burnett's permission.

Chapter 5

1. Alexander Solzhenitsyn beautifully describes his intuitive sensor which enabled him to survive in Russian prison camps by identifying "stool pigeons" who could not be trusted, see *Gulag Archipelago, 1918–1956* (New York: Harper & Row, 1974), pp. 184–185.

2. See Z. Rubin, *Liking and Loving* (New York: Holt, Rinehart & Winston, 1973). Also *Doing Unto Others, Joining, Molding, Conforming, Helping, Loving* (Englewood Cliffs, N.J.: Prentice-Hall, 1975).

3. I. Sarnoff and P. G. Zimbardo, "Anxiety, Fear, and Social Affiliation," *Journal of Abnormal and Social Psychology* 62 (1961):356–363.

4. S. M. Jourard, *The Transparent Self* (Princeton: Van Nostrand, 1964), pp. iii, 46. See also A. L. Chaikin and V. J. Derlega, "Self-disclosure," in J. W. Thibaut, J. T. Spence, and R. C. Carson, eds., *Contemporary Topics in Social Psychology* (Morristown, N.Y.: General Learning Press, 1976), pp. 117–120.

5. See D. E. Linder, "Personal space," in J. W. Thibaut, J. T. Spence, and R. C. Carson, eds., *Contemporary Topics in Social Psychology* (Morristown, N.J.: General Learning Press, 1976), pp. 455–477.

6. These initial differences in behavioral reactions to snakes by people who label themselves as "snake phobics" are observed in the research by my colleague, Albert Bandura, *Principles of Behavior Modification* (New York: Holt, Rinehart & Winston, 1969). Indeed, in order to demonstrate that a given treatment

is effective in overcoming such a phobia, it is necessary to first eliminate those people who are phobic in name only.

7. P. Ellsworth and L. Ross, "Intimacy in Response to Direct Gaze," *Journal of Experimental Social Psychology* 11 (1975):592–613.

8. L. M. Horowitz, "Two Classes of Concomitant Change in a Psychotherapy," in N. Freedman and S. Grand, eds., *Communicative Structures and Psychic Structures* (New York: Plenum, in press).

9. Richard Beery's analysis of the conceptual relationship of fear of academic failure to fear of social failure comes from a personal communication, 5 January 1977. See R. G. Beery, "Fear of Failure in the Student Experience," *Personnel and Guidance Journal* 54 (1975):191–203.

10. R. Keyes, *Is There Life after High School?* (Boston: Little Brown, 1976).

11. See R. E. Glasgow and H. Arkowitz, "The Behavioral Assessment of Male and Female Social Competence in Dyadic Heterosexual Interventions," *Behavior Therapy* 6 (1975):488–498; K. B. McGovern, H. Arkowitz, and S. K. Gilmore, "Evaluation of Social Skill Training Programs for College Dating Inhibitions," *Journal of Counseling Psychology* 22 (1975):505–512; C. T. Twentyman and R. M. McFall, "Behavioral Training of Social Skills in Shy Males," *Journal of Consulting and Cinical Psychology* 43 (1975): 384–395.

12. See P. G. Zimbardo, *The Cognitive Control of Motivation* (Glenview, Ill.: Scott Foresman, 1969).

13. Therapists working in student health centers at several major universities on the East and West coasts have reported an increase in sexual impotence among males. They trace the cause of this inability to have satisfactory sexual intercourse to performance anxiety and role confusion these young men experience when female students openly suggest making it together. There is also guilt involved in some cases where the males do not really want "to go all the way" for moral or religious reasons, but feel it would be unmanly not to, given the open invitation. Effective counseling involves not only helping a male come to grips with his sexual identity, but also teaching the female to be more subtle and less threatening in her approach.

14. Control is another issue that concerns shy people when they meet someone new. In a study just completed (with 160 students), we found that twice as many shys as not shys report "worrying about someone else gaining control over you." One way they cope with such anxiety is by not letting anyone get close enough so that they are in a position to exert that imagined control.

15. L. Forer, *The Birth Order Factor* (New York: McKay, 1976), p. 171.

16. G. V. Solomon and J. C. Solomon, "Shyness and Sex," *Medical Aspects of Human Sexuality* 5 (1971):16.

17. R. May, *Love and Will* (New York: Norton, 1969), pp. 145, 156.

18. N. Kazantzakis, *Zorba the Greek* (New York: Simon & Schuster, 1953).

Chapter 6

1. H. Nawy, "In the Pursuit of Happiness: Consumers of Erotica in San Francisco," *Journal of Social Issues* 29 (1973):147–161.

2. *First Special Report to the U.S. Congress on Alcohol and Health from the Secretary of H.E.W.* (December 1971), DHEW pub. no. HSM 72–9099 USGPO, p. v.

3. Jimmy Breslin, quoted in *Time,* 28 February 1969, p. 76.

4. S. Brownmiller, *Against Our Will: Men, Women, and Rape* (New York: Simon and Schuster, 1975).

5. M. J. Goldstein, "Exposure to Erotic Stimuli and Sexual Deviance," *Journal of Social Issues* 29 (1973):197–219.

6. E. Magargee, "Undercontrolled and Overcontrolled Personality Types in Extreme Anti-social Aggression," *Psychological Monographs* (1966): No. 11, entire issue.

7. Ibid. See also J. Prater and S. Malouf, "The Sudden Murderer: A Study on the Relationship between Shyness and Violence" (Unpublished honors thesis, Stanford University, 1976).

8. See C. Maslach, "The Personal and Social Basis of Individuation," *Journal of Personality and Social Psychology* 29 (1974):411–425.

9. E. Fromm, *Escape from Freedom* (New York: Farrar and Rinehard, 1941).

10. E. H. Schein, with I. Schneier and C. H. Barker, *Coercive Persuasion: A Sociopsychological Analysis of the "Brainwashing" of American Civilian Prisoners by the Chinese Communists* (New York: Norton, 1961).

Part II Introduction

1. C. Bakker, "Why People Don't Change," mimeographed paper (University of Washington School of Medicine, Seattle, Washington, January 1972).

Chapter 7

1. See S. Duval and R. A. Wicklund, *A Theory of Objective Self Awareness* (New York: Academic Press, 1972) for a provocative analysis of the psychology of self-awareness.

Chapter 8

1. Johnny Carson, quoted in Christina Kirk, "TV News Queen Barbara Walters Reveals: My Battle with Shyness," *The Star* (Washington, D.C.), 26 October 1976.

Chapter 9

1. See the research reported by Ziller, cited in Chapter 3.

2. Unpublished research by Trudy Solomon reveals a significant correlation between shyness and self-esteem ($r = -.48$) for 250 sales and managerial personnel of a large firm; and also a significant relationship between shyness and feelings of being worthless ($r = .31$) among forty-three Ph.D. candidates in clinical psychology studying to be professional therapists.

3. See A. Bandura, "Self-Efficacy: Towards a Unifying Theory of Behavior Change," *Psychological Review,* 1977, in press.

4. For fuller reports on relaxation strategies and their effects, see D. A. Bernstein and T. A. Borkovec, *Progressive Relaxation Training* (Champaign, Ill.: Research Press, 1973); and H. Benson, *The Relaxation Response* (West Caldwell, N.J.: William Morrow, 1975).

Chapter 10

1. Quote from Lawrence Welk excerpted from personal correspondence, 23 December 1976.

2. See P. G. Zimbardo, E. B. Ebbesen, and C. Maslach, *Influencing Attitudes and Changing Behavior,* 2d ed. (Reading, Mass.: Addison-Wesley, 1977).

3. Quote by Richard Hatch from article by Andee Beck, "New Man on 'S. F. Streets,'" *San Francisco Sunday Examiner and Chronicle,* 15 August 1976.

4. See L. P. Cercell, P. T. Berwick, and A. Beigal, "The Effects of Assertion Training on Self Concept and Anxiety," *Archives of General Psychiatry* 31 (1974):502–504.

5. M. L. Knapp, R. P. Hart, G. W. Friederich, and G. M. Shulman, "The Rhetoric of Goodbye: Verbal and Nonverbal Correlates of Human Leave-Taking," *Speech Monographs* 40 (1973):182–198.

6. These exercises are adapted from the informative assertion guide by my friends Sharon and Gordon Bower, *Asserting Yourself: A Practical Guide for Positive Change* (Reading, Mass.: Addison-Wesley, 1976), pp. 222–223.

7. Ibid.

Chapter 11

1. Roosevelt Grier's account of his debt to Robert Kennedy was quoted in *Family Circle,* February 1976. Reprinted by permission.

2. Francis Ford Coppola did not want his shy younger sister, Talia Shire, to try for a part in his epic *The Godfather, Part II.* After being nominated for best supporting actress for her role in the picture, her big brother could not bring himself to compliment her. A *New York Times* feature story about Ms. Shire (December 12, 1976) quotes her as saying, "You know Francis never did say anything about my Oscar nomination. . . . He's never told me to this day whether he thinks I can act. My sister-in-law will say, 'Francis says you have some abilities,' but *he* just can't say it." [Say it, F.F.C., because it is deserved, and your compliments mean much to her—and to others you work with.]

3. Quote from Dr. Alice Ginott about little Alfred's revenge fantasies is taken from her article, "The Impact of Words," in the *Sunday San Francisco Examiner and Chronicle,* 9 February 1976.

4. This jig-sawing technique for teaching children the benefits of cooperation has been developed and extensively tested by Elliot Aronson, "Therapy for a Competitive Society," in P. G. Zimbardo, *Psychology and Life,* 9th ed. (Glenview, Ill.: Scott Foresman, 1977), "Research Frontiers Section," 12A–12D.

5. Speech therapist James White's new book to help adults communicate better with children is, *Talking with a Child* (New York: Macmillan, 1977).

6. For the report on ways to increase a child's sociometric rating in a peer group, see S. Oden and S. R. Asher, "Coaching Children in Social Skills for Friendship-Making," *Child Development,* 1977, in press.

7. The association between lack of physical contact and social pathology is interestingly developed by James Prescott, "Body pleasure and the origins of violence," in P. G. Zimbardo and C. Maslach, eds., *Psychology for Our Times,* 2d ed. (Glenview, Ill.: Scott Foresman, 1977), pp. 336–344.

8. Khalil Gibran, *The Prophet* (New York: Knopf, 1923), pp. 15–16.

9. Dr Gerald Phillips' treatment program has been successful with over 50 percent of his clients, according to a recent report of the clinic's five years of operation. See "The Friendship Clinic: The Treatment of Reticence" (Paper presented to the Eastern Communication Association, March 13, 1975).

10. Dr. Smith described the shyness workshop she has inaugurated in southern California in a personal communication, 4 October 1976.

Chapter 12

1. Reducing violence through restructuring the situation is described in the report of Harold L. Cohen in Harold L. Cohen and James Filipczak, *A New Learning Environment* (San Francisco: Josey-Bass, 1971).

2. Cultural variations in help giving are reported in R. Feldman, "Response to Compatriot and Foreigner Who Seek Assistance," *Journal of Personality and Social Psychology* 10 (1968):202–214.

3. Differences in reactions to surgical pain by cultural subgroups in the United States are described in M. Zborowski, *People in Pain* (San Francisco: Josey-Bass, 1969).

4. W. A. Caudill and C. Schooler, "Child Behavior and Child Rearing in Japan and the United States: An Interim Report." *The Journal of Nervous and Mental Disease* 157 (1973):240–257; W. A. Caudill, "General Culture: The Influence of Social Structure and Culture on Human Behavior in Modern Japan," *The Journal of Nervous and Mental Disease* 157 (1973):240–257.

5. For the impact of cultural values on psychopathology in Japan and Taiwan, see R. Hsien, C. Schooler, and W. A. Caudill, "Symptomatology and Hospitalization: Culture, Social Structure and Psychopathology in Taiwan and Japan," *The Journal of Nervous and Mental Disorders* 157 (1973):296–321.

6. Dr. Hatano's comparison of shy and shame in Japanese is contained in a personal communication, November 12, 1976. He recommends to us Ruth Benedict's classic analysis of the social structure of Japanese culture, *The Chrysanthemum and the Sword.* Independent support for the high degree of shyness among the Japanese comes from a detailed survey study by Michiru Sugawa of 614 Japanese and 351 Americans in Japan. Ms. Sugawa's unpublished dissertation data are in close agreement with our own. She sees shyness among Americans as an expression of a personality or temperament style, while for the Japanese shyness reflects anxiety over deviating from social norms of appropriateness.

7. This impressive report of the American delegation studying early development in the People's Republic of China is edited by William Kessen, *Childhood in China* (New Haven: Yale University Press, 1975).

8. See the fascinating account of D. Y. F. Ho, "Prevention and Treatment of Mental Illness in the People's Republic of China," *American Journal of Orthopsychiatry* 44 (July 1974):620–636.

9. Dr. Ayala Pines's characterization of the cultural values that prevent or undermine the development of shyness is given in an unpublished report prepared for our shyness program, "Why Are Sabra (Israeli) Children Less Shy?" October 12, 1976.

10. For an excellent overview of the historical, social, and psychological issues that help us understand the Israeli attitude toward shyness, I recommend A. Jarus, J. Marcus, J. Oren, and Ch. Rapaport, eds., *Children and Families in Israel: Some Mental Health Perspectives* (New York: Gordon and Breach, 1970).

11. See the reports of the social and intellectual consequences of Synanon's communal rearing on its children in E. A. Missakian, "Social Behavior of Communally-Reared Children," Department of Health, Education and Welfare grant proposal, 1976; and L. W. Burke, "The Effects of Communal Rearing in Synanon," DHEW grant proposal, 1975.

12. An entire dissertation devoted to analyzing the Synanon Game was undertaken by S. I. Simon, *The Synanon Game* (Ph.D. dissertation, Harvard University, 1973). Reprinted in *Dissertation Abstracts International,* vol. 36 (1975).

13.

Cross-cultural comparisons of shyness
(ages 18-21, unless noted otherwise)

	Prevalence of shyness (now)	Ever shy (now and/or past)	Never shy	Shy men (of total men)	Shy women (of total women)	Shyness is a personal problem
	%	%	%	%	%	%
2482 American students	42	73	7	44	39	60
123 Oriental Americans	48	88	0	50	44	59
136 Hawaiian Orientals	44	89	2	47	42	61
28 Hawaiian Hawaiians	60	85	7	75	39	68
291 Taiwanese	55	84	0.4	59	51	58
305 Japanese	60	82	2	60	43	75
84 Germans	50	92	1	45	55	91
167 Students from India	47	66	10	46	52	82
307 Mexicans	39	81	3	30	56	75
231 Israelis	31	70	10	28	43	42
152 Jewish Americans	24	70	2	30	16	68
163 Obesity clinic clients*	40	68	7	33	40	73
540 Navy personnel†	33	68	9	33	33	46
‡	39	75	4	40	33	44

* This is a sample obtained at a clinic for obese individuals; average age is 35.

† This is a sample from the U.S. Navy.
   The top line describes the overall sample with an average age of 26.

‡ The bottom line describes a subgroup of 18–21 year olds.

general
references

Adler, A. *Neurotic Constitution.* New York: Moffat, Ward, 1917.

Bach, G. R., and R. M. Deutsch. *Pairing.* New York: Avon Books, 1971.

Bach, G. R., and H. Goldberg. *Creative Aggression: The Art of Assertive Living.* New York: Avon Books, 1975.

Bernstein, D. A., and T. A. Borkovec. *Progressive Relaxation Training.* Champaign, Ill.: Research Press, 1973.

Bower, S. A., and G. H. Bower. *Asserting Yourself.* Reading, Mass.: Addison-Wesley, 1976.

Brager, J., and L. Brager. *Children and Adults: Activities for Growing Together.* Englewood Cliffs, N.J.: Prentice-Hall, 1976.

Egan, G. *Exercises in Helping Skills.* Belmont, Ca.: Wadsworth, 1975.

Ellis, A. *A Guide to Rational Living.* North Hollywood, Ca.: Wilshire Book Co., 1974.

Ellis, A., S. Moseley, and J. L. Wolfe. *How to Prevent Your Child from Becoming a Neurotic Adult.* New York: Crown, 1966.

Erikson, E. H. *Childhood and Society.* 2d ed. New York: Norton, 1963.

Frankl, V. *Man's Search for Meaning: An Introduction to Logotherapy.* Boston: Beacon Press, 1959, 1962.

Maslow, A. H. *Motivation and Personality.* New York: Viking Press, 1971.

Freud, S. *Psychology of Everyday Life.* 2d ed. London: Ernest Benn, Ltd., 1954.

Gagnon, J., and N. Simon, eds. *Sexual Conduct: A Human Source of Sexuality.* New York: Aldine, 1973.

Greenwald, J. *Creative Intimacy.* New York: Simon & Schuster, 1975.

Horney, K. *The Collected Works of Karen Horney.* New York: Norton, 1945.

Jackson, T. A. *Structuring Your Self Confidence*. Scarsdale, N.Y.: Harwood Bldg., 1970.

Johnson, D. W. *Reaching Out*. Englewood Cliffs: Prentice-Hall, 1972.

Jongeward, D., and D. Scott. *Women as Winners*. Reading, Mass.: Addison-Wesley, 1976.

Katchadourian, H. A., and D. T. Lunde. *Fundamentals of Human Sexuality*. New York: Holt, Rinehart & Winston, 1972.

Keen, S., and A. V. Fox. *Telling Your Story*. New York: The New American Library, Signet Books, 1973.

Kelly, G. A. *The Psychology of Personal Constructs*. New York: Norton, 1955.

Kennedy, E. *If You Really Knew Me, Would You Still Like Me?* Niles, Ill.: Argus Communications, 1975.

Liberman, R. P., L. W. King, W. J. DeRisi, and M. McCann. *Personal Effectiveness*. Champaign, Ill.: Research Press, 1975.

Maslow, A. H. *Motivation and Personality*. New York: Viking, 1971.

May, Rollo. *Love and Will*. 2d ed. New York: Norton, 1977.

Morris, D. *Intimate Behavior*. New York: Random House, 1973.

Moustakas, C. E. *The Touch of Loneliness*. Englewood Cliffs, N.J.: Prentice-Hall, 1975.

Newman, M., and B. Berkowitz. *How to Be Your Own Best Friend*. New York: Ballantine Books, 1971.

Perls, F., R. F. Hefferline, and P. Goodman. *Gestalt Therapy*. New York: Dell, 1951.

Rayner, C. *The Shy Person's Book*. New York: McKay, 1973.

Rubin, Z. *Liking and Loving*. New York: Holt, Rinehart & Winston, 1973.

Shaver, K. G. *An Introduction to Attribution Processes*. Cambridge, Mass.: Winthrop Publications, 1975.

Smith, H. C. *Sensitivity to People*. New York: McGraw-Hill, 1966.

Van Fleet, J. K. *Power with People*. New York: Parker, 1970.

Watts, A. *The Wisdom of Insecurity: A Message for an Age of Anxiety*. New York: Pantheon, 1951.

specialized references

Anxiety (including social anxiety) and its management

Cattell, R. B., and F. W. Warburton. "A cross-cultural comparison of patterns of extraversion and anxiety." *British Journal of Psychology* **52** (1961):3–16.

Clark, J. V., and H. Arkowitz. "Social anxiety and self-evaluation of interpersonal performance." *Psychological Reports* **36** (1975):211–221.

Dixon, J. J., C. deMonchaux, and J. Sandler. "Patterns of anxiety: an analysis of social anxieties." *British Journal of Medical Psychology* **30** (1957):102–112.

D'Zurilla, T. J., G. T. Wilson, and R. Nelson. "A preliminary study of the effectiveness of graduated prolonged exposure in the treatment of irrational fear." *Behavior Therapy* **4**, no. 5 (1973):672–685.

Fremouw, W. J., and M. B. Hermatz. "A helper model for behavioral treatment of speech anxiety." *J. of Consulting and Clinical Psychology* **43** (1975):163–164.

Higgins, A. L., and G. A. Marlatt. "Fear of interpersonal evaluation as a determination of alcohol consumption in male social drinkers." *J. of Abnormal Psychology* **94** (1975):644–651.

Karst, T. O., and L. D. Trexler. "Initial study using fixed-role and rational-emotive therapy in treating public-speaking anxiety." *Journal of Consulting and Clinical Psychology* **34**, no. 3 (1970): 360–366.

Lick, J., and R. Bootzin. "Expectancy factors in the treatment of fear; methodological and theoretical issues." *Psychological Bulletin* **82**, no. 6 (1975):917–931.

May, R. *The Meaning of Anxiety.* New York: Ronald Press, 1950.

McGovern, L. P. "Dispositional social anxiety and helping behavior under three conditions of threat." *Journal of Personality* **44**, no. 1 (1976):84–97.

Meichenbaum, D. H., J. B. Gilmore, and A. Fedoravicius. "Group insight versus group desensitization in treating speech anxiety." *Journal of Consulting and Clinical Psychology* **36**, no. 3 (1971):410–421.

Murray, D. C. "Talk, silence and anxiety." *Psychological Bulletin* 75, no. 4. (1971): 244–260.

Odier, C. *Anxiety and Magic Thinking.* New York: International Universities Press, 1956.

Rehm, L. P., and A. R. Marston. "Reduction of social anxiety through modification of self-reinforcement: an instigation therapy technique." *Journal of Consulting and Clinical Psychology* 32, no. 5 (1968):565–574.

Sarason, I. G. "The effect of anxiety, motivation, instruction and failure on social learning." *Journal of Experimental Psychology* 51 (1956):253–260.

Smith, R. E., and I. G. Sarason. "Social anxiety and the evaluation of negative interpersonal feedback." *J. of Consulting and Clinical Psychology* 43 (1975):429.

Watson, D., and R. Friend. "Measurement of social-evaluative anxiety." *Journal of Consulting and Clinical Psychology* 33, no. 4 (1969):448–457.

Weissberg, M. "Anxiety-inhibiting statements and relaxation combined in two cases of speech anxiety." *J. of Behavior Therapy and Experimental Psychiatry* 6 (1975):163–164.

Zimbardo, P. G., G. F. Mahl, and J. W. Barnard. "The measurement of speech disturbances in anxious children." *Journal of Speech and Hearing Disorders* 28 (1963):362–370.

Assertiveness, social skills training, and assessment

Argyle, M., P. E. Trower, and B. M. Bryant. "Explorations in the treatment of personality disorders and neuroses by social skills training." *British Journal of Medical Psychology* 47 (1974):63–72.

Arkowitz, H., E. Lichtenstein, K. McGovern, and P. Hines. "The behavioral assessment of social competence in males." *Behavior Therapy* 6 (1975):3–13.

Borkovec, T. D., N. M. Stone, G. T. O'Brien, and D. G. Kaloupek. "Identification and measurement of a clinically relevant target behavior for analogue outcome research." *Behavior Therapy* 5 (1974):503–513.

Bouffard, D. L. "A comparison of response acquisition and desensitization approaches to assertation training." *Dissertation Abstracts International* 34 (1974) 9-B, 4654.

Bugental, D. B., and B. Henker. "Attributional antecedents of verbal and vocal assertiveness." *Journal of Personality and Social Psychology* 34, no. 3 (1976):405–411.

Christensen, A., and H. Arkowitz. "Preliminary report on practice dating and feedback as treatment for college dating problems." *Journal of Counseling Psychology* 21, no. 2 (1974):92–95.

Christensen, A., H. Arkowitz, and J. Anderson. "Practice dating as treatment for college dating inhibitions." *Behavior Research and Therapy* 13 (1975):321–331.

Curran, J. P. "Skills training as an approach to the treatment of heterosexual-social anxiety: a review." *Psychological Bulletin* 84 (1977):140–157.

Curran, J. P., and F. S. Gilbert. "A test of the relative effectiveness of a systematic desensitization program and an interpersonal skills training program with date anxious subjects." *Behavior Therapy* 6 (1975):510–521.

Frazier, J. R., and J. E. Frazier. "Some comments on the problem of defining assertive training." *Comprehensive Psychiatry* 16 (1975):369–373.

Gambrill, E. D., and C. A. Richey. "An assertion inventory for use in assessment and research." *Behavior Therapy* 6 (1975):550–561.

Glasgow, R. E., and H. Arkowitz. "The behavioral assessment of male and female social competence in dyadic heterosexual interactions." *Behavior Therapy* 6 (1975): 488–498.

Hersen, M., and A. L. S. Bellack. "Assessment of social skills." In A. R. Ciminero, K. S. Calhoun, and H. E. Adams, eds., *Handbook for Behavioral Assessment*. New York: Wiley, in press.

Hersen, M., and R. M. Eisler. "Social skills training." In W. E. Craighead, A. E. Kazdin, and M. J. Mahoney, eds., *Behavior Modification: Principles, Issues, and Applications*. Boston: Houghton Mifflin, 1976.

Joaning, H. H. "Behavioral reversal versus traditional therapy in the group treatment of socially non-aggressive individuals." *Dissertation Abstracts International* 34 (9-B):4665–4666.

Kazdin, A. E. "Covert modeling, imagery assessment and assertive behavior." *J. of Consulting and Clinical Psychology* 48 (1975):716–724.

Lanyon, R. I. "Measurement of social competence in college males." *Journal of Consulting and Clinical Psychology* 31 (1967):495–498.

MacDonald, M. L. "Teaching assertion: A paradigm for therapeutic intervention." *Psychotherapy Theory, Research and Practice* 12 (1975):60–67.

MacDonald, M. L. et al. "Social skills training: behavior rehearsal in groups and dating skills." *J. of Counseling Psychology* 22 (1975):224–230.

McFall, R. M., and A. R. Marston. "An experimental investigation of behavior rehearsal in assertion training." *Journal of Abnormal Psychology* 76 (1970):295–303.

McGovern, K. B., H. Arkowitz, and S. K. Gilmore. "Evaluation of social skill training programs for college dating inhibitions." *Journal of Counseling Psychology* 22, no. 6 (1975):505–512.

Orenstein, M., E. Orenstein, and J. E. Carr. "Assertiveness and anxiety: a correlational study." *J. of Behavior Therapy and Experimental Psychiatry* 6 (1975):203–207.

Osborn, S. M., and G. G. Harris. *Assertive Training for Women*. Springfield, Ill.: Thomas, 1975.

Robinson, N. W. "Visual social modeling and rehearsal in assertive training." *Dissertation Abstracts International* 34 (12-B), 1974, pp. 6222–6223.

Rose, S. D. "In pursuit of social competence." *Social Work* 20 (1975):33–39.

Smith, M. J. *When I Say No, I Feel Guilty.* New York: Bantam Books, 1975.

Springer, J., S. Springer, and B. Aaronson. "An approach to teaching a course on dating behavior." *Family Coordinator* 24 (1975):13–19.

Twentyman, C. T., and R. M. McFall. "Behavioral training of social skills in shy males." *Journal of Consulting and Clinical Psychology* 43, no. 3 (1975):384–395.

Yost, E. J. "The development and evaluation of a social skills training program for college males." *Dissertation Abstracts International* 34(10-B), 1974, 5182.

Attribution and labeling

Calvert-Boyanowsky, J., and H. Leventhal. "The role of information in attenuating behavioral responses to stress: a reinterpretation of the misattribution phenomenon." *Journal of Personality and Social Psychology* 32, no. 2 (1975):214–221.

Farina, A., C. H. Holland, and K. Ring. "The role of stigma and set in interpersonal interaction." *Journal of Abnormal Psychology* 71 (1966):421–428.

Goffman, E. *Stigma: Notes on the Management of Spoiled Identity.* Englewood Cliffs, N.J.: Prentice-Hall, 1963.

Jones, E. E. "How do people perceive the causes of behavior?" *American Scientist* 64 (1976):300–305.

Jones, E. E., and R. E. Nisbett. *The Actor and the Observer: Divergent Perceptions of the Causes of Behavior.* New York: General Learning Press, 1971.

Kelley, H. H. *Attribution in Social Interaction.* Morristown, NJ: General Learning Press, 1971.

Kelley, H. H. "The processes of causal attribution." *American Psychologist* 28 (1973):107–128.

Knapp, M. L., R. P. Hart, G. W. Friederich, and G. M. Shulman, "The rhetoric of goodbye: verbal and nonverbal correlates of human leave-taking," *Speech Monographs* 40 (1973):182–198.

McArthur, L. A. "The how and what of why some determinants and consequences of causal attribution." *Journal of Personality and Social Psychology* 22 (1972): 171–193.

McGee, M. G., and M. Snyder. "Attribution and behavior." *Journal of Personality and Social Psychology* 32, no. 1 (1975):185–190.

Nisbett, R. E., and S. Valins. *Perceiving the Causes of One's Own Behavior.* New York: General Learning Press, 1971.

Ross, L., J. Rodin, and P. G. Zimbardo. "Toward an attribution therapy: the reduction of fear through induced cognitive-emotional misattribution." *Journal of Personality and Social Psychology* 12 (1969):279–288.

Valins, S., and R. E. Nisbett. *Attribution Processes in the Development and Treatment of Emotional Disorders.* New York: General Learning Press, 1971.

Wicker, A. W. "Attitudes versus actions: the relationship of verbal and overt behavioral responses to attitude objects." *Journal of Social Issues* 25 (1969):41–78.

Weiner, M., and W. Samuel. "The effect of attributing internal arousal to an external source upon test anxiety and performance." *J. of Social Psychology* 96 (1975):225–265.

Wolosin, R. J., S. J. Sherman, and A. Bann. "Predictions of own and other's conformity." *J. of Personality* 43 (1975):357–378.

Avoidance reactions and fear of failure

Beery, R. G. "Fear of Failure in the Student Experience." *Personnel and Guidance Journal* 54 (1975):191–203.

Bennett, D. M., and D. S. Holmes. "Influence of denial (situation redefinition) and projection on anxiety associated with threat to self esteem." *J. of Personality and Social Psychology* 92 (1975):915–921.

Bernstein, D. A., and M. T. Nietzel. "Procedural variation in behavioral avoidance tests." *Journal of Consulting and Clinical Psychology* 41, no. 2 (1973):165–174.

Cohen, R. J., R. E. Becker, and R. C. Teevan. "Perceived somatic reactions to stress and hostile pressure." *Psychological Reports* 37 (1975):676–678.

Condry, J., and S. Dyer. "Fear of success: attribution of cause to the victim." In D. N. Ruble, I. H. Frieze, and J. E. Parsons, "Sex roles: persistence and change," *Journal of Social Issues* 32 (1976):63–84.

Douglas, D., and H. Anisman. "Helplessness or expectation incongruency: effects of aversive stimulation on subsequent performance." *J. of Experimental Psychology: Human Perception and Performance* 104 (1975):411–417.

Ferster, C. B. "A functional analysis of depression." *American Psychologist* 28, no. 10 (1973):857–870.

Fromm, E. "Man would as soon flee as fight." *Psychology Today* 7, no. 3 (1973): 35–39.

Good, L. R., and K. C. Good. "An objective measure of the motive to avoid failure." *Psychology* 12 (1975):11–14.

Hiroto, D. S. "Locus of control and learned helplessness." *J. of Experimental Psychology* 102, no. 2 (1974):187–193.

Horner, M. "Femininity and successful achievement: a basic inconsistency." In J. Bardwick, E. Douvan, M. Horner, and D. Gutmann, eds., *Feminine Personality and Conflict*. Belmont, Ca.: Wadsworth, 1970.

Isen, A. "Success, failure, attention, and reaction to others: The warm glow of success." *Journal of Personality and Social Psychology* 15 (1970):294–302.

Kazdin, A. E. "Covert modeling and the reduction of avoidance behavior." *Journal of Abnormal Psychology* 81, no. 1 (1973):87–95.

Longstreth, L. "Birth order and avoidance of dangerous activities." *Developmental Psychology* 1 (1970):154

Murray, E. J. "Resolution of complex decision conflicts as a function of avoidance." *J. of Research in Personality* 9 (1975):177–190.

O'Leary, S. G. "Children's avoidance responses to three probabilities of theoretical consequences." *Dissertation Abstracts International* 34 (1-B), 1973, 420.

Smith, B. D., and L. Gehl. "Multiple-exposure effects of resolutions of four basic conflict types." *J. of Experimental Psychology* 102, no. 1 (1974):50–55.

Tori, C., and L. Worell. "Reduction of human avoidant behavior: comparison of counterconditioning, expectancy and cognitive information approaches." *J. of Consulting and Clinical Psychology* 41, no. 2 (1973):269–278.

Valins, S., and A. A. Ray. "Effects of cognitive desensitization on avoidance behavior." *Journal of Personality and Social Psychology* 7, no. 4 (1967):345–350.

Wilkins, W. "Systematic desensitization and implosion: a theoretical rapprochement." *Psychotherapy: Theory, Research & Practice* 10, no. 4 (1973):312–314.

Behavior modification and cognitive change

Ascher, L. M., and D. Phillips. "Guided behavior rehearsal." *J. of Behavior Therapy and Experimental Psychiatry* 6 (1975):215–218.

Bandura, A. *Principles of Behavior Modification.* New York: Holt, Rinehart & Winston, 1969.

Bandura, A. "Self-efficacy: towards a unifying theory of behavior change. *Psychological Review,* 1977, in press.

Bandura, A. *Social Learning Theory.* Englewood Cliffs, N.J.: Prentice-Hall, 1977.

Bandura, A., R. W. Jeffery, and E. Gajdos. "Generalizing change through participant modeling with self-directed mastery." *Behaviour Research and Therapy* 13 (1975):141–152.

Evers, W. L., and J. C. Schwarz. "Modifying social withdrawal in preschoolers: The effects of filmed modeling and teacher praise." *Journal of Abnormal Child Psychology* 1 (1973):248–256.

Hosford, R. E., and D. L. Sorenson. "Participating in classroom discussion." In *Behavioral Counseling: Cases and Techniques.* J. D. Krumboltz and C. E. Thoresen, eds. New York: Holt, Rinehart & Winston, 1969, pp. 202–207.

Kazdin, A. E. "Effects of covert modeling and model reinforcement on assertive behavior." *Journal of Abnormal Psychology* 83, no. 3 (1974):240–252.

Kazdin, A. E. "Effects of covert modeling, multiple models, and model reinforcement on assertive behavior." *Behavior Therapy* 7 (1976):211–222.

Keller, M. F., and P. M. Carlson. "The use of symbolic modeling to promote social skills in preschool children with low levels of social responsiveness." *Child Development* 45 (1974):912–919.

Kopel, S., and H. Arkowitz. "The role of attention and self-perception in behavior change: implications for behavior therapy." *Genetic Psychology Monographs* 92 (1975):175–212.

Krumboltz, J. D. and C. E. Thoresen. *Behavioral Counseling.* New York: Holt, Rinehart & Winston, 1969.

Krumboltz, J. D., and C. E. Thoresen. *Counseling Methods*. New York: Holt, Rinehart & Winston, 1976.

Lilly, M. S. "Improving social acceptance of low sociometric status, low achieving students." *Exceptional Children* 37 (1971):341–347.

Mahoney, M. J. *Cognition and Behavior Modification*. Cambridge, Mass.: Ballinger, 1974.

Meichenbaum, D. *Therapist Manual for Cognitive Behavior Modification*. Reprint from therapist manual used in study of "Cognitive modification of test anxious college students." *Journal of Consulting and Clinical Psychology* 39 (1972):370–380.

Meichenbaum, D., and R. Cameron. "The clinical potential of modifying what clients say to themselves." *Psychotherapy: Theory, Research & Practice* 11 (1974):103–117.

O'Connor, R. D. "Relative efficacy of modeling, shaping, and the combined procedures for modification of social withdrawal." *Journal of Abnormal Psychology* 79 (1972):327–334.

Oden, S., and S. R. Asher. "Coaching children in social skills for friendship-making." *Child Development,* 1977, in press.

Potter, E. B. "The use of group operant techniques to modify shy boys' behavior." Ph.D. dissertation, University of Denver, 1971. *Dissertation Abstracts International* 32 (5–6), 1971, 3623B–3624B. (University microfilms No. 71-25, 019)

Thoresen, C. E., and M .J. Mahoney. *Behavioral Self-Control*. New York: Holt, Rinehart & Winston, 1974.

Wolpe, J. *The Practice of Behavior Therapy*. New York: Pergamon Press, 1973.

Yamagami, T. "The treatment of an obsession by thought stopping." *Behavior Therapy and Experimental Psychiatry* 2 (1971):133–135.

Zimbardo, P. G. *The Cognitive Control of Motivation*. Glenview, Ill.: Scott Foresman, 1969.

Emotions, thought, and behavior

Donnerstein, E., M. Don, and G. Munger. "Helping behavior as a function of pictorially induced moods." *J. of Social Psychology* 97 (1975):221–225.

Easterbrook, J. A. "The effect of emotion on cue utilization and the organization of behavior." *Psychological Review* 66, no. 3 (1959):183–201.

Eysenck, M. W. "Arousal and speed of recall." *British J. of Social/Clinical Psychology* 4 (1975):269–277.

Eysenck, M. W. "Extroversion, verbal learning and memory." *Psychological Bulletin* 88 (1976):75–90.

Friedman, J. J. "Depression, failure and guilt." *New York State Journal of Medicine* 73, no. 12 (1973):1700–1704.

Hale, W. D., and D. B. Strickland. "Induction of mood states and their effects on cognitive and social behaviors." *J. of Consulting and Clinical Psychology* **64** (1976):155.

Harris, M. B., and C. E. Siebel. "Affect, aggression, and altruism." *Developmental Psychology* **11** (1975):623–627.

Harris, V. A., and E. S. Katkin. "Primary and secondary emotional behavior: an analysis of the role of autonomic feedback on affect, arousal, and attribution." *Psychological Bulletin* **82** (1975): 904–916.

Hatvany, N. "Shyness, emotional arousal, and information processing." M.A. thesis, Stanford University, 1976.

Izard, C. E. *The Face of Emotion.* New York: Appleton-Century-Crofts, 1971.

Schachter, S. "The interaction of cognitive and physiological determinants of emotional state." In L. Berkowitz, ed., *Advances in Experimental Social Psychology.* Vol. 1. New York: Academic Press, 1964.

Schachter, S., and J. Rodin. *Obese Humans and Rats.* Potomac, Md.: Lawrence Erlbaum Associates, 1974.

Schachter, S., and J. E. Singer. "Cognitive, social, and physiological determinants of emotional state." *Psychological Review* **69** (1962):379–399.

Schiffenbauer, A., S. Sherman, and P. G. Zimbardo. "The modification of selective recall of central and incidental task features by emotional arousal." *O.N.R. Technical Report,* Z-02, 1970.

Underwood, W. C. "The effect of mood state on self-evaluation and self-reward." *Dissertation Abstracts International* **84** (9-B), 1974, 4722.

White, Kinnard. "Anxiety, extraversion-introversion, and divergent thinking ability." *Journal of Creative Behavior* **2**, no. 2 (1968):119–127.

Interpersonal relations

Aronson, E. "Some antecedents of interpersonal attraction." In W. J. Arnold and D. Levine, eds. *Nebraska Symposium on Motivation.* Lincoln: University of Nebraska Press, 1969.

Asher, S. R., S. L. Oden, and J. M. Gottman. "Children's friendships in school settings." In L. G. Katz, ed., *Current Topics in Early Childhood Education.* Vol. 1. Hillsdale, N.J.: Lawrence Erlbaum Associates, 1976.

Berscheid, E., and E. H. Walster. *Interpersonal Attraction.* Reading, Mass.: Addison-Wesley, 1969.

Berscheid, E., and E. Walster. "Physical attractiveness." In L. Berkowitz, ed., *Advances in Experimental Social Psychology.* Vol. 7. New York: Academic Press, 1974.

Brehm, J. W. *A Theory of Psychological Reactance.* New York: Academic Press, 1966.

Brislin, R. W., W. J. Lenner, and R. M. Thorndike. *Cross Cultural Research Methods*. New York: Wiley, 1973.

Clove, G. L., N. H. Wiggins, and S. Itkin. "Gain and loss in attraction: attributions from nonverbal behavior." *J. of Personality and Social Psychology* 31 (1975): 706–712.

Goffman, E. *Interaction Ritual*. New York: Anchor, 1967.

Heider, F. *The Psychology of Interpersonal Relations*. New York: Wiley, 1958, Ch. 3.

Mehrabian, G. *Tactics of Social Influence*. Englewood Cliffs, N.J.: Prentice-Hall, 1970.

Rosenfeld, H. M. "Approval-seeking and approval-inducing functions of verbal and nonverbal responses in the dyad." *Journal of Personality and Social Psychology* 4 (1966):597–605.

Sorrentino, R. M., and R. G. Boutillier. "The effect of quantity and quality of verbal interaction on ratings of leadership ability." *Journal of Experimental Social Psychology* 11 (1975):403–411.

Stone, G. P., and H. A. Farberman, eds. *Social Psychology through Symbolic Interaction*. Toronto: Xerox College Publication, 1970.

White, J. *Talking with a Child*. New York: Macmillan, 1977.

Wicklund, R. A. *Freedom and Reactance*. New York: L. Erlbaum Associates, 1974.

Intimacy and sexuality

Berman, J., and D. Osborn. "Specific self-esteem and sexual permissiveness." *Psychological Reports* 36, no. 1 (1975):323–326.

Chaikin, A. L., and V. J. Derlega. "Variables affecting the appropriateness of self-disclosure." *J. of Consulting and Clinical Psychology* 42, no. 4 (1974):588–593.

Davis, J. D., and A. E. Skinner. "Reciprocity of self-disclosure in interviews: modeling or social change?" *J. of Personality and Social Psychology* 29, no. 6 (1974): 779–784.

Dietch, J., and J. House. "Affiliative conflict and individual differences in self-disclosure." *Representative Research in Social Psychology* 6 (1975):69–75.

Ehrenberg, D. B. "The intimate edge in therapeutic relatedness." *Contemporary Psychoanalysis* 10, no. 4 (1974):423–437.

Ellison, C. W., and I. J. Firestone. "Development of interpersonal trust as a function of self-esteem, target status and target style." *J. of Personality and Social Psychology* 29, no. 5 (1974):655–663.

Eysenck, H. J. "Introverts, extroverts and sex." *Psychology Today,* January 1971, pp. 48–51.

Gadpaille, W. J. "A young adult with sexual fears." *Medical Aspects of Human Sexuality* **8**, no. 4 (1974):199–200.

Jourard, S. M. *The Transparent Self.* 2d ed. New York: Van Nostrand Reinhold, 1971.

Lomranz, J., and A. Shapira. "Communicatiye patterns of self-disclosure and touching behavior." *Journal of Psychology* **88**, no. 2 (1974):223–227.

Lowenthal, M. F., and L. Weiss. "Intimacy and crises in adulthood." *The Counseling Psychologist* **6**, no. 1 (1976):10–15.

Perlman, D. "Self-esteem and sexual permissiveness." *J. of Marriage and the Family* **36**, no. 3 (1974):470–473.

Rubin, Z. "Disclosing oneself to a stranger: reciprocity and its limits." *Journal of Experimental Social Psychology* **11**, no. 3 (1975): 233–260.

Rubin, Z. *Doing Unto Others: Joining, Molding, Conforming, Helping, Loving.* Englewood Cliffs, N.J.: Prentice-Hall, 1975.

Loneliness

Bradley, R. "Measuring Loneliness." Ph.D. Dissertation. Ann Arbor, Michigan: University Microfilms, 1969.

Gaev, D. M. *The Psychology of Loneliness.* Chicago: Adams, 1976.

Loucks, S. "The dimensions of loneliness: a psychological study of affect, self concept and object relations." *Dissertation Abstracts International* **35** (6-B), 1974, 3024.

Moore, J. A. "Loneliness: personality, self-discrepancy, aηd demographic variables." *Dissertation Abstracts International,* **34** (5-B), 1973, 2287.

Moustakas, C. E. *Loneliness and Love.* Englewood Cliffs, N.J.: Prentice-Hall, 1972.

Moustakas, C. E. *Portraits of Loneliness and Love.* Englewood Cliffs, N.J.: Prentice-Hall, 1975.

Weigert, E. "Loneliness and trust." *Psychiatry* **23** (1960):121–132.

Weiss, R. S. *Loneliness: The Experience of Emotional and Social Isolation.* Cambridge, Mass.: MIT Press, 1973.

Nonverbal and expressive behavior

Clare, G. L., N. H. Wiggins, and S. Itkin. "Judging attraction from non-verbal behavior: the gain phenomenon." *J. of Consulting and Clinical Psychology* **43**, no. 4 (1975):491–497.

Ekman, P., and W. Friesen. "Detecting deception from the body or face." *Journal of Personality and Social Psychology* **29** (1974):288–298.

Ekman, P., and W. V. Friesen. *Unmasking the Face.* Englewood Cliffs, N.J.: Prentice-Hall, 1975.

Ellsworth, P. C., and J. M. Carlsmith. "Effects of eye contact and verbal contact on affective response to a dyadic interaction." *Journal of Personality and Social Psychology* 10 (1968):15–20.

Gladstein, G. A. "Nonverbal communication and counseling psychotherapy: a review." *Counseling Psychologist* 4, no. 3 (1974): 34–57.

Graham, J. A., and M. A. Argyle. Cross-cultural study of the communication of extra-verbal meaning by gestures." *International J. of Psychology* 10 (1975):57–67.

Hackney, H. "Facial gestures and subject expression of feelings." *J. of Counseling Psychology* 21, no. 3 (1974):173–178.

Jurich, A. P., and J. A. Jurich. "Correlations among nonverbal expressions of anxiety." *Psychological Reports* 34, no. 1 (1974):199–204.

Knapp, M. L. *Nonverbal Communication in Human Interaction.* New York: Holt, Rinehart & Winston, 1972.

Lanzetta, J. T., and R. E. Kleck. "Encoding and decoding of nonverbal affect in humans." *Journal of Personality and Social Psychology* 16 (1970):12–19.

Mehrabian, G. *Nonverbal Communication.* Chicago: Aldine-Atherton, 1972.

Rosenfeld, H. M. "Instrumental affiliative functions of facial and gestural expressions." *Journal of Personality and Social Psychology* 4 (1966):65–72.

Speer, D. C., ed. *Nonverbal Communication.* Beverly Hills, Ca.: Sage, 1972.

Waldron, J. "Judgment of like-dislike from facial expression and body posture." *Perceptual Motor Skills* 41 (1975):799–894.

Walker, B. N. "A dyadic interaction model for nonverbal touching behavior in encounter groups." *Small Group Behavior* 6 (1975):308–324.

Weitz, S., ed. "Nonverbal communication: readings with commentary." New York: Oxford University Press, 1974.

Zuckerman, M., N. S. Lipets, J. M. Koirumaki, and R. Rosenthal. "Encoding and decoding nonverbal cues of emotion." *J. of Personality and Social Psychology* 32 (1975):1068–1076.

Personality theory

Allport, G. W. *Becoming: Basic Considerations for a Psychology of Personality.* New Haven, Conn.: Yale University Press, 1955.

Allport, G. W. *Personality and Social Encounter.* New York: Harper & Row, 1964.

Allport, G. W. *The Nature of Personality.* Westport, Conn.: Greenwood, 1950.

Bem, D. J., and A. Allen. "On predicting some of the people some of the time: the search for cross-situational consistencies in behavior." *Psychological Review* 81 (1974):506–520.

Cattell, R. B. *The Scientific Analysis of Personality.* New York: Penguin, 1965.

Comrey, A. L. *Manual for the Comrey personality scales.* San Diego, Ca.: Educational and Industrial Testing Service, 1970.

Endleman, R. *Personality and Social Life*. New York: Random House, 1967.

Eysenck, H. J., and S. B. G. Eysenck. *Personality Structure and Measurement*. San Diego: Robert R. Knapp, 1969.

Geiwitz, J. P. *Non-Freudian Personality Theories*. Belmont, Cal.: Brooks/Cole, 1969.

Mischel, W. *Personality and Assessment*. New York: Wiley, 1968.

Mischel, W. "Toward a cognitive social learning reconceptualization of personality." *Psychological Review* 80 (1973):252–283.

Rotter, J. B. "Generalized expectancies for internal versus external control of reinforcement." *Psychological Monographs* 80, no. 1, no. 609 entire issue (1966).

Self-awareness, self-monitoring, self-perception, self-consciousness, self-concept, and self-esteem

Bem, D. J. "Self-perception theory." In L. Berkowitz, ed. *Advances in Experimental Social Psychology*. Vol. 6. New York: Academic Press, 1972.

Carver, C. S., and D. C. Glass. "The self consciousness scale: a discriminant validity study." *Journal of Personality Assessment* 40, no. 2 (1976): 169–172.

Cottle, T. J. *Perceiving Time: A Psychological Investigation with Men and Women*. New York: Wiley, 1976.

Duval, S., and R. A. Wicklund. *A Theory of Objective Self Awareness*. New York: Academic Press, 1972.

Fenigstein, A., M. F. Scheier, and A. H. Buss. "Public and private self consciousness: assessment and theory." *Journal of Consulting and Clinical Psychology* 43, no. 4 (1975):522–527.

Festinger, L., A. Pepitone, and T. Newcomb. "Some consequences of de-individualization in a group." *Journal of Abnormal and Social Psychology* 47 (1952):382–389.

French, F. C. "Group self-consciousness: a stage in the evolution of the mind." *Psychological Review* 15 (1906).

Geller, V., and P. Shaver. "Cognitive consequences of self-awareness." *Journal of Experimental Social Psychology* 12 (1976):99–108.

Good, L. R., and K. C. Good. "A measure of self-esteem." *Psychology* 12 (1975): 32–34.

Goodheart, E. *The Cult of the Ego: The Self in Modern Literature*. Chicago: University of Chicago Press, 1968.

Gordon, C., and J. G. Gergen. *The Self in Social Interaction*. New York: Wiley, 1968.

Kafka, E. "On the development of the experience of mental self, the bodily self, and self-consciousness." *Psychoanalytic Study of the Child* 26 (1971):217–240.

Kettner, M. G. "The ugly duckling complex: a symposium." *Psychological Perspectives* 5 (1974):177–130.

Liebling, B. A., and P. Shaver. "Evaluation, self-awareness and task performance." *Journal of Experimental Social Psychology* 9 (1973):297–306.

Maslach, C. "Social and personal bases of individuation." *Journal of Personality and Social Psychology* 29 (1974):411–425.

Modigliani, A. "Embarrassment, face-work, and eye-contact: testing a theory of embarrassment." *Journal of Personality and Social Psychology* 17 (1971):15–24.

Nadler, A. *Objective Self Awareness, Self-Esteem and Causal Attributions for Success and Failure.* Office of Naval Research, Organizational Effectiveness Research Programs (Code 452), Contract No. N00014-67—226-0030, NR 177-946.

Sears, R. R. "Experimental Studies of Projection: II. Ideas of Reference." *The Journal of Social Psychology* 8 (1937):189–400.

Sears, R. R. "Relation of early socialization experiences to self-concepts and gender role in middle childhood." *Child Development* 41, no. 2 (1970):267–288.

Snyder, M. "Self-monitoring of expressive behavior." *Journal of Personality and Social Psychology* 30 (1974):526–537.

Thorngate, W. "Must we always think before we act?" *Personality and Social Psychology Bulletin* 2 (1976):31–35.

Zimbardo, P. G. "The human choice: individuation, reason, and order versus deindividuation, impulse and chaos." In W. J. Arnold and D. Levine, eds., *Nebraska Symposium on Motivation, 1969.* Lincoln: University of Nebraska Press, 1970, pp. 237–307.

Shyness: theory, research, treatment

Campbell, H. "Morbid shyness." *British Medical Journal* 2 (1896):805–807.

Cattell, R. B. *Personality and Mood by Questionnaire.* San Francisco: Josey-Bass, 1973.

Comrey, A. L., and K. Jamison. "Verification of six personality factors." *Educational and Psychological Measurement* 26 (1966):945–953.

Davis, H. R. "Cognitive and behavioral components of shyness." Senior Honors Thesis, Stanford University, 1976.

Distenfeld, V. "Shyness as a mediator of change in encounter groups." Masters thesis, California State University, Hayward, 1976.

Elliott, F. "Shy middle graders." *Elementary School Journal,* 1968, pp. 297–300.

Hampton, F. A. "Shyness." *Journal of Neurology and Psychopathology* 8 (1927–1928):124–131.

Kaplan, D. M. "On shyness." *International Journal of Psychoanalysis* 53 (1972): 439–453.

Lewinsky, H. "The nature of shyness." *British Journal of Psychology* 32 (1941): 105–113.

Lingren, R. H. "An attempted replication of emotional indicators in human drawing by shy and aggressive children." *Psychological Reports* 29 (1971):35–39.

MacFarlane, J. W. "Studies in child guidance. 1. Methodology of data collection and organization." *Monographs of the Society for Research in Child Development* 3 (1938): No. 6, entire issue.

MacFarlane, J. W., L. Allen, and M. P. Honzik. *A Developmental Study of the Behavior Problems of Normal Children Between Twenty-one Months and Fourteen Years.* Berkeley, Ca.: University of California Press, 1962.

Maslach, C., and T. Solomon. "Shyness as a mediator of social pressures toward dehumanization." Unpublished manuscript, University of California, Berkeley, 1977.

McDougall, W. *Outline of Abnormal Psychology.* New York: Scribner's, 1926, pp. 381–396.

Marnell, M. E. "Shyness: a definition and social learning therapy." (Shyness Research Project). Unpublished manuscript, Stanford University, 1976.

Phillips, G. "The Friendship Clinic: The treatment of reticence." Paper presented to the Eastern Communication Association, March 13, 1975.

Phillips, G. M., and N. J. Metzger. "The reticent syndrome: some theoretical considerations about etiology and treatment." *Speech Monographs* 40, no. 3 (1973).

Pilkonis, P. A. "Shyness: Public behavior and private." Ph.D. dissertation, Stanford University, 1976.

Potapow, M. "Timidity." *O Hospital* 75 (1969):1493–1494.

Prater, J., and S. Malouf. "Sudden murder: a study on the relationship between shyness and violence." Senior Honors Thesis, Stanford University, 1976.

Ross, H. "The shy child." *Public Affairs Pamphlets,* no. 239.

Ryerson, E. S. "The riddle of shyness." M.A. thesis, California State University, Los Angeles, 1975.

Siegelman, M. "Origins of extraversion-introversion." *Journal of Psychology* 69 (1968):85–91.

Solomon, G. V., and J. C. Solomon. "Shyness and sex." *Medical Aspects of Human Sexuality* 5 (1971):10–19.

Tong, D. Y. F. "Interview interactions between shy and non-shy persons." Senior Honors Thesis, Stanford University, 1976.

Zimbardo, P. G. "NIMH Research Proposal for the causes and correlates of shyness." Unpublished manuscript, Stanford University.

Zimbardo, P. G., P. A. Pilkonis, and R. M. Norwood. *The Silent Prison of Shyness* (ONR Tech. Rep. Z-17). Stanford, Ca.: Stanford University, November 1974.

index